CONSCIOUSNESS AND LEARNING RESEARCH

CONSCIOUSNESS AND LEARNING RESEARCH

SUSAN K. TURRINI
EDITOR

Nova Science Publishers, Inc.
New York

NOTICE TO THE READER

The Publisher has taken reasonable care in the preparation of this book, but makes no expressed or implied warranty of any kind and assumes no responsibility for any errors or omissions. No liability is assumed for incidental or consequential damages in connection with or arising out of information contained in this book. The Publisher shall not be liable for any special, consequential, or exemplary damages resulting, in whole or in part, from the readers' use of, or reliance upon, this material.

Independent verification should be sought for any data, advice or recommendations contained in this book. In addition, no responsibility is assumed by the publisher for any injury and/or damage to persons or property arising from any methods, products, instructions, ideas or otherwise contained in this publication.

This publication is designed to provide accurate and authoritative information with regard to the subject matter covered herein. It is sold with the clear understanding that the Publisher is not engaged in rendering legal or any other professional services. If legal or any other expert assistance is required, the services of a competent person should be sought. FROM A DECLARATION OF PARTICIPANTS JOINTLY ADOPTED BY A COMMITTEE OF THE AMERICAN BAR ASSOCIATION AND A COMMITTEE OF PUBLISHERS.

LIBRARY OF CONGRESS CATALOGING-IN-PUBLICATION DATA
Turrini, Susan K.
Consciousness and learning research / Susan K. Turrini, editor.
   p. cm.
Includes bibliographical references and index.
ISBN 13 978-1-60021-333-5
ISBN 10 1-60021-333-2
1. Consciousness--Research. 2. Learning, Psychology of--Research. I. Turrini, Susan K. II. Title.
BF311.T82   2006
153--dc22   2006020951

Published by Nova Science Publishers, Inc. ✤ New York

CONTENTS

PREFACE

Consciousness is a quality of the mind generally regarded to comprise such as subjectivity, self-awareness, sentience, sapience, and the ability to perceive the relationship between oneself and one's environment. It is a subject of much research in philosophy of mind, psychology, neurology, and cognitive science. This book gathers a compilation of new and significant research on many facets of consciousness research. These include memory studies, evolution of consciousness, paranormal experiences, phenomenal consciousness, meditation, human emotion and psychopathology.

Chapter 1 - The proposed theory of consciousness is based on formulation of a protophenomenal fundamental as a singular common denominator of the plurality of consciousness manifestations. The main approach stands on the postulation that *any* living entity, as long as it is alive, possesses an innate protoconscious quality. Accordingly, as initial target, an abstract definition of life based on a novel "morphic" principle is introduced. The central postulate is set to the immanent *non-congruence* between the postulated abstract species-specific geometrical form of a living cell and its physical (structural-molecular) constitution. Such non-congruence is "felt" by the cell ("geometrical feeling" or "morphic sensation") that is the essence of the postulated protophenomenal fundamental (protoconsciousness). Actual degree of the non-congruence is dynamically fluctuating, depending on external factors that make disturbing influence on cell's material substrate, thus upsetting the balance and increasing non-congruence. This causes immediate spatial rearrangements of the cell's material substrate toward minimization of the non-congruence that is designated as a "rudimentary psychic act". The formulated protophenomenal fundamental as elementary, axiomatic, strictly defined, homogeneous, and measurable entity meets all the conditions ordered to the established physical fundamentals while it preserves phenomenal quality.

Combination of the suggested concept of the abstract protophenomenal fundamental with Alexander Gurwitsch's theory of irreducible biological field has appeared appropriate for describing higher forms of consciousness (primordial consciousness and human consciousness *per se*) as well as for explaining the Free Will enigma inevitably associated with violation of the established physical laws. In the frame of the proposed theory, the Free Will is not an illusion but a source of mental causation.

The Gurwitschian biological field, irreducible to the known physical fields, has connected the proposed theory with the vitalistic doctrine which is highly unpopular (and even suppressed) by the contemporary science imbued with dominating reductionist approach. Such abnormal situation is analyzed in the article as a historical aberration.

Chapter 2 - A fundamental issue in memory research is whether performance based on conscious and unconscious mental processes can be experimentally distinguished in unimpaired individuals. Although Jacoby's (1991) process dissociation procedure (PDP) appears to be successful in assessing the separate contributions to memory performance of these two processes, the procedure is controversial because of evidence that requisite assumptions of independence between the processes may not hold. Studies by Curren and Hintzman (1995) have demonstrated that violating a particular independence assumption can cause the PDP to yield invalid estimates of unconscious processes. The studies described here question the generality of Curren and Hintzman's conclusions. It is suggested that their results may have been due to a minority of their stimuli having unusually low probabilities of being produced in a word stem completion task by conscious and unconscious processes. Using existing data of Stern, McNaught-Davis, and Barker (2003) that utilized the PDP to estimate conscious and unconscious contributions to a memory task, the effects of including items with low probabilities of being output through these two processes are examined. As the proportion of the low probability items is increased, outcomes similar to those described by Curren and Hintzman are obtained that characterize violations of the crucial independence assumption. A model is introduced to help explain these outcomes. It is concluded that violating an underlying assumption of independence is not an inevitable consequence of applying the PDP but, rather, may represent a special circumstance that can be avoided or corrected.

Chapter 3 - This chapter explores the consequence of fear and anxiety on student learning in clinical settings. Student identified clinical incidents and their emotional corollary, particularly the emotions of fear and anxiety, provide the focus of the study. Mental health settings were selected because community attitudes towards the mentally ill frequently equate mental illness with the potential for violence, criminality and even homicide. It can be anticipated therefore that health care students undertaking clinical education in mental health settings are likely to be apprehensive and fearful and may confront considerable difficulty attempting to assimilate theory into practice in these learning environments. Data were gathered from one hundred and thirty students undertaking clinical experience in mental health settings. Two hundred and sixty critical incident reports were read and their content analyzed within three broad categories: description of incident, affect produced and effect on student learning. Immediate emotional and cognitive responses and perceived levels of fear and anxiety triggered in the students by the critical incident are reported. The impact of these emotions and cognitions was ascertained through small group debriefing and reflection exercises with the students. The findings from the study demonstrate the need for educators to integrate into the clinical curriculum learning activities aimed at assisting students manage fear and anxiety.

Chapter 4 - Clinical research points out that there is a comorbid relationship between drug addiction and high-risk sexual behavior. Much of this relationship has been explained as the use of sexual behavior as a way to exchange for drugs of abuse. However, studies using animal models have implicated neural and psychological mechanisms that may link drug abuse and risky sexual behavior. Both drug taking and sexual behavior involve overlapping neural circuitry, and both events also evoke dopamine efflux in the nucleus accumbens. This neural overlap appears to be sufficient to induce cross-sensitization. However, this cross-sensitization appears to be unilateral with chronic drug exposure resulting in the enhancement of sexual motivation and sexual behavior, but not the reverse. In contrast to the cross-sensitization literature, the findings of reinstatement studies have suggested that the neural overlap and involvement of dopamine may not be sufficient for the reinstatement of drug-seeking behavior following a sexual event that presumably primes the system. The purpose of the present chapter is to review this empirical literature and to discuss the possible role of learning as a link between the two, with particular emphasis on the incentive sensitization view of drug addiction.

Chapter 5 - Consciousness will be understood for the purpose of this chapter as the capacity to discriminate between the self and the environment. In this sense, it is an attribute that mammals, including man, share. But, just as in a play of collective creation the message is both constructed and conveyed through actors and scenic props, consciousness is a process that is built in successive stages in response to stimuli that come from inside and from the environment through the recruitment of certain neurons to construct neuron circuits glued together by proteins. The circuits are constructed in stages in response to external stimuli and are built upon to construct new and ever expanding circuits that will fire in step when the same stimulus is registered by the brain. In this way, different circuits involving different neurons will be built and will respond to different stimuli allowing for discrimination between stimuli. This is the first of a series of similar processes that will successively be accrued by the brain and that will allow in man for the more complex mental processes that differentiate *Homo sapiens* from other species. We will argue that the main protein involved in the construction of these circuits is the ionotropic glutamate receptor activated by N-Methyl-D-Aspartate (iGluR-NMDA). iGluR-NMDA is a three to five subunit membrane spanning voltage gated Ca^{++} channel. The actual number of subunits is not known, but from theoretical and preliminary electron microscopy considerations we believe the five unit ensemble is preferred in most brain regions. There are three different types of subunits from which one, NR1, must always be present for the channel to operate. NR2 and NR3 come in four and two types respectively, thus allowing for a very large number of potential five member receptor combinations. While not all combinations are possible, this potentiality, combined with differential neuron to neuron distribution, would explain the individual build up of neuronal circuits that make the response to similar stimuli unique to each individual. This is further compounded by the observation that the response to glutamate can be modulated by several agonists and antagonists, making the response to the neurotransmitter different in different neuronal molecular ambient occurring in a given area of the brain. The molecular events that lead to circuit build-up would start by the voltage gated opening of the iGluR-NMDA Ca^{++} channel in a postsynaptic neuron in the presence of glutamate and certain agonists such as glycine. Ca^{++} influx would result in expression of certain proteins such as ligins and cadhesins and their mobilization to the synapse where they would build protein bridges that will make permanent links between the participating neurons. Apart from these considerations, there are several lines of evidence supporting this proposal: The number of iGluR-NMDA's is different in different parts of the brain, the number of iGluR-NMDA's in cerebellum is large at birth and diminishes with age, hippocampal iGluR-NMDA's seem to be important in memory construction and, under anesthesia, there is inactivation of iGluR-NMDA.

Chapter 6 - In this chapter, we make an overview of the literature on the learning styles, approaches to studying and the role of gender and handedness on second language (L2) learning and we report our findings from a three-fold research we undertook at the university of Thessaly in a sample of 452 undergraduate students. In the first part of our research we investigated the influence of gender, handedness and Faculty choice on the performance of phonological, syntactical and semantic tasks in L2. In the second part we examined further how Greek students' approaches to studying in combination with gender, academic discipline and professional degree in English affect performance on verbal fluency tasks in English as a second language. In the third part of our research we investigated the relationship between Greek students' learning styles and performance in English phonological, syntactic and semantic tasks, in combination with their gender and discipline.

Our results showed that handedness alone did not influence the students' performance on L2 tasks. Gender was found to play an important role in our results with females performing better than males in both syntax and semantics. Approaches to studying alone or in combination with students' gender and professional degree in L2 influenced students' performance on syntactical L2 tasks, in which they used a deep or strategic approach, but not on phonological or semantic ones. Concerning learning styles, our study revealed that university students have a tendency to prefer a divergent learning style while performing phonological and semantic tasks and an accommodative learning style while performing syntactical tasks in L2.

In conclusion, our research findings suggest that individual differences influence the way people learn and succeed in language study. However, more research is needed in the field in order to make individual differences practical in the classroom and enable the most learners possible to learn a foreign language in their preferred styles using their own approaches to studying.

Chapter 7 - Nineteenth century England was pervaded by a sense of progress engendered by the steam-powered industrial revolution. This sense of progress made itself felt in the worlds of science and philosophy. In particular, the worlds of biology and the other life sciences were pervaded by evolutionary ideas. In this contribution I discuss the consequences of these ideas for the problem of mind. Evolutionary thought took many forms in the nineteenth century but all of them saw man as part of the living world. This placed enormous stress on the mind-matter dualisms of earlier centuries which, in general, saw man not as part of Nature, but apart from Nature. The response to this stress took the form of various types of dual-aspect, parallelistic and epiphenomenalist theories. I examine these responses in the work of Richard Owen, Herbert Spencer, John Hughlings Jackson, and Thomas Henry Huxley. The evolutionary tradition, emerging from early nineteenth-century transcendental biology and associated with German Romantic thought and Samuel Taylor Coleridge, influenced the greatest of mid-century comparative anatomists, Richard Owen. Another early evolutionary tradition, stemming from the embryological thought of Karl von Baer, influenced the work of Herbert Spencer, the 'philosopher of evolution', and through him the neurology and neurophilosophy of John Hughlings Jackson, the 'father' of British neurology. Finally, a third tradition, originating in the work of natural historians during the European diaspora, culminated in the work of Charles Darwin and his champion Thomas Henry Huxley. The conflict between Huxley and Owen is well known and centred on differing understandings of the brain and mind. Huxley, by common consent, won the encounter. The Darwin-Huxley 'paradigm' consequently became the immensely successful orthodoxy of twentieth century life science. Yet the very success of this paradigm only increases the sharpness of the mind-body conundrum. This chapter discusses these nineteenth century controversies and interpretations with a view to gaining perspective on the problem of consciousness as we begin the twenty-first century.

Chapter 8 - Human beings are enormously successful in interacting with their environment. The two most important developments allowing us to do this are consciousness and the ability to create a variety of voluntary new or novel intentional actions. The two are intimately connected, as one does not occur without the other. Consciousness is subjective; subjective may be defined as the having of or the adopting of a particular point of view or perspective. Voluntary new or novel intentional actions are actions which are newly created at the time through the choice or free will (voluntary) of the person for some specific purpose (intentional). A detailed description of various different types of voluntary new or novel intentional actions and where and how they are generated in the brain is given. These actions are always created with respect to the point of view or perspective of the person and this point of view or perspective is shown to be equivalent to consciousness. Hence consciousness is a point of view or perspective created in the brain from perception which is utilized to create and generate specific voluntary new or novel intentional actions. A basic nonlinear emergent mechanism, responsible for a large number of natural phenomena, is described and utilized to explain the generation of consciousness and the creation and generation of voluntary new or novel intentional action. This mechanism results in the formation of new or novel explicit stable states which are shown to be equivalent to consciousness and are able to generate voluntary new or novel intentional actions. A detailed comparison of the properties of these nonlinear explicit stable states and the properties of consciousness results in the conclusion that the two are identical. Since these states are physical, consciousness is given a physical basis and can have physical effects. The link between consciousness and voluntary new or novel intentional action is also established. Consciousness is shown to be natural, material, and functional. It is a physical development which has evolved for a special purpose: the creation of voluntary new or novel intentional actions. These actions allow the person to respond in a rapid, versatile, and purposeful manner to changes in the environment. This is extremely important for the survival and success of the individual in a rapidly changing and complex environment. Supporting empirical evidence and ideas for future research are also given.

In: Consciousness and Learning Research
Editor: Susan K. Turrini, pp. 1-45

ISBN 1-60021-333-2
© 2007 Nova Science Publishers, Inc.

Chapter 1

FORMULATION OF PROTOPHENOMENAL FUNDAMENTAL AND RUDIMENTARY PSYCHIC ACT: VITALISTIC THEORY OF CONSCIOUSNESS

Michael Lipkind

Unit of Molecular Virology, Kimron Veterinary Institute,
Beit Dagan, P.O. Box 12, 50250 Israel
International Institute of Biophysics, Neuss-Hombroich,
D-41472, Germany

> *"...If there exists some single brain property P that is necessary and sufficient,
> or just necessary, for all conscious experience, then there exists a lawlike link
> between property P and all conscious experiences."*
>
> O. Flanagan
> "Consciousness Reconsidered", 1992

ABSTRACT

The proposed theory of consciousness is based on formulation of a protophenomenal fundamental as a singular common denominator of the plurality of consciousness manifestations. The main approach stands on the postulation that *any* living entity, as long as it is alive, possesses an innate protoconscious quality. Accordingly, as initial target, an abstract definition of life based on a novel "morphic" principle is introduced. The central postulate is set to the immanent *non-congruence* between the postulated abstract species-specific geometrical form of a living cell and its physical (structural-molecular) constitution. Such non-congruence is "felt" by the cell ("geometrical feeling" or "morphic sensation") that is the essence of the postulated protophenomenal fundamental (protoconsciousness). Actual degree of the non-congruence is dynamically fluctuating, depending on external factors that make disturbing influence on cell's material substrate, thus upsetting the balance and increasing non-congruence. This causes immediate spatial rearrangements of the cell's material substrate toward minimization of the non-congruence that is designated as a "rudimentary psychic act". The formulated protophenomenal fundamental as elementary, axiomatic, strictly defined, homogeneous, and measurable entity meets all the conditions ordered to the established physical fundamentals while it preserves phenomenal quality.

Combination of the suggested concept of the abstract protophenomenal fundamental with Alexander Gurwitsch's theory of irreducible biological field has appeared appropriate for describing higher forms of consciousness (primordial consciousness and human consciousness *per se*) as well as for explaining the Free Will enigma inevitably associated with violation of the established physical laws. In the frame of the proposed theory, the Free Will is not an illusion but a source of mental causation.

The Gurwitschian biological field, irreducible to the known physical fields, has connected the proposed theory with the vitalistic doctrine which is highly unpopular (and even suppressed) by the contemporary science imbued with dominating reductionist approach. Such abnormal situation is analyzed in the article as a historical aberration.

INTRODUCTION

The aim of the present studies, fully corresponding to the above epigraph, is to formulate such a *basic property*, which is necessary and sufficient for all the highly heterogeneous consciousness manifestations ("hodgepodge" of consciousness, according to O. Flanagan's saying [Flanagan, 1992, p. 213-214]). In fact, the numerous consciousness expressions are either almost *synonymous*, e.g., awareness, experience, mind, mentality; or *metaphoric,* e.g., self, "I", psyche, psi, soul, etc.; or manifesting various *attributes* of consciousness, e.g., feeling, cognition, comprehension, intention, volition, intuition, thought, mood, purposefulness, decision-making, hesitation, meditation, imagination, creativity, morality, etc. etc., the content of the list depending on one's fantasy and mood. Consequently, the task is to formulate such a "protophenomenal" fundamental, which, as a singular denominator, could cover all the attributes and manifestations of consciousness (Lipkind, submitted). In this respect, an especial care should be taken against the main danger for any definition – tautological shadow, which might creep into formulation. Therefore, by my conclusion, in order to keep the strictest and unequivocal character of the formulation, the protophenomenal fundamental to be postulated must meet the conditions characteristic for the established physical fundamentals: mass, charge, and space-time. In accordance with this, the sought-for protophenomenal fundamental must be *elementary* (further unsplittable), *axiomatic* (further unquestionable), strictly and unequivocally *defined*, qualitatively *uniform* (homogeneous), and *measurable*. It is quite clear that neither consciousness *as it is*, which is notoriously known as escaping any definition (Sutherland, 1989; Lipkind, 1998c, 2003), nor any of its numerous *attributes* and manifestations meet the hard limits of the above obligatory demands to the protophenomenal fundamental. Amongst the incredible obstacles concerning the proposed formulation, the most striking one is a substantial difference between the hypothetical protophenomenal fundamental to be proposed and any physical fundamental. Namely, a physical fundamental, e.g., mass, is *constant* in its axiomatic properties in every physical entity in any state, let it be the mass of an electron, a protein molecule, a piece of rock, the Earth, the Sun, a Galaxy, or any living entity. Contrary to that, the properties of consciousness manifestations are changing and interchanging in the course of time, in any combinations, e.g., feeling might be followed by imagination or thinking, then exchanged for hesitation while performing volitional acts, etc, etc. The situation is perfectly described by M.

Delbrück in respect of a living organism: "A mature physicist, acquainting himself for the first time with problems of biology, is puzzled by the circumstance that there are no 'absolute phenomena' in biology. Everything is time-bound and space-bound. The animal or plant or microorganism he is working with is but a link in an evolutionary chain of changing forms, none of which has *any permanent validity*" (Delbrück, 1949, cited from Mayr (1961, p. 1502, *boldface* is mine). This utterance concerning living properties relates in full measure to mental properties, which seem to be even more complicated, unpredictable, and going far away from the "*permanent validity*".

Thus, in accordance with the declared task, the protophenomenal fundamental to be postulated *must* be a *common basis* for *any* manifestation of the consciousness hodgepodge. Since the difficulties of such endeavor look insuperable within the present paradigm, any success on this way is possible only in case of the development of an entirely novel approach for attacking the consciousness enigma. Such an approach has been suggested (Lipkind, 1998c) and further elaborated (Lipkind, 2003), and the present exposition is a necessary step consisting in axiomatic analysis of the newness of the suggested approach.

The irreducibility of consciousness to the established physical laws is considered in the light of the recent version of the dualistic approach to consciousness problem that is associated with the concept of irreducible "extra ingredient" (Chalmers, 1995). The latter, used as a "working" tool, was represented by the suggested *morphic* principle (Lipkind, 1998c, 2003), according to which the species-specific *Form (Morpha)* of a living entity is taken as a basis for an abstract definition of life as the first step for further formulation of the protophenomenal fundamental. The reason for such a choice is in accordance with my conviction, that namely morphology can be accounted as an intrinsic feature of any living system that cannot be derived from any properties whatsoever of its physical constituents based on canonic properties of the involved molecules[1].

However, if the concept of the *extra ingredient* considered as an *irreducible* fundamental, additional to the established physical fundamentals, is specifically associated with *life* as a realm, the whole idea belongs – *just formally* – to the framework of the vitalistic trend, which with fatal inevitability induces traditional dislike *before* any specific consideration. Such an abnormal situation dictates to start the whole exposition, related to the postulated here theory of consciousness, from the analysis of the vitalistic principle.

1. ANALYSIS OF THE VITALISTIC PRINCIPLE

The present state of art concerning the vitalistic trend in biology displays a unique picture in the history of science.

---

[1] Such a view can be disputed: it is possible to claim that the morphological shape can, in principle, be inferred from the properties of the whole totality of all the molecules involved into a living system having that shape. However, such a case must be compatible with isomorphic identity between the three levels of biological organization (molecular, cellular, and morphological) that is not the case (Lipkind, submitted) as it will be considered later.

1.1. Vitalism under Anathema

The term "vitalism" has become a synonym of something, which, in the best sense, is mystical but in general is merely "anti-scientific". However, for mysticism *per se,* e.g., parapsychology, there is quite a decent place in modern interdisciplinary disputes on the "scientific basis of consciousness". Such notions as "soul", "psyche", psychon", "suspended animation", "conscious mental field", "psi"-phenomena, "ghost in the machine", "unembodied mind" – in general, all the spectrum of terms belonging to dualistic and spiritualistic glossary – have a privilege of being discussed in the most scientifically oriented meetings on consciousness, whereas there is a strong taboo against any mention of the word "vitalism". Vitalism is literally under anathema: any use of the heretical word, even in a neutral sense, may induce a medieval suspicion of being defiled by this evil. Actually, vitalism is one more victim of "wishful-and-fearful thinking" (Griffin, 1998, p. 98). Another victim of the situation is theoretical biology that turned out to be in a unique situation. A Physicist theorizing on the most general and "hot" problems of the Universe, Life, and Consciousness has a full right and freedom to include in her/his theoretical considerations any notions – such as Cosmic Free Will, Universal Mind, Act of Creation that are *beyond* the established physical laws – without being labeled as a Mystic. A Biologist has no such right and freedom: if her/his theoretical considerations are beyond the dogmas of molecular genetics – the Bible and the physicalist bulwark of modern biology – s/he may be very easily blamed and ostracized as a Vitalist.

Such an unbearable situation is associated with a primitive idea about vitalism. Namely, according to the commonplace opinion, the vitalistic principle is conceived as a kind of an abstract metaphysical omnipotent "vital spirit" (*vis vitalis,* élan vital, etc.), which "organizes" ("animates") the material components of a living system (organism), thus determining its structural appearance and coherent functioning. Such a simplified (or, better to say, vulgar), evidently tautological, "phlogiston-like" view on the vitalism has neither explanatory power, nor scientific value, being a smeared caricature of the great principle.

Therefore, an especial endeavor is needed for overcoming historical negation of vitalism considered in the main-stream science as a heresy. Therefore, the above-declared condition, stating that the irreducible protophenomenal fundamental to be proposed *must* meet all the demands made to the established physical fundamentals, presents a crucial examination to any such proposition.

The denial of the vitalistic principle is due not only to the bad historical reputation of vitalism, but also to poor knowledge and oversimplified ideas of modern philosophers about factual biological reality. This is manifested in a remarkable utterance by D. Chalmers, when he claims that "one cannot explain conscious experience on the cheap" whereas "one can explain most biological and cognitive phenomena on the cheap" (Chalmers, 1995, p. 208). However, such a belletristic "cheap attitude" to the Life phenomena was formulated by Chalmers later in a quite strict form, in his definition of the supervenience as applied to biological facts (Chalmers, 1996). In accordance with this definition, "the physical facts about the world seem to determine the biological facts, for instance, in that once all the physical facts about the world are fixed, there is no room for the biological facts to vary. (Fixing all the physical facts will simultaneously fix which objects are alive)" [Chalmers, 1996, p. 32-33]. This is a clear-cut and serious expression of the anti-vitalistic principle, based on down-top causation (Hofstadter, 1979) which, however, being only a postulated assertion, must be proven by reference to biological facts. The peculiarity of the situation is that Chalmers takes for granted that the modern molecular genetics has solved all the biological enigmas, i.e., the Almighty DNA has extirpated the notorious "vital spirit" forever, being able, in principle, to explain all the biological phenomena. Hence, the life is nothing else but a part of the physical world based on the same physical fundamentals. Such a view can be challenged.

1.2. Classic Vitalism *versus* Classic Dualism

While the reductionist philosophy is based on the pure physical laws, the dualistic philosophy makes a jump from the physical sphere directly to the sphere of consciousness (conceivable in the highest form of human psychological, intellectual, and spiritual expressions), thus skipping over the phenomenon of life, i.e., considering it as a part (or derivative) of the physical world. The classic (Cartesian) dualism establishes a principal gap between conscious and non-conscious realms. The latter includes both physical and biological phenomena, with the conviction that the living state can be reduced to (comprehensively explained by) the same physical laws. Vitalism establishes a principal gap between living and non-living phenomena, i.e., all forms of life versus the whole ("dead") physical world, with the conviction that consciousness can be reduced to (comprehensively explained by) the autonomous principles of life. In the present-day science, the dualistic view is considered as legitimate whereas the vitalistic view is intolerable and faced with determined inclination to exorcise this evil from the science.

Such a simple but crucial shift of the division between the realms (location of the "gap") is the most important step in the suggested approach. It means, that the primary question is "What is life?" and the question "What is consciousness?" becomes the secondary one. Accordingly, this shift provides a larger formal system (life *versus* consciousness) which, by breaking the limits of "Gödel's ring" (Gödel, 1931; Antoniou, 1992), would make the notorious "hard problem" solvable by shifting it into the category of the "easy problems" (Chalmers, 1995).

Anyhow, vitalism is radical dualism, which means that, in principle, life cannot spontaneously originate from physical matter, however great its degree of complexity. This is perfectly expressed by the classic *"Omne vivum ex ovo"* by William Harvey supported experimentally by the "no self-conception" principle of Louis Pasteur. In accordance with this, the vitalistic essence of the suggested extra ingredient is that its "extra-ness" (irreducibility to the physical fundamentals) is related not to the conscious mind but to any living entity.

However, the Aristotelian notion of *entelechy (εντελεχεια)*, which means "having its goal in itself", i.e., in a more specific sense, purposefulness, is closely associated with the Aristotelian *causa finalis*, which has a mental significance. That is why according to H. Driesch, a founder of the modern, scientific, vitalism (Driesch, 1908), a synonym for the revived notion of entelechy is psychoid (Driesch, 1915). The Drieschean concept of entelechy was based on his classic experiments on "harmonic regulations" (Driesch 1891), which showed unequivocally the absence of isomorphic identity in embryonic development. Thus, the Drieschian entelechy is of "psychic nature" associated with the purposeful *causa finalis*, i.e., it is more advanced than the tautological notions of *vis vitalis*, élan vital, etc. Nevertheless, the Drieschian entelechy is defined in a highly abstract way without implying any connection of entelechy with biological structural-functional reality as described by the physical laws. Entelechy's mode of action is vaguely determined: it does not operate in space but acts into space, influencing the directionality of morphogenetic processes (Driesch, 1915, 1929). "The notion of entelechy as a factor regulating diversity in distribution of elements is reminiscent of Maxwell's famous fiction about 'demons' able to interfere in molecules' distribution resulting in heat transfer from a place of a lower temperature into a place of a higher temperature, i.e. in violation of the 2nd law of thermodynamics. The mode of the entelechy's action is realized according to the principle underlying the Maxwell's fiction." (Driesch, 1915, p. 260)[2].

Any attempt of elaboration of a theory based on the urge to bring the vitalistic trend closer to the biological reality means creation of working hypothesis employing comprehensively elaborated concepts whose scientific fruitfulness has been already proven. The concept of field seems to be the best candidate.

The existing theories of consciousness employing the field principle have been comprehensively reviewed (Lipkind, 2005). It was indicated that the explaining power of the theories based on the established physical fields, e.g., electromagnetic field and quantum mechanical approach implementing the field principle, is limited to revealing the physical basis of neural correlates of consciousness. The theories based on the notion of an autonomous field irreducible to physical fundamentals promises its possible identification with the hypothesized extra ingredient. The detailed analysis of the field principle will be dwelt on later; meanwhile only A. Gurwitsch's theory of biological field will be touched in connection with the vitalistic doctrine.

1.3. "Practical Vitalism": A. Gurwitsch's Theory of Biological Field

The latest version of Gurwitsch's theory of the vectorial biological field (Gurwitsch, 1944, 1947a, 1947b, 1954, 1991) is a unique combination of the logical structure of vitalistic principle, expressed in its full philosophical integrity, with specific postulations based on the whole life phenomenology as manifested on all the three levels of biological organization – molecular, cellular and morphological. This theory can be considered as an unprecedented example of "practical vitalism", by Gurwitsch expression (1915). In the framework of the theory suggested in the present article, Gurwitsch's theory of the vectorial biological field was employed as a basis for the development of the naturalistic notion of the protophenomenal fundamental.

The theory of biological field was elaborated by Gurwitsch throughout his life. He was the first to introduce the field principle into biology (Gurwitsch, 1912), that was acknowledged in contemporary reviews (Bertalanffy, 1933; McDougall, 1938; Weiss, 1939) as well as in more recent works by the biologists who employed the concept of field in their theoretical considerations (Waddington, 1966, 1968; Haraway 1976; Sheldrake, 1986; Goodwin, 1986; Welch, 1992; Laszlo, 1993; Gilbert et al., 1996). The initial abstract version of Gurwitsch's field theory (which was called by the author "embryonal field") was developed using various biological models (Gurwitsch, 1914, 1915, 1922, 1927, 1929, 1930)

---

[2] Driesch, himself, renounced any attempt for scientific explanation of life phenomenology, ontogenesis in particular.

and was published in German with the only exception (Gurwitsch, 1915)[3]. The last version of the theory, which concerned cellular vectorial field related to all the levels of biological organization, was elaborated by Gurwitsch in the 1940s in Soviet Russia; it was published mainly in Russian (Gurwitsch, 1944, 1947b) and in French (Gurwitsch, 1947a), and has remained practically unknown to Western science. The latest version was described in the manuscript which was completed in 1954 (just before Gurwitsch passed away) but it could be published only after Gorbachyov's "perestroika" in original Russian (Gurwitsch, 1991)[4]. The first review of Gurwitsch's field theory was published in Russian in 1963 (Beloussov, 1963). The first comprehensive review of Gurwitsch's field theory written in a Western European language (German) was published in 1987 (Lipkind 1987a, 1987b), and the first English review on the theory was published in 1992 (Lipkind, 1992). Some excerpts from the Gurwitsch's book (written in 1954 and published in 1991 in Russian) were translated into English and published in 1994 (Beloussov, 1994). The most detailed English reviews were published just recently (Lipkind 1998a, 1998b) together with the latest attempts to apply Gurwitsch's field theory to a scientific approach to the consciousness problem (Lipkind, 1996, 1998c, 2003, 2006).

2. THEORETICAL PREMISES FOR THE PROPOSED VITALISTIC THEORY OF CONSCIOUSNESS

A puzzling constellation of some basic problems of the mind-matter relationships has to be dwelt on before the exposition of the proposed theory.

2.1. Hard Problem

The hard problem of consciousness was formulated (Chalmers, 1994, 1995, 1996) by exposing a simple question to which there was (and has yet been) no answer in the contemporary state of art: Why does neural activity give rise to subjective experience? This question can be paraphrased in a more general form: How at all can consciousness emerge from a physical system of whatever high degree of complexity? In this context, the "physical system" is meant to be fully described by the established physical laws. According to modern natural science, which is free of any vitalistic inclination, any biological system is considered as a physical system of an especial sort. Hence, the above question calls into doubt the very possibility of the emergence of a conscious flash from the entrails of a physical system. By critical consideration of a number of works on consciousness, which are of theoretical significance (Jackendoff, 1987; Allport, 1988; Wilkes, 1988; Baars, 1988; Edelman, 1989; Crick and Koch, 1990; Crick, 1994a; Dennett, 1991; Flohr, 1992; Humphrey, 1992; Clark,

---

[3] This article (the only one written by Gurwitsch in English by invitation from the journal "American Naturalist") suffered anecdotic fate: all the copies of the journal issue that included Gurwitsch's article "On practical vitalism" were shipped to Europe, and the ship sank.

[4] Therefore, in further citations, the reference to 1954 will be preceded the reference to 1991 (the posthumous publication) to display the chronological occurrence of Gurwitsch's pioneering endeavors.

1992; Hardin, 1992), Chalmers demonstrates their impotency to solve the Hard Problem (Chalmers, 1995, p. 207).

However, I take into consideration an "opposite" phenomenon expressed in the next question: How can the emerged consciousness exert any effect upon the physical stuff? The initial "recipient" of such a sprung-up conscious "impulse" is a molecular substrate in the physical vicinity (though it were a neuron or neuronal associations) in which an arisen conscious impulse is to be further transformed into a neural (efferent) impulse. Since "the emergence of experience goes beyond what can be derived from the physical theory" (Chalmers, 1995, p. 208), in order "to account for conscious experience, we need an extra ingredient in the explanation" (Chalmers, 1995, p. 207). Evidently, the concept of the extra ingredient, itself, means that the consciousness is irreducible to the established physical fundamentals. "This position qualifies as a variety of dualism, as it postulates basic properties over and above the properties invoked by physics. But it is an innocent version of dualism, entirely compatible with the scientific view of the world. Nothing in this approach contradicts anything in physical theory; we simply need to add further bridging principles to explain how experience arises from physical processes. ... If the position is to have a name, a good choice might be naturalistic dualism" (Chalmers, 1995, p. 210). Based on these dualistic utterances, Chalmers dwells on possible candidates for such an extra ingredient, namely, non-algorithmic processing, nonlinear and chaotic dynamics (Penrose, 1989, 1994), quantum mechanics (Hameroff, 1994), and even "future discoveries" in neurophysiology. He convincingly proves that there is "nothing extra" in those ingredients as far as their explaining power is concerned, i.e., the same question remains unanswered: why should any of those processes give rise to experience?

2.2. Binding Problem

Historically, the binding problem was connected first with psychology being dependent on general philosophical views on spatial-temporal contiguity of mental representation of the external world (Hume, 1735/1958, 1777/1975). The modern version of the binding problem is expressed on neurological level being based on the well established evidence on the disjunctive way of processing of visible percepts realized within different brain cortex areas. In spite of such spatially segregated processing of particular features of the object, it is perceived as unitary, i.e. the whole dynamically changing world appears as integral and coherent. Therefore, the synthesis of all the disjointed, dispersed, and separately processed elements (components, features) of the complex signals from the continually changing picture of the external world must be realized by *binding* together neurological states occurring in different brain areas. In particular, the visual data are processed separately within about fifty functionally segregated specialized cortical areas (Hubel and Livingstone, 1987; Livingstone and Hubel, 1987), each one being responsible for a specific feature, like movement, colour, texture, size, curvature, some topological properties like height/width ratio, stereoscopic depth, orientation of lines and edges, and so on (Treisman, 1986; Ramachandran and Anstis, 1986; Hubel and Livingstone, 1987; Livingstone and Hubel, 1987; Ramachandran, 1990; Zeki, 1992, 2000). At the same time, multi-modal association areas in the cortex in which single perceptual features could be unified into a final perceptual image have not been found, so there is no explanation how the disjointed features of any perceived object are linked together. This binding problem looks more keen since there is *no* locus in the cortex, which could be called either *"master map"* (Treisman, 1986), or *multi-modal association areas* (Damasio, 1989), or *central cortical "information exchange"* (Hardcastle, 1994). Nevertheless, still there is a certain (rather emotional) hope for future finding of "grandmother" neurons and convergence zones (Hardcastle, 1994).

The binding problem is particularly complicated in the case of the visual system. The histological fact is that about 300 retinal rods (the 1st neuron of the visual network way) are structurally (histologically) connected via bipolar cells (the 2nd neuron) with one ganglion cell (the 3d neuron). Consequently, these 300 adjacent rods form a microarea within retina which during the vision process may contain heterogeneous picture as projected from a (micro)part of the visible object. Thus, the axon of the ganglion cell must conduct forward an impulse carrying such complex (integrated) visual information. This already is incompatible with the classic neuronal theory according to which the neuron firing means only the *conduction* of a signal that is realized according to the 'all-or-none' principle.

Thus, apart from the binding problem seemingly realized at the cortical level, two opposite processes associated with the same current visual signal go on simultaneously through the whole way from receptors to brain. One of them consists of the anatomically determined *confluence* of distinct signals related to different spatial parts of the perceived object into a *single but complex* signal, its complexity being based on the additivity (puzzle-like summation) principle – integration of different parts into a certain whole. The other one consists of the above-described *splitting* of the perceived object's image into dozens of quite different object's features, like shape, movement, color etc. which are processed separately in distinct cortical areas. The possibility of the coexistence and simultaneous realization of these two antidromic processes within the same anatomic unit (system) is totally incomprehensible. On one hand, confluence (merging, junction, maybe synthesis) of a number (hundreds!) of axonal impulses reflecting *parts* (portions, pieces) of the object, and, on the other hand, disjunction (splitting, breaking, maybe analysis) of the object as a whole – *not into parts* (portions, pieces) – but into so drastically different (somewhat category-like) and causally disconnected features, like color, form, texture, movement, spatial relationships, etc. And after (or in parallel to) that, there is binding of such disjoined features into an integral coherent image. Such antidromic way of stimuli processing within the neural networks displays the bias/variance dilemma that is incompatible with the neuronal theory, presenting an insuperable obstacle for the presumption of computational mechanism of the brain functioning. According to the modern computational language, the problem is formulated as claiming that the objects or their different aspects have to be represented (to co-exist) within the same physical "hardware" (brain), that resulting in the *"superposition catastrophe"* (Von der Malsburg, 1987). Therefore, if to define the main postulate of the neuronal theory in the way that each mental representation ("symbol") of the external objects is represented by the corresponding subsets of coactive neurons within the same brain structure, then if more than one of such "symbols" become active at a moment (that must occur within the real functioning pattern), they become superimposed by co-activation (structural "overlapping" of the activated subsets). In such a case, any information carried by the "overlapping" subsets must be lost, that being the mortal verdict for the whole foundations of the classic neuronal theory.

Consequently, the binding problem, being not a purely theoretical construction but arisen from the very heart of the neurobiological and psychological reality, looks incomprehensible within the framework of the anatomic structure and physiological regularities associated with perception. An especial question concerns the relation of the binding problem *per se* (apart from the above integration of signals within the retina's neurons) to the somato-mental gap, which is so fathomless in the case of the hard problem. In this respect, the main question concerns the "localization" of the events associated with splitting of the signals into different components (constituents, features) and their consequent binding, or, better to say, timing of this signal processing in relation to the somato-mental gap (before or after?). A reasonable supposition is that, the integration of the initial signals within the retina level precedes their further splitting which, hence, occurs still within somatic level (thalamo-cortical framework), i.e. *before* the gap, while the binding is realized within the mental level, i.e. *after* jumping over the gap. The in principle possibility that *both* the splitting and binding take place within the mental sphere (*after* the Gap) is hardly probable since the anatomical areas in the brain cortex correspond to the already split components/features (Hubel and Livingstone, 1987, Livingstone and Hubel, 1987; Ramachandran and Anstis, 1986; Treisman, 1986; Ramachandran, 1990; Zeki, 1992), so that the splitting seems to occur before the signals reach the final 5th (cortical) neuron.

Thus, all the above considerations connected with both the hard problem and the binding problem are closely associated with some particular actual questions formulated in the sphere of the experimental neuroscience (John, 2001), e.g. the synchronization of neural units activities within a brain area, coherent activity between the brain areas, the role of coherent oscillations in binding, the functional significance of distributed coherence, spatiotemporal patterns of coherence, and the role of coherence in brain encoding of information. In this respect, the field concept looks as a very promising notion for explanation.

2.3. Gödel's Theorem

If the hard problem - binding problem entanglement is considered from the point of view of mathematical formalism, the "hardness" of the problem falls under limitations to the decidability or verifiability pointed out by Gödel's theorem (Gödel, 1931; Nagel and Newman, 1958). According to Gödel's theorem, no formal system (within itself) can fulfil the following three conditions altogether, namely, it cannot be (a) finitely describable, (b) consistent (free of contradictions), and (c) complete (be proven to be true or false). The Chalmers' "hard problem" falls into the trap of the "undecidable Gödel sentences", thus, bringing the problem to the "Gödel's Gate" (Antoniou, 1992), from which there are several paths depending on which from the above three conditions is given up. The path based on giving up the second condition (consistency, absence of contradiction) should be beyond consideration as incompatible with scientific method in general. The path based on giving up the third condition (completeness) means choosing the consistency and finiteness and, thus, dealing only with constructive proofs (Beeson, 1985). Then, whenever the one choosing this path meets unavoidable incompleteness, s/he stops studying the taken problem and transfers to another task of the same logical sort (consistency and finiteness without completeness). The tasks decidable by this path belong, using Chalmers' terminology, to the sort of "easy" problems. The path based on giving up the first condition (finite description) means choosing the consistency and completeness and, hence, losing the finite description, so that the one choosing this path gets no constructive proofs and, thus, obtains the notorious hard problem, which, according to the Gödel's theorem, is non-solvable within the frame of the considered formal system. The golden middle path between the finite but incomplete ("easy problems") and infinite but complete ("hard problem") is to try to go beyond the theory (beyond the given formal system) by constructing a larger one. "Any apparent disharmony can be removed only by appropriately widening of the conceptual framework" (Bohr, 1958).

2.4. Supervenience and Isomorphism

The idea of supervenience initially mentioned by Moore (1922) and later employed by Hare (1952) in philosophical debates was applied to the mind-body problem by Davidson (1970). The modern concept of supervenience (Kim, 1978, 1984, 1987, 1990, 1993; Horgan, 1978, 1982, 1984, 1993; Hare, 1984) is outlined by Chalmers (1996) by the following way: "The notion of supervenience formalizes the intuitive idea that one set of facts can fully determine another set of facts" (Chalmers, 1996, p. 32). However, further consideration reveals a certain contradiction. On the one hand, "[i]t is widely believed that the most fundamental facts about our universe are physical facts, and all other facts are dependent on these", whereas, on the other hand, "the kind of dependence relation that holds in one domain, such as biology, may not hold in another, such as that of conscious experience" (Chalmers, 1996, p. 32). Accordingly, "[t]he physical facts about the world seem to determine the biological facts, for instance, in that once all the physical facts about the world are fixed, there is no room for the biological facts to vary. ... This provides a rough characterization of the sense in which biological properties supervene on physical properties" (Chalmers, 1996, p. 32-33).

This means that in the framework of the supervenience concept, the morphological (organismic) high-level properties (B-properties) can be considered as supervenient on the cellular low-level properties (A-properties). Together with this, by Chalmers consideration, life is supervenient on the physical world, whereas consciousness may not be supervenient on life that is the ground of Chalmers' "innocent dualism" (Chalmers, 1995, p. 210)[5]. Meanwhile, it is important for the further analysis to dwell on a problematic connection between the concepts of supervenience and isomorphism.

Formally, isomorphism means likeness or similarity and, according to a certain intuitive feeling, it may be associated, somehow, with either reduction, or even definition. According to the statement by Hofstadter, the "*isomorphism* [is] another name for coding" (Hofstadter, 1985, p. 445), which sounds intriguing while needing clarification. For example, as far as life is concerned, the genetic triplet code could be considered as the "isomorphic prototype" of life that is not true since life as a domain is much richer and not confined to the genetic code. As to the consciousness, the question is concentrated on what its "isomorphic prototype" is, i.e., what is that which "codes" consciousness.

This question resulting from the combination of the above two notions – supervenience and isomorphism – becomes the culminating point: the above *isomorphic prototype* of consciousness seems to become a knot fixing the source of the whole enigma. "The problem of isomorphism is that if consciousness literally resides in the brain, then there must be *something* in the brain that literally resembles or is similar to consciousness – that is to say

---

[5] This assertion, inconsistent with the spirit of the present article, will be discussed in detail later.

consciousness itself. But we have no idea how that could be the case" (Revonsuo, 2000, p. 67). Searching for the nature of this "something" may look simply like a paraphrase of the initial problem. Any claim that this "something" is somehow "simpler" (less sophisticated) than the consciousness *per se* would look like a pure speculation.

In this respect, the experiments by Driesch (1891) have been of crucial significance, clearly demonstrating the absence of unequivocal connection between the cellular and morphological levels in the course of the ontogenetic development of morphological traits, which is realized neither by the Lego toy (puzzle) mosaic principle, nor by the stimulus-response reactivity chain. This disproves any claim that the morphological level is supervenient on the movement trajectories of individual cells which means that the morphogenesis is determined not by internal properties of the cells but by the regularities associated with the developing "whole" related to the morphological level itself, i.e., to the high-level B-properties. Such a conclusion is, essentially, an expression of the vitalistic principle (Driesch, 1891, 1908, 1915, 1929).

However, apart from all the philosophical and biological grounds associated with the vitalistic trend, I want to indicate the robust evidence demonstrating the *absence of isomorphic identity* between the living manifestations expressed on different levels of biological organization: organismic (morphological), cellular, and molecular. Accordingly, any macro-expression of a developing morphological organ, e.g., its evolving species-specific morphological contours, may be realized via a number of different structural patterns observed on the cellular (microscopic) level. Similarly, a macro-expression of any living state observed on both the morphological and the cellular levels demonstrates the same absence of isomorphic identity with the corresponding processes that occur on the molecular level, e.g., current chemical (enzymatic) reactions. The claim is that the same living manifestation that is observed (and described by strict criteria) on a higher level can be expressed via a (rather large) number of quite *different* possible microstates expressed on the lower level. Such a higher level may be the morphological (organismic) level *versus* the cellular one as well as both the cellular and morphological levels *versus* the molecular one. It is important to emphasize that the absence of isomorphic identity is not due to the "ordinary" statistical fluctuations, which would be assumed within the framework of cellular-*versus*-molecular levels. Indeed, it is possible to argue that since the whole mass of molecules constituting any cell are under chaotic movements, which are superimposed upon any observable "organized" molecular movements that cause a structurally specific cell morphology, the absence of the absolutely strict isomorphic identity may always be considered as being due to such statistical fluctuations. In this respect, the framework of the cellular-*versus*-morphological levels is the most unequivocal since within this framework the acting units are cells, which, in contrast to molecules, are not subjects to chaotic movements. Therefore, the fact of the absence of isomorphic identity during the formation of geometrically specific contours on the morphological level from equipotential elements – cells (this fact usually is neglected in most molecular biological theoretical considerations) is strong evidence that the life phenomenology cannot be explained "on the cheap" (Chalmers, 1995, p.208) by mere reduction to the physical fundamentals.

Thus, the biological reality demonstrates the absence of isomorphic identity between morphological (organismic) macro-expression (high-level B-properties) and the respective processes realized on the cellular micro-expression (low-level A-properties). Similarly, there is no isomorphic identity between the cellular level, if it is considered as a macro-expression (high-level B-properties), and the molecular level, including current chemical (enzymatic) reactions as well as any other no matter how far micro- and submicro-processes (low-level A-properties). In the framework of the suggested theory, such influence of a higher level of a living entity (high-level B-properties) on a lower level (low-level A-properties) in both the morphological-cellular and cellular-molecular contrapositions is an expression of the up-down causation (Hofstadter, 1982, p.197). At the molecular level, the supervenience results in restraining chaotic movements of the excited molecules by influencing on their trajectories or specific orientation – "vectorization" – according to Gurwitsch's designation (Gurwitsch, 1944). Such "vectorization" is closely associated with the vectorial *field* concept.

2.5. Free Will Dilemma: An Illusion or the Source of Mental Causation?

The dilemma is perfectly uttered by D. Wegner, namely: "Do we consciously cause what we do, or do our actions happen to us?" (Wegner, 2002, p. ix). These two alternative approaches to the free will problem are so radically contrasting that one of them simply rejects the existence of the free will, which is declared as an illusion, while the other, defending existence of the free will, has to confront it versus the whole edifice of natural sciences grounded on the physical laws-based deterministic causality.

Consequently, the first step in this way is a concise consideration of the main arguments dealing with the question whether the free will is an illusion or it is an existing and decisive free choice-based factor determining actual behavior. Only in the case of the latter alternative, a potential applicability of the concept of irreducible field for the analysis of the free will may be suitable.

2.5.1. Free Will Dilemma Is an Illusion

This alternative affirms that mind is totally reducible to the physical fundamentals. Then, according to the radical materialist formula, mental state *is* brain state, i.e., the mind is nothing more than the functioning brain. In neuroscience, the materialistic explanation of the free will is based on the behaviorist doctrine, according to which any psychic act, which is felt as voluntary, is, in fact, a response to a theoretically endless causal chain of the consecutive stimulus-response blocks described by the physical language, i.e., any cause of a mental manifestation is a physical act, which was caused by another physical act, which had been caused by another physical act, etc., etc. ("causal closure", Montero, 2003). The physical circular causality is realized either by deterministic regularity (classic physics), or probabilistic randomness (quantum physics). In the view of the classic physics, an individual at every moment has only *one* option of acting with *no choice.* This means that theoretically it is possible to reveal all the causal chain in the past (up to infinity) and predict the future outcome (up to infinity). In the view of the quantum physics, an individual can behave in many different ways due to the *blind chance mode*, i.e., again, with *no choice* since the probability is definitely determined. Thus, both the *strict regularity* (classic physics) and the *uncertainty* (quantum physics) are governed by the physical laws with *no* interference of the free will. Correspondingly, the brain-mind causation is realized by that the brain is always going to do what it is caused to do by local mechanical disturbances, so that the idea that one's "will" is actually able to cause anything at all, is illusory. In this respect, the neuronal network is a reflection of the deterministic regularity of the physical world in the physiologically functioning brain. The mental events have physical effects because they, themselves (under different description), are physical events. The brain is a material object, while the mind is its epiphenomenal shadow like "the noise of the engine, the smoke from the fire", by W. Freeman's expression (Freeman, 1999) as cited by S. Pockett (Pockett, 2002, p. 53).

According to this view, any human act, except clear reflex ones, is *accompanied* by internal conviction and general emotional feeling that this very act is a result of realization of a previous intention, proceeding under individual's full control, and, thus, apprehended by the individual as volitional. The key word here is *"accompanied"* indicating that the *real main* act by its nature is a purely physiological (physical, in the end) process. Hence, the free will is an illusion, and the processes, which anatomically and physiologically are distinct from those by which the mind creates action, induce the emotional feeling of its existence. Such conclusion means *denial of mental causation* that is in the spirit of the materialist philosophy.

All the argumentation concentrates on proving that the free will is not a force of the mind causing body action via somatic brain. The free will as a psychological phenomenon is subject's *experience* of consciously willing and intentionally performing an action that has nothing to do with the causative connection of the action with the person's conscious mind. This has been perfectly expressed, rather long ago, by David Hume who defined the will as nothing but the *internal impression* we feel and are conscious of, when we knowingly give rise to any new motion of our body, or new perception of our mind (Hume, 1739/1888).

Apart from philosophical argumentation, scientific evidence (to be shortly accounted here) is based mainly on the neuropathological data gained by both clinical observations of different syndromes and experimental approaches. This includes the "alien hand" syndrome and phantom limb movements as well as different modes of brain stimulation[6].

The important impact into experimental studies on the free will was the discovery of electric readiness potentials for voluntary actions (Kornhuber and Deecke, 1965), which revealed that brain electrical activity starts increasing about 0.8 seconds *before* the voluntary movement. These experiments were further developed by B. Libet and colleagues (Libet, 1985, 1992, 1993; Libet et al., 1983) by including into experimental scheme the registration of the volitional moment expressed in experiencing conscious awareness of "wanting" to perform a given self-initiated movement. The results have shown that the experience of conscious free will appears at some point *after* the brain has already started preparing for the action that was demonstrated by appearance of the readiness potentials. This means that the brain starts *first*, followed by the experience of conscious will and then by action (Libet, 1992). An important fact in this respect is that the readiness potentials do not occur for involuntary movements such as tics or reflex actions (Obeso et al., 1981).

The conclusion is expressed by the following utterance: "A microanalysis of the time interval before and after action indicates that consciousness pops in and out of the picture and doesn't really seem to do anything" (Wegner, 2002, p. 59).

---

[6] The "alien hand" syndrome (Banks et al., 1989; Gasquone, 1993; Leiguarda et al., 1993) is a neuropsychological disorder in which a person experiences one hand as operating autonomously as if with a mind of its own. This syndrome is often linked with damage to the middle of the frontal lobe on the side of the brain opposite the affected hand (Jones, 1988), suggesting that such autonomous "mental behavior", fully resembling the normal behavior (which is believed to be free will-caused) but without subjective emotional feeling of free will operation, is simply caused by stimulation from the affected brain part. The phantom limb movements always occur consciously, i.e., are not spontaneously made (Leiguarda et al., 1993); this also seems to substantiate the idea that a signal sent to the absent limb is somehow conscious.

2.5.2. Free Will Dilemma is the Source of Mental Causation

The other alternative is grounded on dualistic philosophy originating from the classical Cartesian bifurcation between *res extensa* and *res cogitans*. In accordance with this, the approach rests on the following basic premises: mind, although being intimately connected with the activity of the somatic brain, appears to be a non-material entity, which, in turn, can make influence on the material brain causing it to start certain physical actions (libertarian imperative). Besides such causal influence upon the material brain, the non-material mind has its own *non-material activity* ("internal life"), which is expressed in self-reflection, thinking, intentions, decision-making, meditation, and many other manifestations of consciousness. Anyhow, just formally, the causal influence of the non-material mind on the material brain means violation of the established physical laws[7].

All the pro and contra arguments about the status of the free will as ontological entity have been outlined in detail (Lipkind, 2006, in press).

One of the arguments that the free will is not an illusion is based on the assertion that "volition acts by selecting among the possibilities in a random event" (Burns, 1999). If a certain chain of voluntary acts is suggested to occur due to the deterministic physical causality, a calculated probability of such occurrence (depending on the complication of the acts) is very low that is in rough disagreement with the probability of their practical realization.

Another argument was based on the above-described experiments by B. Libet and colleagues ((Libet, 1985, 1992, 1993; Libet et al., 1983), which were shown to support the unconscious origin of the volitional act. However, although volitional process is initiated unconsciously, because the readiness potentials appear 350-400 ms *before* a subject becomes aware of intention to act, the awareness still appears 200 ms before the motor act. Therefore, the free will action cannot be excluded but its involvement is limited to control the final outcome, i.e. the free will can *veto* the act and, thus, *control* performance of the act (Libet, 1999). Libet attempted to extrapolate the original experimental data concerning spontaneous motor acts by encompassing more complex volitional acts with deliberation about what choice of action to adopt including pre-planning of when to act on such a choice (e.g., beginning to speak or to write). The results have shown that the time interval between conscious deliberation about the choice of action and the final decision to "act now" (of about 200 ms) was similar to the time interval between the conscious awareness of the intention to act and the act itself in the case of fully spontaneous voluntary acts. Such coincidence is considered by Libet as a substantial reason for accepting seriously a non-deterministic alternative of the free will. A particular topic designated as "timing of mental events" (Libet, 2002) needs an especial consideration, which is beyond the limits of this article.

Anyhow, the existence of the free will means violation of the established physical laws leading to immediate intrusion of chaotic components into the unshakable network of the physical circular causality. This signifies that the phenomenon of the free will-caused violation of the physical laws is as natural as the phenomena of gravitation or electromagnetism. This, in turn, bears a global problem of causal realization and maintenance of the general reality in conditions of the co-existence of the physical world and the free will-

---

[7] The expression "the established physical laws" means the laws of the present-day physics grounded on the established fundamentals (mass, charge, space-time), but not a notion of "physical" as an essential idea (Montero, 2003).

possessing living entities. In fact, such physical world - free will co-existence means *continuous* violation of the physical laws. Moreover, due to heterogeneous spread of the whole plenty of the living creatures highly differing by qualitative complexity and variable intensity of the free will manifestations, such violation of the physical laws is *irregular.* Consequently, the question is how the realization of the universal reality can be possible in conditions when the physical laws are *continuously while irregularly* violated.

The answer would be achieved by means of a strict definition of the free will using the *physical* glossary. Such a condition becomes obligatory for determination of the ontological status of the free will and its combination with the physical world within a general architecture of the universal reality.

In this respect, a task of an especial interest is to analyze in detail at which particular biological (neurophysiological) site(s) such violation could occur. The studies initiated in this direction and defined as *mind-brain interaction mechanisms* (Wilson, 1999) have been determined by answering the following questions: Which physical laws are violated? How minimal can be such a violation? Would such violations be detectable? In this respect, there are two possibilities: (1) A non-physical mind is to *supply* such energy during volitional acts, and (2) A non-physical mind is to *harness*, rather than supply, such energy during volitional acts.

In those studies, the starting question was concentrated on what a minimal level of energy is required to cause nerve cells in the brain to fire action potentials (to initiate neural stimulation). A crucial point in this respect concerns the possibility that the claimed violation of the physical laws is so negligible that might occur *undetected.* This means that if the required energy, coupled with the time during which it would need to be available, were low enough, it could be "hidden" under Heisenberg principle of quantum-mechanical uncertainty. Hence, the practical calculation task was to find out what minimal energy would be required from a non-physical mind to trigger a *single* action potential in a *single* neuron. Such calculation was performed by taking into account all the possible stages of the action potentials formation (initiation of the nerve impulse), on which the energy would be needed, namely: (1) Opening sodium channels, (2) Altering voltage gradients, (3) Synaptic transmission, (4) Neuronal modulation, and (5) Self-generation of action potentials by neurons (Wilson, 1999).

An appropriate calculation, based on a single ion channel as a source of formation of a *single* action potential as a cause of a physiological neural impulse and attempted for any site of a possible influence of a non-physical mind on physical brain, has shown that the needed energy is by *orders-of-magnitude higher* than that minimal value which would be hidden under quantum mechanical uncertainty principle and remained undetected. Moreover, induction of an action potential would usually require the opening of *more* than a single channel. Besides, physiological evidence shows that transmitter release from a considerable number of synapses in a single neuron may be required (Hille, 1992), and a volitional act to be performed needs involvement of at least a few if not many neurons. Consequently, the final conclusion is that if a non-physical mind is supposed to influence brain-directed neural processes, this would mean *violation of fundamental physical laws*.

Thus, the confrontation of the two alternatives shows that the considered evidence still leaves open the main question whether the actual behavior is under deterministic prediction (i.e. the free will is an illusion), or the actual behavior is due to conscious intention to perform certain acts by making choice ("libertarian imperative" associated with the free will-based mental causation). The deterministic alternative, although being in harmony with the physical laws, exposes the explanatory gap (Levine, 1983) between the physical determinism and the free will phenomenology. However, according to the reductionist view, the explanatory gap will eventually become explainable in some future by means of certain in principle new scientific regularities to be discovered that will make up the deficiencies of the established physical laws. Such a hope is a kind of faith, but even this faith may be shaken by what has come to be known as Hempel's dilemma (Hempel, 1980), which concentrates on strictly formal investigation of what *physical means*. Anyhow, in the current discussions on explanation of the free will, the materialistic approach has been dominating, while the suppressed dualistic approach is just making initial attempts to hold on scientific grounds.

2.6. The Concept of Field

The field concept is the universal notion involving the whole physical world from elementary particles to cosmic level. The notions of "field" and "wave" first uttered by Faraday for explanation of electric and magnetic phenomena were further developed and formalized by Maxwell as electromagnetic field. Further development of the field principle has resulted in profound generalization of physical reality based on the strictest formalism (equations by Maxwell, Lorentz, Planck, Einstein, Lagrange, Schrödinger, and others). All that concerned the "classic" period of the field concept development, which was symbolized by Einstein's life-time efforts toward a unitary field theory incorporating electromagnetic and gravitational fields (Bergmann, 1979). The modern theoretical summits based on hyper-dimensional spaces (Pagels, 1985, Kaku, 1994) including "reflection space" and "catastrophe structures" (Sirag, 1993, 1996) were crowned by the Ultimate Theory of Everything based on the "superstring revolution" (Callender and Huggett, 2001) that has resulted in "a quantum-mechanically consistent description of all forces and all matter" (Greene, 1999, p. 368). Naturally, such theory has an attractive taste of the Promised Land – quite a reasonable belief that such "Everything" must include consciousness as well.

2.6.1. The Usage of the Field Concept in the Contemporary Theories of Consciousness
The concept of field was employed in contemporary models of consciousness as a tool for solving the hard problem (Lipkind, 2005). The considered models comprised those grounded on the established physical fields, including electromagnetic field (Pockett, 1999, 2000, 2002a; McFadden, 2000, 2002a, 2002b; John, 2001, 2002; Romijn, 2002) and quantum mechanical approach implementing the field principle (Hameroff, 1994, 1997, 1998, 2001; Penrose, 1996a, 1996b, 2001; Penrose and Hameroff, 1995; Hameroff and Penrose, 1996a, 1996b), as well as those based on the autonomous fields, irreducible to the physical fundamentals (Sheldrake, 1981, 1986, 1993, 1994a, 1994b; Libet, 1994, 2001; Searle, 2000a, 2000b, 2000c). According to the analysis of the above theories (Lipkind, 2005), the explaining power of the physical field-based theories is limited to revealing the physical basis of the neural correlates of consciousness leaving the hard problem unsolvable, while the notion of the autonomous field can be theoretically connected with the notion of "extra ingredient" (Chalmers,1995), which is the kernel of the hard problem. As to the existing autonomous field-based models of consciousness, the field principle has been used in a rather *symbolic* manner without strict field-specific postulation that resulted in either tautological

definition (B. Libet), or metaphoric description (J. Searle), or esoteric speculation (R. Sheldrake). Besides, there are examples of the vain usage of the field principle, e.g., the "integrated field of consciousness" (Kinsbourne, 1988), which, in fact, means multimodality (i.e. constellation of different brain areas) and the "field of consciousness" (Hasker, 1999, p. 195-196), in which the word "field" has an idle meaning and can be easily replaced by various substitutions, like "stream", "state", "phenomenon", "process", etc.

Thus, the real situation is that the physical field-based theories cannot in principle solve the hard problem, in contrast to the potential capacity of the autonomous field-based theories, although the existing theories are not properly postulated. However, an essential contribution to the consciousness problem came namely from the sphere of the electromagnetic field-based theories: the experimental results have demonstrated that synchronization of the 40 Hz oscillations occurring in different brain regions proceeds with *zero time delay* (Desmedt and Tomberg, 1994; John, 2001). Such oscillations synchrony between the *distant* brain regions is unexplainable by the classic neuronal doctrine (discrete synaptic transactions) and may be considered as a strong argument for the involvement of a *field-like* factor. This argument supports and encourages further consciousness theorizing using the field principle as a tool for solving the hard problem. A rational trend for the theorizing should consist in starting new initiatives in the autonomous field sphere, the main effort being directed to a proper postulation of the field in a suggested theory.

Therefore, before any consideration of the irreducible field-based theories, I have attempted to characterize the field principle in a generalized abstract form, *irrespective of the physical nature* of any of the established fields (gravitational, electromagnetic, weak nuclear, and strong nuclear).

2.6.2. The Necessary Field Attributes

The above-declared attempt has resulted in summarizing the following formal prerogative features of the field principle:

(1) Implication of actual field source(s).

(2) Action-at-a-distance from the field source upon sensitive-to-field entities (substrate) – as opposed to direct ("mechanical") contact (collisions).

(3) Unboundedness – absence of any distinct boundaries of the field influence, which, hence, theoretically is infinite.

(4) Field integrity, i.e. continuity "where the hole cannot be" (Campbell, 1990, p. 145).

(5) Dependence of certain parameters of any in-field-occurring process on its coordinates within a certain whole, which is under significant field influence.

(6) Field "direction", which may have different expressions from the "classic" scalar and vectorial fields till the modern highly complicated expressions (tensor-string-twistor, etc.) associated with "over-classic" number of dimensions.

(7) Field measurability, i.e. quantitative estimation of certain field particulars, like intensity, decrement (distance dependence), fluctuation, and other parameters.

From the above postulates, the 5th one seems to be the most indicative: empirically found dependence of any parameters of a process on its coordinates in a certain whole is direct indication that this process is realized within an actual field.

Any physical field-based theory includes the above postulates into its formulation. The same rule should be kept toward any version of the autonomous field theory; otherwise, it will remain merely metaphoric. Therefore, this is a necessary premise for formulation of the suggested geometrical theory of consciousness to be discussed later.

3. The Abstract Geometrical Theory of Consciousness

The general pre-requisite of the proposed theory is irreducibility of consciousness to the established physical fundamentals. According to particular postulation, any living entity possesses conscious quality in dependence on its species-specific degree of complexity. This means that consciousness originates from life, or, better to say, coexists with life. Therefore, the definition of life precedes the formulation of the protophenomenal fundamental.

3.1. Morphic Principle and the Abstract Definition of Life

By the majority of the authors dealing with the consciousness problem, including "New Mysterians" (Chalmers, 1995, 1996), "Liberal Naturalists" (Rosenberg, 1996), and devoted materialists (Dennett, 1991, Hardcastle, 1996), life is not strictly defined but is described by a set of various life manifestations. There is a mere enumeration of arbitrarily chosen life manifestations, the choice depending on the authors' educational background, taste and emotional inclination, for example: "DNA, adaptation, reproduction, and so on" (Chalmers, 1995), in one case, and "reproduction, development, growth, self-repair, immunological self-defense and the like" (Dennett, 1996), in another one. Such situation (especially, those "and so on" and "and the like") is intolerable in physics and is in full contradiction to the conditions for a valid definition (Lipkind, 2006, in press), which must not be tautological or synonymous; must not be reduced to a mere listing of attributes, properties, and features of an entity to be defined; must be valid syntactically, i.e., contain a subject (the Defined) and a predicate (the Defining); and should be constructed in accordance with the "minimization principle", i.e., contain only necessary and sufficient conditions.

Accordingly, as opposed to the above invalid "set-like" kind of the life definitions, the central point of the proposed definition is based on a morphic principle, according to which the species-specific Form (*Morpha*) of a living entity is considered as a fundamental irreducible property. Such choice has been dictated by my conviction that morphology of a living entity cannot be reduced to the physical fundamentals.

In accordance with the morphic principle, I suggest the following definition of life:

> LIFE (any living system) is evolving and aging species-specific non-equilibrial (i.e. needing incessant energy influx) self-preserving and self-reproducing GEOMETRICAL FORM, which is continuously refilled by specific substances.

From the formal point of view, the suggested definition is neither tautological, nor synonymic, while the main advantage, as compared to the above-mentioned 'set-like' ones, is its syntax. Namely, instead of enumeration of manifestations of the life as the defined subject, the definition has one predicate *("FORM")* around which there are necessary attributes (including a subordinate clause) hierarchically subordinated to the predicate. The definition is constructed in accordance with the "minimization principle", i.e. contains only necessary and sufficient conditions. The minimization principle is secured by the abstract nature of the definition in which no specific property of life is mentioned. However, any of the genuine life manifestations like metabolism, reproduction, heredity, growth, differentiation, morphogenesis, etc. are *covered* by this definition, not mentioning the above-cited picked up at random life qualities like "DNA, adaptation, reproduction, and so on" (Chalmers, 1995), and "reproduction, development, growth, self-repair, immunological self-defense and the like" (Dennett, 1996). For example, a wide spectrum of different life properties realized at cytological level (mitosis), genetic level (DNA triplet code), ontogenetic level (gene expression during embryological development and cell differentiation), biochemical level (DNA transcription, RNA translation, protein post-translational modifications), physiological level (coordinated functioning of different living systems owing to neurological or hormonal regulations), and ecological level (adaptation to environmental conditions providing individual survival) – all these life manifestations are covered by the abstract expression *"self-preserving and self-reproducing GEOMETRICAL FORM"* taken from the suggested definition. In the definition, however, there is a certain inevitable logical "misbalance" amongst the attributes to the predicate "Form". Namely, some of the attributes are related to the notion of Life as related to a living individual (e.g. "evolving and aging") while the others are related to the general notion of Life as a cosmic phenomenon (e.g. "non-equilibrial").

Apart from the formal accuracy, the crucial point of the above definition – the *morphic* principle – is not trivial. Usually, the other Life manifestations, like metabolism, heredity, reproduction, internal mileau constancy, evolution, and, accordingly, different principles like biochemical, biophysical, genetic, thermodynamic, synergetic (self-organization) have been regarded as being of the paramount importance (Loeb, 1906, 1912; Lotka, 1925; Szent-Gyorgi, 1957; Monod, 1971; Dawkins, 1976; Haken, 1977; Cairns-Smith, 1982; Caplan and Essig, 1983; Prigogine and Stengers, 1984; Babloyantz, 1986; Lifson, 1987; Waechterhauser, 1988; Eigen, 1992, 1993; Elitsur, 1994; Dennett, 1995; Kauffman, 1996; Dolev and Elitzur, 2000). These principles are clearly associated with reductionist trend of explanation contrary to the morphic principle: the *form* in my definition is that biological entity which cannot be derived from the physical fundamentals.

3.2. "Pre-Naturalistic" Definition of Protoconsciousness Based on the Morphic Principle

The proposed morphic definition of life was a basis for further definition of the protophenomenal fundamental.

3.2.1. The Psychic Ontogenesis

The basic assertion is that the ontogenetic development of the somatic and mental spheres goes in inalienable association. Then, the question is how this inalienability is realized.

I have used analytical approach consisting in imaginable backward (retrospective) evolution. The starting point is the stage of a mature individual's consciousness *per se* associated with the functioning brain that can be expressed as a continual stream of variegated experiences (only partly depending on the environments) laying upon a certain personal "psychic background", which is slowly changing and advancing along with the age and which can be identified with the individual *"I"*. The current "stream of experience" contributes to the "I" which is changing and aging. The psychic ontogenesis relates to this psychic background.

The consistent analysis of such backward evolution (retrospective involution) of the psychic phenomenology reveals impossibility to indicate a moment of the first appearance (emergence) of the initial psychic phenomenology during the brain development. Moreover, the conceivable retrospective involution cannot be limited to the developing brain but must continue deep into earlier stages of the developing embryo (before cell differentiation). Consistently performed retrospective analysis inevitably brings to the initial point of the individual psychic development that is the individual's *zygote* – the fertilized egg.

The above involution evidently must be followed by successive "simplification" of the psychic phenomenology. It is not *a priori* clear till what level such conceivable involution is realizable, especially during the early – "pre-cerebral" (before cell differentiation) period of the development, i.e. till what level the corresponding "simplified" ("rudimentary") psychic phenomenology would still have its specific attributes ("psychic gleams"). The success in this way depends on formulation of such *rudimentary psychic act*, which would be taken for the further analysis of the notion of *protoconsciousness* to be postulated and defined. Such rudimentary psychic phenomenon has been suggested (Gurwitsch, 1954, 1991): this is *knowledge*. The choice of this notion was conditioned by two evident advantages: (a) the knowledge can be considered as the ground of any expression of the psychic phenomenology; (b) the notion of the knowledge permits quantitative estimation like "less – more" throughout the evolution process, so that no "break of continuity" (Gurwitsch, 1954, 1991) could occur along this way.

Thus, at this point of the analysis, two conclusions are taken together: in the human individual psychic development, the initial point is the zygote where the psychic activity is reduced to the *knowledge*[8]. But *what* is this knowledge about? This is a crucial point determining whether the proposed formulation of the extra ingredient is indeed non-tautological. In the Drieschian style, it would sound as follows: "An embryo (in our case, a zygote) *knows its own state*" (Driesch, 1908). The tautology here is clearly evident, being connected with the word "state" which is too general. Therefore, if the "knowledge" is accepted as a rudiment of consciousness, the main task, in order to escape the tautology, is to indicate such specific quality of the notion of *"state"* to which the *"knowledge"* must be related. Such quality is suggested (Lipkind, 2003), being expressed by the notion of *form* taken in a strictly defined manner. Accordingly, the utterance "the zygote knows its own *state*" is changed for the utterance "the zygote knows its own *form*". Such expression of the rudimentary consciousness is *not* tautological and can serve as a basis for the definition of consciousness to be formulated.

---

[8] This is to emphasize the difference between the notion of knowledge in this context and the notion of information suggested by Chalmers (1995). The latter has a certain abstract mathematical cybernetical meaning and can be applied to the "dead" world as well. In the present context, the knowledge means (is inalienable of) its immediate experience, i.e. the knowledge of a momentary "state" means a kind of its "possession" and the possession is already a feeling of belonging to a certain possessor which is a kind of the "Self".

3.2.2. The Auxiliary Definitions of Protoconsciousness

The suggested definition of protoconsciousness is based on the same morphic principle as the above life definition, and relates to any living cell of any origin[9]. The expression "any living entity" means any species-specific cell as an elementary living system. As the first step, I suggest the first auxiliary definition of the Protoconsciousness, which is as follows:

> PROTOCONSCIOUNESS is the embodied immanent capacity of any living cell to FEEL its own evolving dynamically fluctuating species-specific GEOMETRICAL FORM.

I designate this capacity as "geometrical feeling" (or "morphic sensation" as a synonym).

From the formal point of view, the advantage of this definition is that it is not tautological: the capacity to "feel" namely and only form and nothing else gives those limitations, which express the difference between mathematical equation and mathematical identity (sameness)[10]. Therefore, the aim of this step is to escape what is the most dangerous for any definition – tautology. In accordance with this definition, the protoconsciousness is an inalienable attribute of life, i.e. any cell as far as it is alive *feels its own geometry.*

The most comprehensive conception of geometrical feeling concerns not only external shape of the cell (morphological contours): the geometrical feeling transpierces through the whole living cell body, i.e. each geometrical (stereometrical) dot within the three-dimensional cell body is felt, sensed, being aware of by the cell.

The deficiency of the definition is that its Defined component – *protoconsciousness* – as well as the Defining part – *capacity to feel form* – are *phenomenal*, while the attribute *"embodied"*, which is associated with *physical,* is only declared but does not *"work"* in the equation. Therefore, the psycho-physical collision (discrepancy, gap) is not properly expressed here. In this definition, the predicate has abstract geometrical meaning without any connection with somatic "flesh".

The second auxiliary definition takes into account one of the attributes of the predicate in the definition of life ("geometrical form"), namely, that the latter "is continuously refilled by specific substances". Consequently, if the abstract geometrical form is "filled" (moreover, "continuously refilled") by material stuff, there is a non-congruence (disharmony) between the geometry (morphology) of this "ideal" form and the real distribution of the physical substrate which "fills" (constitutes) this morphic (geometrical) "receptacle". This "physical substrate" includes, essentially, the whole totality of all the intracellular molecular stuff and processes that are under "usual" biochemical and genetic regularities. Consequently, it is not passive stuffing inside the "ideal form" but biochemically highly active medley of different substances including numerous enzymes involved into dynamic network of metabolic pathways. Besides, this physical substrate is partly included into different subcellular structures (e.g. cytoskeleton) that, although "solid", are not rigid but dynamically flexible, being under continual regulatory and restitutional changes. Therefore, the material substrate filling (occupying) the geometrically ideal morphic "receptacle" is in the state of incredible dynamic heterogeneity and turbulence, thus "gushing over" the external and internal geometrical "borders" of the ideal form. Just this dynamic *non-congruence* between the ideal geometrical form and the real continual spatial distributions of the material substances within

---

[9] That is, belonging to any Kingdom of Life: animal, plant, bacterial, fungal.
[10] A tautological version of such a definition would be as follows: "The protoconsciousness is the immanent capacity of any living system to feel its own state" (instead of form).

this form is currently felt ("experienced") by the cell. Therefore, the second auxiliary definition of the protoconsciousness is exchanged for the corrected version that is as follows:

> PROTOCONSCIOUSNESS is the embodied immanent capacity of any living cell to FEEL any spatial NON-CONGRUENCE between the cell's evolving species-specific 'ideal' geometric FORM, on one hand, and the real distribution of the material STUFF 'filling' this form, on the other hand.

From the formal point of view, the main advantage of this definition is that here the physical component within the definition becomes to be "working": the Defining part contains both the *phenomenal* component ("capacity to *feel*") and the *physical* component ("distribution of the *material* stuff 'filling' the abstract form").

The essence of this definition is that now the "geometrical feeling" is not the feeling of the geometrical form but the feeling of the non-congruence between this ideal geometrical form and its physical (material) realization. Namely, any current non-congruence between the ideal geometrical frame determining the species-specific macro-morphology, on one hand, and the dynamically fluctuating distribution of the physical "meat" filling this frame, on the other hand, is "felt" by the living entity. By other words, the living cell "feels" the three-dimensional shape of its own body as soon as the metabolically active (dynamically "boiling") material stuff constituting this body "violates" the geometrical abstract borders of this shape. However, since the absolute coincidence of physical and geometrical is ontologically impossible (only asymptotic approximation to the never reachable coincidence is to be imagined), the discrepancy (non-congruence) between the both will never cease, and so will the feeling of this non-congruence by a living cell. Consequently, such "non-congruence" is, essentially, a formalized expression of the psycho-somatic gap which, allegorically, is analogous to the discrepancy between the ideal geometry and its physical imitation (abstract mathematics *versus* solid physics), e.g. geographical meridian upon the globe of natural size *versus* the corresponding particular relief on the Earth. Hence, the protoconsciousness can be imagined as current awareness by the living cell about the eternal gap between the ideal geometrical form and its physical prototype.

In the light of this idea, the living process in general can be expressed as continuous dynamic approximation of the real physical form to its geometrical ideal.

However, the above definition of protoconsciousness still has an internal ontological deficiency, which is as follows:

According to the general intention of the present studies, the definition of protoconsciousness is an initial basis for the final definition of consciousness *per se*. In such a case, the final definition of protoconsciousness must take into account some "active" features from the hodgepodge manifestations of consciousness *per se* to be defined later, namely those somehow associated with free will, e.g. volition, decision, intention, etc. These qualities should be somehow "reflected" in the suggested definition of the protophenomenal fundamental.

3.2.3. Final Definition of Protoconsciousness and Rudimentary Psychic Act

The state of the geometrical-physical non-congruence in living cell is unbalanced (non-equilibrial), constantly fluctuating in accordance with dynamics of metabolically active intracellular processes, so that the degree of the non-congruence is continually changing. Here comes another postulated attribute of protoconsciousness connected with the capacity of living cell *to preserve* its own species-specific morphology. In the frame of the considered postulation, such capacity is realized by *smoothing* the non-congruence between the "ideal" geometrical form and physical stuff "materializing" it. This (re)action may be described as follows.

Any living system tends to approximate to the minimal non-congruence between the species-specific geometrical form and its physical realization, which is under continual pressure and turbulence of numerous metabolic pathways. These fluctuations are "brushed up" by the immovable stability[11] of the invisible geometrical contours of the species-specific frame. Such brushing up process leading to smoothing the non-congruence is a certain background state of a "non-excited" cell whose "on-rest" protoconsciousness (geometrical feeling of "undisturbed" living cell) can be compared with Jamesian "stream of consciousness" (James, 1890, 1892). However, if there is any external disturbance leading to a certain (reversible) disorganization of the cell's physical structure drastically increasing the non-congruence degree, this causes morphological reaction of the cell leading to restoration of its damaged physical morphology approximating to the abstract geometrical form and return to minimal non-congruence. This means that if any physical factor acts upon the material substrate which "fills" (constitutes) the species-specific form of a living cell, this upsets the current balance by causing 'tension' between the "ideal" species-specific geometry (stereometry) of the cell and the real spatial distribution of the material stuff within this "ideal" form. This tension is "felt" by the cell, which "reacts" morphogenically "to smooth" the non-congruence. The restored morphology decreases the degree of the non-congruence, thus returning the cell to the background state of the dynamic rest. Consequently, the combination: *"geometrical feeling"* – *"morphogenic reaction"* can be considered as a *rudimentary psychic act* (*"morphological mentality"*).

In accordance with this, the final comprehensive definition of protoconsciousness is as follows:

> PROTOCONSCIOUSNESS is the embodied immanent capacity of any living cell to FEEL and MINIMIZE any spatial NON-CONGRUENCE between the cell's evolving species-specific "ideal" geometrical FORM and the real distribution of the material STUFF 'filling' (constituting) this form.

The advantage of this definition is that by combining two capacities *("…to feel and minimize any spatial non-congruence…")* it represents both the enigmas associated with consciousness: its origination within the physical stuff of the brain and its further influence upon the physical stuff of a respective neuron initiating efferent impulse.

3.2.4. Reflections on the Abstract Pre-naturalistic Definition of Protoconsciousness

The above-declared advantage of the final definition of Protoconsciousness may bear a certain doubt, namely, such double-potential capacity – to feel and minimize non-congruence

---

[11] This 'immovable stability' of the species-specific geometrical form of a cell as an elementary living entity is ideal case when the morphology of the cell can be accounted as unchanged for a certain period. In general, however, in the above-given definition of Life, the expression "evolving and aging … geometrical form" means that the abstract geometrical frame is not constant but evolving. This is especially expressed in the case of Primordial (embryonic) Consciousness to be defined further.

– may look incompatible with the first demand to any fundamental – to be elementary (further unsplittable). "To feel and to minimize" seems to include different mechanisms, namely, "to feel" non-congruence is immediately clear, while "to minimize" the non-congruence means to "act", i.e. to "move" physically (on the molecular level) the material stuff to reach maximal approximation of the physical mould to its geometrical prototype. Hence, it would seem that these two aspects of the suggested concept of protoconsciousness correspond to different fundamentals, e.g. the postulated geometrical feeling corresponds to the common capacity "to feel", while the capacity to minimize non-congruence concerns something like a reaction to feeling associated somehow with intention and realization of a volitional act. However, by my intuitive conviction, essential consciousness necessarily includes both the aspects, i.e. feeling is necessarily fraught with inevitable consequences. I believe, a "pure feeling" does not exist – it always is immediately associated with its experience. This experience would be expressed by different states: from volition resulting in active behavior till an internal state expressed, for example, by deep intellectual reflection, or ecstatic delight, or imagination, etc. Therefore, if on the conscious level, feeling and its *immediate* experience are inseparable, i.e. they are part and parcel of the same phenomenal quality, such a principle must be correct also for the level of the postulated protoconsciousness. Then, the capacity to feel *and* minimize the non-congruence can be prerogative qualities of a single protophenomenal fundamental.

Such situation is perfectly illustrated by Le Chatelier's principle concerning conditions of the chemical dynamic equilibrium state in solutions and gazes. According to Le Chatelier's principle which states that "if a system at equilibrium is subjected to a disturbance or stress that changes any of the factors determining the state of equilibrium, the system will react in such a way as to *minimize* the effect of the disturbance" (Mahan and Myers, 1987, p. 171, *boldface* is mine). I believe this is not only an illustration but also an expression of a deep ontological analogy. The analogy, however, concerns only the "mode of (re)action": certainly there is no analogy between the dynamic state of the non-congruence between the abstract geometrical and solid physics "experienced" by a living cell, on the one hand, and the state of the dynamic chemical equilibrium in solutions, on the other hand. The analogy becomes evident namely at the stage of reaction, which is realized by the minimization of the effect of any disturbance caused either by any factors changing the chemical equilibrium (Le Chatelier's principle), or by any factors upsetting the balance of the non-congruence (the protoconsciousness concept). However, the reaction of the chemical equilibrium system expressed "in such a way as to minimize the effect of the disturbance" proceeds as if automatically, according to the natural law. "The condition of a system at equilibrium represents a compromise between two opposing tendencies: the *drive* for molecules to assume the state of lowest energy and the *urge* toward molecular chaos or maximum entropy" (Mahan and Myers, 1987, p. 109, *boldface* is mine). Therefore, although the suggested definition of protoconsciousness is extravagant enough, the above analogy between the "reactive" part of the protophenomenal fundamental (minimization of the "non-congruence") and the Le Chatelier's principle associated with the general laws of thermodynamics supports scientific validity of the suggested definition.

4. VITALISTIC THEORY OF CONSCIOUSNESS

The abstract definition of protoconsciousness and the postulated geometrical feeling are considered now as a basis for further theorizing toward a definition that covers the full phenomenological bouquet of the human consciousness *per se*. However, since the pre-naturalistic definition was intended to overcome the psychophysical gap, both the defined protoconsciousness and the consciousness *per se* to be defined belong to the same ontological level – after the "break of continuity". Namely, both, being described by the same psychic vocabulary, have at least one common attribute – feeling – which is either the postulated "geometrical feeling" as an expression of the protophenomenal fundamental (protoconsciousness), or the "ordinary" feeling as a basic constituent of any one out of the full spectrum of manifestations of the consciousness *per se*. However, it is not at all self-evident that the abstract morphic principle, which has been used for the definitions of life and protoconsciousness, would be sufficient for the description of the consciousness *per se*. Moreover, although the geometrical feeling, at least formally, has common language with the "ordinary" feeling, the postulated "minimization of non-congruence" (a part of the final definition of protoconsciousness), considered as a "rudimentary psychic act", has no analogue in the glossary of the science of consciousness. This postulation – designated as a reaction of a living cell to a physical stimulus that disturbs the relative harmony between the abstract geometrical form of a cell (including neuron) and the physical stuff "filling" (constituting) this abstract form – still remains on an absolutely abstract level. According to the postulation, such a "reaction" is realized on the molecular level continually, and now the main question concerns the nature of that "force" which "moves" (influences) the molecular substrate, causing it to approximate more closely to the minimal non-congruence. The expression "the force which moves" invites the idea of a field (Lipkind, 2005). Within the limits of the above purpose, the association of a newly suggested notion of geometrical feeling that expresses the extra ingredient by means of the scientifically well-established and strictly formalized field principle seems promising.

4.1. "Naturalization" of the Abstract Definitions of Life and Protoconsciousness by Means of A. Gurwitsch's Theory of Biological Field

Thus, the general task is to develop a definition of the consciousness *per se* based on the formulated concept of geometrical feeling, i.e., to come from the fundamental protoconsciousness, as an inalienable attribute of any form of life, to the consciousness *per se* as related to the brain of a normal, mature human individual. This means to provide a way to elucidate the "nature" of the abstract geometrical form, which is the predicate in the life and protoconsciousness definitions. This, in turn, means that the abstract morphic principle, which could be considered as an epistemological tool, must be expressed in an ontological sense. In other words, the main task is to formulate a naturalistic factor that determines the species-specific morphology of a living entity, and specifically for this aim, it is intended to use the concept of field. Consequently, I want to impart a "naturalistic" meaning to the postulated irreducible notion of the protophenomenal fundamental (geometrical feeling) via an irreducible field model that is strictly and unequivocally formulated. The meaning I am attributing to the word "naturalistic" concerns association of the hypothetical field with the biological reality, which does not always fit the laws of the today's physics. As a model of such a hypothetical field, the theory of the cellular vectorial field, formulated by Alexander Gurwitsch (1944, 1947a, 1947b, 1954, 1991) was the choice that provided a combination of the strictly formalized irreducible field principle with biological regularities.

The declared irreducibility of the field to be explored as a model that accommodates the postulated protoconsciousness together with the new definition of life means combining the above-defined protophenomenal fundamental with the firmly established physical fundamentals (mass, charge, time/space). That would mean an entirely new paradigm including a non-physical fundamental.

Such a new paradigm is in discrepancy with the contemporary science based on the reductionist principles of scientific exploration since the time of Galileo and Newton. In particular, the search for the "naturalistic" meaning of the postulated irreducible non-physical extra ingredient may induce an ironical attitude: according to dominating materialist approach, the physical laws have been established (and thus exist) as "natural", so that any irreducibility to these laws looks "unnatural" (*meta*physical). As to the mysterious enigmas like the psycho-physical gap, free will, mental causation leading to violation of the physical laws, etc., the reductionist approach is helpless: the only answer from the reductionist science is a general confidence that all these enigmas will eventually become explainable in some future by means of new radical (but physical, in the end) regularities to be discovered. Such a hope is a kind of faith, which may be challenged.

4.2. The Postulates of the Theory of the Vectorial Biological Field by A. Gurwitsch

In this theory, a notion of the autonomous irreducible field is neither tautological, nor metaphoric, nor allegorical, being based on strictly defined postulates deeply rooted in biological reality. These postulates are as follows:

(1) Each cell is a source of the field generated in the nucleus.
(2) The field is of vectorial nature and the vectors are directed centrifugally from the field source.
(3) The generation of field is associated with certain processes in the nucleus, namely those related to transformations of "chromatin". Extranuclear chromatin (cytochromatin) is also a source of the field.
(4) There are *elementary "flashes" of generated field,* connected with certain elementary acts in the chromatin metabolism. A total number of such flashes per time unit designated as *field intensity* depends immediately on the intensity of the chromatin metabolism and, hence, on the general cell metabolism.
(5) The elementary flashes of generated field can occur only if these acts proceed within the sphere of influence of the already existing field. Essentially, this is the expression of the principles declared by W. Harvey ("*omne vivum ex ovo*") and L. Pasteur (*denial of a spontaneous generation of life*).
(6) The field vectors directed from the nucleus are the resulting values from a total statistical number of the elementary flashes of the field at any moment. Therefore,

the field intensity is a completely dynamic fluctuating parameter subtly reacting to metabolic changes.

(7) The elementary field is *spatially anisotropic* and this is the main postulate. Its meaning is that the isodynamic surface at which all the vectors are equal *is not* merely *spherical* but more complicated. However, this "complication" may be sufficiently simple, e.g. it may be considered as *ellipsoidal*. The anisotropy of the ellipsoid can be expressed as a particular ratio between its three axes and such ratio, being species-specific, is considered as an *invariant species constant*. An infinite number of possible axes ratios cover the potential number of all the possible species.

(8) The field vector has a certain decrement along with the distance from the field source. An exact function of the dependence is a matter of empirical examination. In spite of the decrement, the influence of the field is not limited to the cell boundaries

(9) Field vectors exert influence upon the *excited* protein molecules (those which have just got a portion of metabolic energy and are in the excitation state) transforming a portion of the molecule general excitation energy into *directed kinetic energy*. This is expressed either in the directed movement (flow) of the excited protein molecules along with the vector or in specifically directed deformations of the protein molecules if they are anchored to any structures. This means that in living conditions the field "works" against the chaotic movement (agitation) of the protein molecules.

(10) The intensity of the field at a certain cell point (the length of the vector at this point) determines what share of the whole molecule excitation energy is transformed into the directed kinetic one. E_d / E_t ratio, where E_d is the directed kinetic energy and E_t is the molecule total excitation energy, displays this share. The intensity of the field depends not on the amount of the chromatin but on its *turnover*.

(11) The vectors from separate field sources can be composed geometrically and the resulting vector at the point of composition will determine the direction of the kinetic constituent of the full molecular excitation energy. Therefore, in different parts of the system consisting of a number of cells and, hence, the corresponding number of field sources there is an *integral (actual) field* resulting from the total geometrical composition of all the vectors issued from all the sources (nuclei). Evidently, in such composition both the field intensity (being a function of metabolic activity as well as the distance of the point of the composition from the field sources) and the field anisotropy (relation of the point to the nuclei' axes) make contribution into the value (length) of the resulting vector.

(12) The last postulate is, essentially, the inference from the above postulates, especially the previous one concerning the notion of integral (actual) field. Geometrical configuration of the integral actual field imposing vectorization upon energetically excited protein molecules of intracellular substrate (the object of the field influence) determines dynamic configuration of the protein molecular continuum. Such dynamic associations of the energetically excited protein molecules maintained by continuous metabolic energetic influx are called *"unbalanced (non-equilibrial) molecular constellations"*. These constellations provide dynamic conditions for steric facilitation or hindrance for certain reactions which, hence, are not due to the canonic chemical properties of the molecules – members of the constellation, but to specificity of configuration of the constellation which is determined by the

geometrical configuration of the integral actual field at any considered locus. The unbalanced molecular constellations are considered as a "working substrate" of most biological manifestations.

Although the question about the nature of the biological field is not especially touched upon in the above postulates, two principal comments should be added.

a) Gurwitschian field cannot be reduced to any known physical field: it is an immanent property only of living objects. According to the postulate 5, the elementary flash of the biological field is induced *only by the existing field, so that the field is successive and cannot originate de novo.* This is the full expression of the vitalistic principle.

b) Gurwitschian field *is not energetic* which means that no special energy is focused in the field source. The field vector just transforms a portion of the metabolic energy accumulated in the excited protein molecules into directed kinetic energy moving or deforming the molecules. The energy is not supplied by the field to the spot of its action but the field vector as if *harnesses the local energy accumulated at this spot* (Wilson, 1999).

Thus, the Gurwitschian field is neither tautological, nor metaphoric, while responding to all the demands for any physical field. The explanatory capacity of the theory was tested by Gurwitsch by applying it to different levels of biological organization (Gurwitsch, 1954, 1991): molecular (metabolism), cellular (mitosis, differentiation and histogenesis), and organismic (morphogenesis, neuro-muscular system, brain cortex structure and functioning). The mode of the field action expressed on the morphological level is defined as subjection of equipotential elements (cells) to integral morphogenic field causing the cells' spatial orientation or/and movement. On the molecular level, the field action is expressed as vectorization of the molecules' movement *in vivo* as opposed to the molecules' chaotic movement *in vitro*.

4.3. Definition of Life in the Light of the Gurwitschian Field

A new definition of the protophenomenal fundamental, as compared to its previous – "pre-naturalistic" – definition has to be preceded with a new definition of life made in the light of the Gurwitschian field.

A new definition of life, which I call "naturalistic", is as follows:

LIFE (any living system) is an evolving and aging species-specific non-equilibrial self-preserving and self-reproducing GEOMETRICAL FORM, which is continuously refilled with certain substances coming from its environment and whose spatial configuration is determined by the Gurwitschian FIELD.

Formally, in contrast to the previous, "pre-naturalistic", definition, in the new definition the concrete geometry of the "abstract geometrical form" is specified by Gurwitsch's field theory postulation. To my conviction, such specification makes the new definition "naturalistic". The reason for such assertion is that the postulates of Gurwitsch's field theory, being deeply rooted in biological reality, comprehensively cover the whole life phenomenology. However, the new definition, like the "pre-naturalistic" one, retains the advantage of remaining on the abstract level without reference to any specific life properties. At the same time, the association with the Gurwitschian field concretizes the abstract attributes of the definition, which acquire an explanatory power. For example, the attribute "species-specific" is clarified (detailed, explained) by Gurwitsch's postulate concerning the field anisotropy. Similarly, all the other attributes depend directly on the respective Gurwitsch's field theory postulates, which cover all the essential life manifestations.

4.4. "Naturalistic" Definition of the Protophenomenal Fundamental

In a similar way, the previously formulated definition of protoconsciousness, based on the postulated "geometrical feeling" and "morphogenic mental reaction" has been re-analyzed in the light of Gurwitsch's field theory. Based on such an amalgamation, a *naturalistic* definition of the protoconsciousness has been formulated:

> PROTOCONSCIOUSNESS is the embodied immanent capacity of any living cell to FEEL and immediately MINIMIZE any spatial NON-CONGRUENCE between the abstract geometrical configuration of the cell's Gurwitschian FIELD and the real distribution of the cellular material STUFF exposed to the field influence.

The difference of this definition from the previously given "pre-naturalistic" final definition is that instead of the "species-specific 'ideal' geometrical form" there is the "geometrical configuration of the cell's Gurwitschian field". Again, as in the case of the new definition of life, the "naturalistic" meaning of the new definition of protoconsciousness is due to Gurwitsch's field theory postulates covering all the life properties and manifestations.

However, the non-congruence in the new definition may be imagined differently from that in the pre-naturalistic definition. The "physical" side of the non-congruence – the material stuff – is the same in both the definitions. As to the "geometrical" side of the non-congruence, in the new definition the abstract species-specific "ideal" geometrical form is exchanged for a field, which implies a certain network of *lines of force* determined both by the field species-specific spatial *anisotropy* (postulate #7) and the spatial configuration of the resulted integral actual field (postulate #11). Besides, the "minimization" acquires another meaning: in the previous definition the capacity "to feel and minimize" was considered as a *single (unsplittable)* fundamental quality, so that the minimization was realized "automatically" by analogy with Le Chatelier's principle. In the framework of the new definition, the minimization is more concretized. Now, there is a field-associated law according to which any material entity that is sensitive to the field is subjected to the influence from the field. Since, according to the postulation (postulate # 9), the material entities sensitive to the Gurwitschian field are the *excited* protein molecules (those which have just absorbed a portion of metabolic energy and are in the state of excitation), there is transformation of a portion of the molecule general excitation energy into *directed kinetic energy*, and the direction of the movement is determined by the field vector at the respective spatial point. Such vector-directed movements of the excited protein molecules along the field lines of force will minimize the non-congruence returning to (in the case of a rough disturbance) or preserving (in the case of the background micro-disturbances) maximally reachable[12] harmony between the cell's field tension and the material substrate intracellular distribution. The postulated transformation of a portion of the protein molecule's general excitation energy into *directed kinetic energy* means that under "normal" living conditions, the field "works" against the chaotic movement (agitation) of the protein molecules.

4.5. Definition of the Primordial Consciousness

It has been deduced by backward evolution analysis (section 3.2.1., p. 21) that the initial point of an individual psychic development relates to the zygote. Further analysis is connected with the moment of the first cleavage of the zygote into two blastomeres (embryonic daughter cells), each one being a source of the Gurwitschian field. The great game of the individual development begins, being immanently associated with (led by) the mutually developing *integral* field. The integral field of such a two-cells' system (which from this moment *is* an *embryo*) results from geometrical vectorial composition of the fields[13] of both of the blastomeres. The spatial non-congruence between a new geometrical configuration of the integral Gurwitschian field and the material stuff filling (building, constituting, realizing) this abstract configuration is *felt* by this initial embryo whose physical essence (body) "strives" for approximation to its dynamically predetermined "geometrical ideal". This approximation is realized by the corresponding growth of the embryo's physical body that is put into effect by metabolically mediated increasing of the amount of material stuff coming from the environmental medium and assimilated by the embryo's body. However, it is not just growth as expressed in increases of volume and mass (like swelling) – this is a morphological process, i.e., physical embodiment of the abstract geometrical form that is determined by the "lines of force" of the developing integral embryonic field. The next cleavage causes the same non-congruence and the same morphogenic reaction. Such continuous approximation of the physical "content" (body) of the developing embryo to its (her/his!) developing integral field can be considered as the embryo's "actions" – a continuous series of the embryo's "acts" ("deeds") that can be described as an expression of the embryo's "behavior". The latter can be analyzed by means of the same non-congruence notion: now the non-congruence is between the configuration of the Gurwitschian field, on the one hand, and the distribution of the physical substrate within the field-influenced space, on the other hand. This means that both the factors as if located on the opposite sides of a Gap between the geometrical abstract entity and the respective material substrate. The embryo's reaction to the non-congruence, "aiming" to smooth it, is realized via the field-caused vectorization of the molecular movements. Anyhow, the non-congruence is "felt" because of the same geometrical feeling (morphic sensation) that was described in the abstract definition of protoconsciousness (section 3.2.2., p.23).

Thus, the embryonic development can be imagined as the embryo's behavior. According to Driesch's views, the embryo's entelechy "experiences the current state" and directs morphogenesis purposefully (Driesch 1915), whereas according to Gurwitsch's views, the

---

[12] A full 100% spatial correspondence between the field configuration and the current distribution of the protein molecules cannot be achieved in principle, similarly to the absence of the absolute coincidence between the geometrical prototype and its physical mould.

[13] The postulate #11.

developing embryo "knows his actual field" (Gurwitsch 1954, 1991, p. 280) and "acts morphogenically" toward smoothing geometrical disharmonies (tensions) arising from either "normal" environmental fluctuations, or extravagant interventions, such as Driesch's experiments on "harmonic regulations" (1891). The above difference in views is clearly expressed in the degree of tautology: The Drieschian "experience of the current state", which is vague and indistinct, is confronted by the much more definite Gurwitschian "embryo's knowledge of his own integral field". My suggestion goes further in that direction: the embryo feels non-congruence between the geometrical configuration of her/his developing abstract integral Gurwitschian field and the actual form of her/his physical body, and strives to minimize the non-congruence. The word "strive" has, on the one hand, a clearly qualitative meaning close to intention, aiming, even yearning, but, on the other hand, this "striving" may be imagined as returning immediately (almost automatically) to the initial state like tumbler or tilting doll.

Consequently, the primordial consciousness concerning the developing embryo at early ("pre-cerebral") stages (before the embryonic cells' differentiation) is defined as follows:

> PRIMORDIAL CONSCIOUSNESS is the embodied immanent capacity of an early non-differentiated ("pre-cerebral") embryo to FEEL and immediately MINIMIZE any spatial NON-CONGRUENCE between the geometrical configuration of the embryo's evolving INTEGRAL Gurwitschian FIELD and the actual spatial distribution of the embryo's material STUFF.

Thus, the rudimentary psychic phenomenology during the "pre-cerebral" stages of the embryo development includes the embryo's *experience* of the continuously changing non-congruence between the momentary configuration of the embryo's integral field and the actual distribution of the molecular stuff, on the one hand, and, on the other hand, morphogenic *action* directed to minimize (smooth) the non-congruence. Consequently, the early embryogenesis can be imagined as a chain of the embryo's actions, each one being associated with the embryo's *act of choice* among different possibilities. Such embryonic "free will" becomes evident in the case of the experimental interference that was clearly demonstrated in the classic experiments by H. Driesch ("harmonic regulations"), which led to formulation of the notions of *equipotentiality* and *equifinality,* that means the development of the *same* final species-specific form (equifinality) from equipotential elements (cells) by quite *different* ways (Driesch, 1891, 1908). In the glossary of the modern theory of supervenience (Horgan, 1982; Kim, 1984, 1987, 1999), the equifinality can be expressed as the *absence of the isomorphic identity* during the morphological development: the *same* final species-specific form displayed on the morphological level can be realized via quite *different* processes that occur on the cellular and molecular levels.

4.6. Brain as Geometrical Continuum: Conversion of the Primordial Consciousness into Consciousness *per se*

The development of the brain includes two remarkable features: together with the development of cytoarchitectonics and a highly complicated network of neuronal interconnections, the brain develops as a *morphologically compact geometrical whole*. In view of Gurwitsch's field theory, this leads to the formation of the brain integral field – a kind of field geometrical continuum. As a result, a remarkable combination is established: unsurpassed complexity of the integral field geometrical configuration is combined with incredible sophistication of the neural cytological infrastructure. There are all the anatomical premises for the manifestations of mental phenomenology in its highly developed form. This stage of the development means "resurrection" of the vanished initial embryonic consciousness, but now this is not that "ancient" rudimentary embryo's "knowledge" ("experience") of the non-congruence between the embryo's integral field configuration and the embryo's material body, characterized by slow "morphological action" directed to the closest approximation between the two. At this stage, the integral field of the whole embryo is replaced by the integral field of the embryonic brain, which is exposed to the current stream of diverse signals (impulses) coming from the developing external and internal somatic receptors via a highly complicated neural network becoming more and more sophisticated. All these impulses are conducted in neurophysiological manner, i.e., the physical energy causing specific excitation of the respective receptors is transformed into the neural impulses (described by biophysical and biochemical terms) that transfer the initial signals from the receptors towards the corresponding areas of the developing brain. The current waves of such a stream flow into (are engulfed by) the Gurwitschian integral field of the brain, thus causing dynamic "disharmonies" in the brain field configuration. These disharmonies are due to the same *non-congruence* – this time between the ideal geometry (stereometry) of the whole-brain integral field continuum (internal "lines of force"), on the one hand, and the real (disturbed by incoming impulses) distribution of the structured physical stuff filling (imitating) this geometrical frame, on the other hand. In contrast to the case of the primordial consciousness, in which the non-congruence relates to the embryo as a whole, in the case of the consciousness *per se*, the non-congruence caused by the *physiologically conducted* physical signals, relates not to the whole embryo but to the geometrical continuum of the embryo's whole brain cortex.

4.7. The Final Definition of the Consciousness *per se*

Thus, the definition of the Consciousness *per se*, is as follows:

> CONSCIOUSNESS PER SE is the capacity of a mature human brain to FEEL any NON-CONGRUENCE between the geometrical configuration of the INTEGRAL Gurwitschian FIELD of the BRAIN and the current fluctuations and disturbances of the spatial distribution of the brain material STUFF.

The important elucidation to be added to this definition relates to the expression *"current fluctuations and disturbances of the spatial distribution of the brain material stuff"*. The detailed version reads as follows: *"current fluctuations and disturbances of the spatial distribution of the brain material stuff that are caused by current stream of afferent neural impulses generated in the sense organs (including all the totality of the external, internal, and proprioceptive receptors) and conducted into the brain geometrical field continuum"*. This addition could be syntactically inserted into the complete definition but that would make it too cumbersome. Therefore, it seems to be better arranged in the above form of a supplementary (auxiliary) elucidation.

The aforementioned non-congruence is the same discrepancy between the ideal abstract geometrical form expressed by the Gurwitschian field of the brain and its material realization, i.e., "filling" ("stuffing") the geometrical frame with the physical "content". The expression "*ideal* geometrical form of the brain" is not so easily comprehended, since the rough macroform of brain, although having its characteristic image, is not an example of a strictly external geometrical appearance. However, the internal cytoarchitectonics of the brain cortex has remarkable geometrical characteristics that served as the basis for Gurwitsch's theorizing. Gurwitsch emphasized strict *geometrical* features of the cortex cytoarchitectonics (which are absent from the histological organization of the subcortical centers), namely: the specific structure and *configuration* of the cells that dominate in a given area (pyramid cells, for example), the *lamellar* character of their spatial arrangement and, especially, the strictly *parallel* orientation of the cell axes (Gurwitsch 1954, 1991). Just these geometrical features of the brain are meant in the respective part of the above definition of the consciousness *per se*, namely, "*the geometrical configuration of the INTEGRAL Gurwitschian FIELD of the brain*".

As to the "stuffing" of the abstract geometrical frame with the physical "content" as a factor causing the non-congruence, evidently, the absolute congruence between physical and geometrical cannot be achieved in principle, as in the case of the absolute zero of temperature. Therefore, the maximal conformity, i.e., the practical (not absolute) congruence between the geometrical ideal form and its physical realization, is accomplished with the achievement of minimal fluctuations, e.g., the inevitable weak agitation of the molecules that fill the field-determined geometrical framework. Since, according to the suggested postulation, such non-congruence is felt and experienced, the unattainable least minimal non-congruence would mean on the psychic level something like *nirvana*. Against a background of such quasi-congruence, any physical perturbations within the "molecular substrate" disturb the physical-*versus*-geometrical conformity and cause the non-congruence. The current dynamic stream of the afferent neuronal firing originates from various receptors, which are excited by diverse physical stimuli that cause specific sensations, e.g., mechanical (tactile, equilibrial [balancing], proprioceptive), chemical (olfactory, gustatory), acoustic (auditory), and photonic (visual). The specificity of the conducted impulses is determined by the corresponding physical characteristics of the initial stimuli. Since the current dynamic stream of the impulses causing the non-congruence proceeds from the whole totality of the receptors as they are bombarded ceaselessly by all the possible stimuli coming from the external world as well as from the own body, the experience of this integral non-congruence unequivocally reflects the current state of the world as-perceived.

Thus, the causal chain of the psychical loop is as follows: 1) *Activation* of the receptors by the physical stimuli leading to their excited state; 2) *Conduction* of this excitement, via the neuronal network, into the brain; 3) *Disturbance* by the neuronal firing of the molecular substrate of the respective brain part(s) that upsets *conformity* between the field-determined internal geometrical frame and the molecular substrate (increase of the non-congruence); 4) *Feeling* (experience) of the dynamically changing non-congruence, which reflects a coherent and comprehensive picture of the external world (including the own body) as-perceived by the individual in every detail; 5) *Reaction* to the non-congruence, which is initiated at the micro-level of the interactions between the Gurwitschian field and the molecular substrate and can be expressed at the phenomenological macro-level through the enormously wide spectrum of all the possible psycho-physiological manifestations, ranging from emotional explosions accompanied by any form of behaviour to deep intellectual reflection with Jamesian stream of consciousness as a background.

CONCLUSION

The definitions of protoconsciousness, primordial consciousness, and consciousness *per se* have been formulated in consistent succession being derived from the suggested definition of life based on the morphic principle. The crucial point concerns the concept of the "geometrical feeling" as a protophenomenal axiomatic fundamental based on which the concept of protoconsciousness was uttered as an inalienable attribute of any living system. Accordingly, the consciousness in general, being an immanent property of life, can be realized in a wide spectrum of its expressions, from the "geometrical feeling" – "morphological response" as an elementary psychic act ("morphological mentality") – through the instinctive/reflective behavior – up to the highly developed manifestations of the mature human individual's psychic phenomenology that is the consciousness *per se*.

The morphic principle has been more concretized (and at the same time generalized) by the Gurwitsch's theory of biological field that permitted to express the morphic principle not only on the morphological and cytological levels but also on the molecular one. This means, essentially, the reductionist operation within the holistic conceptual framework. The main achievement of such reductionist operation is the postulate about the "molecular substrate" of the field action that was expressed by the field-directed vectorization of the molecules' movements (or orientation) *in vivo* as opposed to their chaotic movements *in vitro*.

The notion of the non-congruence between an abstract geometrical form and its physical realization has imparted to the protoconsciousness an especial nuance. Namely, the protoconsciousness can be imagined as current awareness by a living cell of the non-congruence expressed as discrepancy, disparity, disharmony, divergence, incompatibility, collision, conflict between the ideal geometrical form and its physical realization that means that the discrepancy between the Ideal Geometry and Robust Physics is "felt" by the cell. The ideal geometry is species-specific, initially pre-existing, and pre-determined, while the robust physics is actually occurring and constantly fluctuating to adapt, to adjust, to fit, to accommodate, to approximate to the ideal geometry. Accordingly, the living process can be expressed as a continuous dynamic approximation of the "real" physical form to its "ideal" geometry. Since this approximation is felt until still there is any non-congruence between physical and geometrical (which can diminish only asymptotically, i.e., the physical will never coincide with geometrical), then the geometrical feeling (protoconsciousness) never ceases, being an inalienable part of any living entity. Hence, the geometrical feeling is suggested for the role of the protophenomenal fundamental alongside the physical fundamentals (mass, charge, space/ time).

The whole analysis has been initiated on the level of purely abstract morphic principle without considering the "nature" of the postulated protoconsciousness. However, on the one hand, the usage of Gurwitsch's field theory, deeply rooted in biological reality, "naturalizes" the abstract protoconsciousness, while, on the other hand, the Gurwitschian biological field, irreducible to the known physical fields, connects the proposed theory with the vitalistic doctrine which is highly unpopular (and even suppressed) by the contemporary science imbued with dominating reductionist approach.

However, if to overcome emotional dislike towards the concept of vitalism, a dryly-rational account shows that the naked kernel of the vitalistic idea is the evident analytic and empirical conclusion that the known physical fundamentals are not sufficient to describe the life phenomenology, so that an additional axiomatic fundamental is needed This is quite an "innocent" statement, which is no more mystical than the widely discussed concept of the *extra ingredient* (Chalmers, 1995). The simplest – just formal – truth is that if at all the concept of the extra ingredient is accepted as valid, its further association with anything from the reality is the necessary condition to make this concept "work". Then, any attempt to search for the extra ingredient within the life realm means in fact the recognition of the vitalistic principle. Hence, formulation of the hard problem with the appeal for the extra ingredient and at the same time rejection of the vitalistic principle as obsolete (Chalmers, 1995) is a conceptual mistake.

However, an abstract vitalistic principle based on vague general notions (*vis vitalis,* élan vital) will remain a toothless declaration unless it has a non-tautological expression, that having been the main task of the present consideration. Such a non-tautological formulation based on the morphic principle has been achieved, that resulting in further deduced notion of geometrical feeling. The latter, expressed as the feeling of the non-congruence between the abstract geometrical form of a living entity and its physical (structural-molecular) body, that being designated as protoconsciousness, was associated with further postulated minimization of the non-congruence, that being designated as a rudimentary psychic act. These notions closely associated with any living entity are irreducible to the established physical fundamentals and, thus, just formally are considered as vitalistic. Since, on the other hand, these notions are non-tautological, the whole theory relates to the "practical vitalism" (Gurwitsch, 1915), which, to my deep conviction, potentially, is a powerful trend which has not yet been explored due to the totalitarian authority of the dominating reductionist approach.

The explaining power of the morphic principle could be disputed: it is possible to claim that the morphological shape of a living entity can be inferred finally from the canonical properties of the whole totality of all the molecules involved into the living system. However, such a case can be in principle realizable only on the basis of isomorphic identity (Horgan, 1982; Kim, 1984, 1987) between the living state in its macro-expression and the respective processes occurring on the molecular level, while the absence of the isomorphic identity is evident at all the levels of biological organization (Lipkind, 1998c). In particular, a number of possible states on the molecular level would correspond to the same living macro-phenomenon observed at a higher level (cellular and morphological). The important point is that such diversity is not a result of statistical distribution, which fluctuates around a principal rigid pivot-like regularity but is a result of the top-down causation typical for the living systems (Lipkind, 1999, 2000).

The suggested new paradigm has a potential capacity to solve some of the consciousness enigmas, this topic being out of the limits of the present paper. One of those problems, concerning the free will and volition, has been explained by means of the present theory (Lipkind, 2006, in press).

REFERENCES

Allport, A. (1988). What concept of consciousness? In A. Marcel and E. Bisiach (Eds.), *Consciousness in Contemporary Science* (Oxford University Press, pp. 159-182). Oxford.

Antoniou, I. (1992). Is consciousness decidable? In *Science and Consciousness, Proceedings of the 2nd International Symposium*, Athens, January 3-7, 1992, pp. 69-91.

Baars, B. J. (1988). *A Cognitive Theory of Consciousness*. Cambridge: Cambridge University Press.

Babloyantz, A. (1986). *Molecules, Dynamics, and Life*. New York: John Wiley and Sons.

Banks, G., Shot, P., Martinez, A. J., Latchaw, R., Rattcliff, G. and Boller, F. (1989). The alien hand syndrome: Clinical and postmortem findings. *Archives of Neurology*. 46, 456-459.

Bergmann, P. (1979). Unitary field theories. *Physics Today*, 32, 44-51.

Beeson, M. (1985). *Foundations of Constructive Mathematics*. Berlin: Springer, E. Bishop.

Beloussov, L. V. (1963). The sources, development, and perspectives of the theory of biological field. In I.V. Nikitinskaya and G.A. Astafieva (Eds.), *Physical and Chemical Foundations of Life Phenomena: Historical Essays* (USSR Academy of Sciences Publishing House, pp. 59-117). Moscow.

Beloussov, L. V. (1994). Alexander Gavrilovitch Gurwitsch (1874-1954). *Rivista di Biologia - Biology Forum*, 87, 119-26.

Bertalanffy, L. von (1933). *Modern Theories of Development: An Introduction to Theoretical Biology*. Oxford: Oxford University Press.

Bohr, N. (1958). *Atomic Physics and Human Knowledge*. New York: Wiley and Sons.

Cairns-Smith, A. G. (1982). *Genetic Takeover and the Mineral Origin of Life*. Cambridge: Cambridge University Press.

Callender, C. and Huggett, N. (Eds.) (2001). Physics Meets Philosophy at the Planck Scale. Cambridge: Cambridge University Press.

Campbell, K. (1990). *Abstract Particulars*. Oxford: Blackwell.

Caplan, S. R. and Essig, A. (1983). *Bioenergetics and Linear Nonequilibrium Thermodynamics*. Cambridge MA: Harvard University Press.

Chalmers, D. J. (1994). Concluding remarks on the Conference 'Toward a Scientific Basis for Consciousness; in Conference Report by Jane Clark. *Journal of Consciousness Studies*, 1, pp.152-154.

Chalmers, D. J. (1995). Facing up to the problem of consciousness. *Journal of Consciousness Studies*, 2, pp.200-219.

Chalmers, D. J. (1996). *Conscious Mind: In Search of a Fundamental Theory*. New York, Oxford: Oxford University Press.

Clark, A. (1992). *Sensory Qualities*. Oxford: Oxford University Press.

Crick, F. H. C. (1994a). *The Astonishing Hypothesis - The Scientific Search for the Soul*. London: Simon and Schuster.

Crick, F. H. C. and Koch, C. (1990). Toward a neurobiological theory of consciousness. *Seminars in the Neurosciences*, 2, 263-275.

Damasio, A. R. (1989). The brain binds entities and events by multiregional activation from convergence zones. *Neural Computation*, 1, 123-132.

Davidson, D. (1970). Mental events. In L. Foster and J. Swanson (Eds.), *Experience and Theory* (University of Massachusetts Press, pp. 79-101). Amherst.

Dawkins, R. (1976). *The Selfish Gene*. Oxford: Oxford University Press; New edition (1989). Oxford: Oxford University Press.

Dennett, D. C. (1991). *Consciousness Explained*. Little-Brown and Co.; 2nd edition (1993): Penguin Books: Harmondsworth.

Dennett, D.C. (1995). *Darwin's Dangerous Idea*. New York: Simon and Schuster.

Dennett, D. C. (1996). Facing backwards on the problem of consciousness. *Journal of Consciousness Studies*, 3, 4-6.

Desmedt, J. D. and Tomberg, C. (1994). Transient phase-locking of 40Hz electrical oscillations in prefrontal and parietal human cortex reflects the process of conscious somatic perception. *Neuroscience Letters*, 168: 126-129.

Dolev, S. and Elitsur, A.C. (2000). Biology and thermodynamics: seemingly-opposite phenomena in search of a unified paradigm. *The Einstein Quaterly: Journal of Biology and Medicine*, 15, 24-33.

Driesch, H. (1891). Entwicklungsmechanische Studien. 1. Der Wert der beiden ersten Fürchungszellen in der Echinodermenentwicklung Experimentelle Erzeugung von Theil- und Doppelbildungen. *Zeitschrift für Zoology*, 53, 160-78. (In German).

Driesch, H. (1908). *Science and Philosophy of the Organism*. London: Adam and Charles Black.

Driesch, H. (1915). *Vitalism: Its History and System*. Russian Edition, Edited and authorized translation from German into Russian by A.G. Gurwitsch). Moscow: Nauka. (In Russian).

Driesch, H. (1929). *The Science and Philosophy of the Organism*. London: Adam and Charles Black.

Edelman, G. (1989). *The Remembered Present: A Biological Theory of Consciousness*. New York: Basic Books.

Eigen, M. (1992). *Steps Towards Life - A Perspective on Evolution*. Oxford: Oxford University Press.

Eigen, M. (1993). The origin of genetic information: viruses as models. *Gene*, 135, 37-47.

Elitzur, A. C. (1994). Let there be life: Thermodynamic reflections on biogenesis and evolution. *Journal of Theoretical Biology*, 164, 429-459.

Flanagan, O. (1992). *Consciousness Reconsidered*. Cambridge MA: MIT Press.

Flohr, H. (1992). Qualia and brain processes. In A. Beckermann, H. Flohr, and J. Kim (Eds.), *Emergence or Reduction? Prospects for Nonreductive Physicalism* (De Gruyter, pp. 220-240). Berlin.

Gasquone, P. G. (1993). Alien hand sign. *Journal of Clinical and Experimental Neuropsychology*, 15, 653-667.

Freeman, W. J. (1999). *How Brains Make Up Their Minds*. London: Weidenfeld and Nicolson.

Gödel, K. (1931). Über formal unentscheidbare Satze der Principia Mathematica und verwandter System. *Monatshefte für Mathematik und Physik*, 38, 173-198 (In German).

Goodwin B.C. (1986); Is biology an historical science? In S. Rose and L. Appignanese (Eds.), *Science and Beyond* (Blackwell, pp. 47-60). Oxford.

Gilbert, S. F., Opitz, J. M. and Raff, R. A. (1996). Resynthesizing evolutionary and developmental Biology. *Developmental Biology*, 173, 357-372.

Green, B. (1999). *The Elegant Universe: Superstrings, Hidden Dimensions, and the Quest for the Ultimate Theory*. New York: Norton.

Griffin, D. R. (1998). *Unsnarling the World-Knot: Consciousness, Freedom, and the Mind-Body Problem.* Berkeley, Los Angeles, London: University of California Press.

Gurwitsch, A. G. (1912). Die Vererbung als Verwirklichungsvorgang. *Biologische Zentralblatt,* 32, 458-486. (In German).

Gurwitsch, A. G. (1914). Der Vererbungsmechanismus der Form. *Roux' Archiv für die Entwicklungsmechanik,* 39, 516-577. (In German).

Gurwitsch, A. G. (1915). *On practical vitalism.* American Naturalism, 15.

Gurwitsch, A. G. (1922). Über den Begriff des embryonalen Feldes. *Roux' Archiv für die Entwicklungsmechanik,* 51, 383-415. (In German).

Gurwitsch, A. G. (1927). Weiterbildung und Verallgemeinerung des Feldbegriffes. *Roux' Archiv für die Entwicklungsmechanik,* 112, 433-454 (Festschrift für H. Driesch). [In German].

Gurwitsch, A. G. (1929). Der Begriff der Äquipotentialität in seiner Anwendung auf physiologische Probleme. *Roux' Archiv für Entwicklungsmechanik,* 116, 20-35. (In German).

Gurwitsch, A. G. (1930). *Die histologischen Grundlagen der Biologie.* G. Fischer Verlag, Jena. (In German).

Gurwitsch, A. G. (1944). *The Theory of the Biological Field.* Moscow: Sovetskaya Nauka. (In Russian).

Gurwitsch, A. G. (1947a). Une theorie du champ biologique cellulaire. *Bibliotheca Biotheoretica,* ser. D, 11, 1-149, Leiden. (In French).

Gurwitsch, A. G. (1947b). The concept of "whole" in the light of the cell field theory. In A.G. Gurwitsch (Ed.), *Collection of Works on Mitogenesis and the Theory of the Biological Field* (USSR Academy of Medical Sciences Publishing House, p.p. 141-147). Moscow. (In Russian).

Gurwitsch, A. G. (1954). *Principles of Analytical Biology and the Theory of Cellular Fields.* Manuscript, Moscow. (In Russian).

Gurwitsch, A. G. (1991). *Principles of Analytical Biology and the Theory of Cellular Fields.* Moscow: Nauka. (In Russian).

Haken, N. (1977). *Synergetics: An Introduction.* Heidelberg: Springer.

Hameroff, S. (1994). Quantum coherence in microtubules: A neural basis for an emergent consciousness? *Journal of Consciousness Studies,* 1, 91-118.

Hameroff, S. R. (1997b). Quantum computing in microtubules – An intra-neural correlate of consciousness? *Japanese Bulletin of Cognitive Science,* 4, 67-92.

Hameroff, S. R. and Penrose, R. (1996). Conscious events as orchestrated space-time selections. *Journal of Consciousness Studies,* 3, 36-53.

Haraway, D. J. (1976). *Cristals, Fabrics, and Fields: Metaphors of Organicism in Twentieth-Century Developmental Biology.* New Haven: Yale University Press.

Hardcastle, V. G. (1994). Psychology's binding problem and possible neurobiological solutions. *Journal of Consciousness Studies,* 1, 66-90.

Hardcastle, V. G. (1996). The why of consciousness: a non-issue for materialists. *Journal of Consciousness Studies,* 3, 7-13.

Hardin, C. L. (1992). Physiology, phenomenology, and Spinoza's true colors. In A. Beckermann, H. Flohr and J. Kim (Eds.), *Emergence or Reduction? Prospects for Nonreductive Physicalism* (De Gruyter, pp. 201-219). Berlin.

Hare, R. M. (1952). *The Language of Moral.* Oxford: Clarendon Press.

Hare, R. M. (1984). Supervenience. *Proceedings of the Aristotelian Society, suppl.*, 58, 1-16.

Hempel, C. G. (1980). Comments on Goodman's ways of worldmaking. *Synthese*, 45, 193-194.

Hille, B. (1992). *Ionic Channels of Excitable Membranes.* Sunderland, MA: Sinauer Associates.

Hameroff, S. (1994). Quantum coherence in microtubules: A neural basis for an emergent consciousness? *Journal of Consciousness Studies*, 1, 91-118.

Hameroff, S. (1997). Fundamental geometry: The Penrose-Hameroff Orch OR model of consciousness. In N. Woodhouse (Ed.), *Geometry and the Foundations of Science: Contributions from an Oxford Conference Honoring Roger Penrose* (Oxford University Press, pp. 103-127). Oxford.

Hameroff, S. (1998). Funda-Mentality: is the conscious mind subtly linked to a basic level of the universe? *Trends in Cognitive Sciences*, 2, 119-124.

Hameroff, S. (2001). Consciousness, the brain, and space-time geometry. In: P.C. Marijuan (Ed.), Cajal and Consciousness: Scientific Approaches to Consciousness on the Centennial of Ramón y Cajal's Textura (*Annals of the New York Academy of Science, 929, 74-104*). New York.

Hameroff, S. and Penrose, R. (1996a). Conscious events as orchestrated space-time selections. *Journal of Consciousness Studies*, 3, 36-53.

Hameroff, S. and Penrose, R. (1996b). Orchestrated reduction of quantum coherence in brain microtubules: A model for consciousness. In S. Hameroff, A. Kaszniak and A. Scott (Eds.), *Toward a Science of Consciousness:The 1ˢᵗ Tucson Discussions and Debates* (Bradford Book, MIT Press, pp. 507-540). Cambridge, MA, and London.

Hameroff, S. and Watt, R. C. (1982). Information processing in microtubules. *Journal of Theoretical Biology,* 98: 549-561.

Hameroff, S., Dayhoff, J. E., Lahos-Beltra, R., Samsonovich, A. and Rasmussen, S. (1992). *Conformational automata in the cytoskeleton: Models for molecular computation. IEEE Computer* (October Special Issue on Molecular Computing), pp. 30-39.

Hofstadter, D. R. (1979). *Gödel, Escher, Bach: an Eternal Golden Braid.* New York: Basic Books.

Hofstadter, D. R. (1982). Prelude … ant fugue. In D. Hofstadter and D. Dennett (Eds.), *The Mind's I: Fantasies and Reflections on Self and Soul* (Penguin Books, pp. 149-201). Harmondsworth, UK.

Hofstadter, D. R. (1985). *Metamagical Themas: Questing for the Essence of Mind and Matter.* New York: Basic Books.

Horgan, T. (1978). Supervenient bridge laws. *Philosophy of Science*, 45, 227-249.

Horgan, T. (1982). Supervenience and microphysics. *Pacific Philosophical Quaterly*, 63, 29-43.

Horgan, T. (1984). Supervenience and cosmic hermeneutics. *Southern Journal of Philosophy,* suppl., 22, 19-38

Horgan, T. (1993). From supervenience to superdupervenience: Meeting the demands of a material world. *Mind*, 102, 555-586.

Hubel, D. H. and Livingstone, M. S. (1987). Segregation of form, color, and stereopsis in primate area 18. *The Journal of Neuroscience*, 7, 3378-3415.

Hume, D. 1735/1958. *A Treatise on Human Nature.* Oxford, New York: Oxford University Press.

Hume, D. (1739/1888). *A treatise of human nature* (edited by L. A. Selby-Bigge). London: Oxford University Press.

Hume, D. (1777/1975). *Enquiries Concerning Human Understanding and Concerning the Principles of Morals.* Oxford, New York: Oxford University Press.

Humphrey, N. (1992). *A History of the Mind.* New York: Simon and Schuster.

Jackendoff, R. (1987). *Consciousness and the Computational Mind.* Cambridge MA: MIT Press.

James, W. (1890). *The Principles of Psychology.* New York: Henry Holt and Co.; republished in 1950 New York: Dover Books.

James, W. (1892*). Psychology.* Cleveland, New York: World.

John, E. R. (2001). A field theory of consciousness. *Consciousness and Cognition,* 10, 184-213.

John, E. R. (2002). The neurophysics of consciousness. *Brain Research Reviews,* 39, 1-28.

Jones, L. A. (1988). What do they reveal about proprioception? *Psychoogical. Bulletin,*103, 72-86

Kaku, M. (1994). *Hyperspace.* New York: Oxford University Press.

Kauffman, S. (1996). *At Home in the Universe: the Search for Laws of Self-Organization and Complexity.* New York: Viking.

Kim, J. (1978). Supervenience and nomological incommensurables. *American Philosophical Quarterly,* 15, 149-156.

Kim, J. (1984). Concepts of supervenience. *Philosophy and Phenomenological Research,* 65, 153-176.

Kim, J. (1987). "Strong" and "global" supervenience revisited. *Philosophy and Phenomenological Research,* 68, 315-326.

Kim, J. (1990). Concepts of supervenience. *Metaphilosophy,* 21, 1-27.

Kim, J. (1993). *Supervenience and Mind: Selected Philosophical Essays.* Cambridge: Cambridge University Press.

Kim, J. (1998). *Mind in a Physical World: An Essay on the Mind-Body Problem and Mental Causation.* Cambridge, MA: MIT Press.

Kim, J. (1999). Supervenient properties and micro-based properties: A reply to Noordhof. *Proceedings of the Aristotelian Society,* 99, 115-117.

Kornhuber, H. H. and Deecke, L. (1965). Hirnpotentialandeerungen bei Wilkurbevegungen und passiv Bewegungendes Menschen: bereitshaftspotential und reafferente Potentiale. *Pflügers Archiv für Gesamte Psychology,* 284, 1-17. (In German).

Laszlo, E. (1993). *The Creative Cosmos: A Unified Science of Matter, Life and Mind.* Edinburgh: Floris Books.

Leiguarda, R., Starkstein, S., Nogues, M.and Berthier, M. (1993). Paroxysmal alien hand syndrome. *Journal of Neurology, Neurosurgery and Psychiatry,* 56, 788-792.

Levine, J. (1983). Materialism and qualia: the explanatory gap. *Pacific Philosophical Quarterly,* 64, 354-361.

Libet, B. (1985). Unconscious cerebral initiative and the role of conscious will in voluntary action. *Behavioral and Brain Sciences,* 8, 529-566.

Libet, B. (1992). The neural time-factor in perception, volition, and free will. *Revue Métaphysique Morale,* 97, 255-272.

Libet, B. (1993). *Neurophysiology of Consciousness.* Boston: Birkhäuser.

Libet, B. (1994). A testable field theory of mind-brain interaction. *Journal of Consciousness Studies*, 1, 119-126.

Libet B. (1999). Do we have free will? *Journal of Consciousness Studies*, 6, 47-57.

Libet B. (2002). The timing of mental events: Libet's experimental findings and their implications. *Consciousness and Cognition*, 11, 292-299.

Libet, B. (2001). Consciousness, free action and the brain: Commentary on John Searle's article (with a short reply from John R. Searle). *Journal of Consciousness Studies*, 8, 59-65.

Libet, B., Gleason, C., Write, E. W., and Pearl, D. K. (1983). Time of conscious intention to act in relation to onset of cerebral activity (readiness potentials): The unconscious initiation of a freely voluntary act. *Brain*, 106, 623-642.

Lifson, S. (1987). Chemical selection, diversity, teleonomy and the second law of thermodynamics: Reflections of Eigen's theory of self-organization of matter. *Biophysical Chemistry*, 26, 303-311.

Lipkind, M. (1987a). Gurwitschs Theorie vom biologischen Feld. Teil I. *Fusion* (German edition) 8, No. 4, 30-49. (In German).

Lipkind, M. (1987b). Gurwitschs Theorie vom biologischen Feld. Teil II. *Fusion* (German edition) 8, No. 5-6, 53-65. (In German).

Lipkind, M. (1992). Can the vitalistic entelechia principle be a working instrument? (The theory of the biological field of Alexander Gurwitsch). In F.-A. Popp, K. H. Li and Q. Gu (Eds.), *Recent Advances in Biophoton Research and its Applications* (World Scientific, pp. 469-494). Singapore, New Jersey, London, Hong Kong.

Lipkind, M. (1996). Application of the theory of biological field by A. Gurwitsch to the problem of consciousness. In C. Zhang, F.-A. Popp, and M. Bischof (Eds.), *Current Development of Biophysics* (Hangzhou University Press, pp. 223-251). Hangzhou.

Lipkind, M. (1998a). Alexander Gurwitsch and the concept of the biological field. Part 1. 21st *Century Science and Technology*, 11, No. 2, pp. 36-51.

Lipkind, M. (1998b). Alexander Gurwitsch and the concept of the biological field. Part 2. 21st *Century Science and Technology*, 11, No. 3, pp. 34-53.

Lipkind, M. (1998c): The concepts of coherence and "binding problem" as applied to life and consciousness realms: Critical consideration with positive alternative. In J.J. Chang, J. Fisch and F.-A. Popp (Eds.), *Biophotons* (Kluwer Academic Publishers, pp. 359-373). Dordrecht.

Lipkind, M. (1998d): Alexandre Gurwitch: La théorie du champ biologique. *Fusion* (French edition), No. 71, pp. 4-26. (In French).

Lipkind, M. (1999). The holistic quality in biology: ontology, epistemology, and causation. *Coherence – International Journal of Integrated Medicine*, No. 2, 4-18.

Lipkind, M. (2000). The holistic quality in biology in view of the Gurwitschian field principle: ontology, epistemology, and causation. In L. Beloussov, F.-A. Popp, V. Voeikov, and R. Van Wijk (Eds.), *Biophotonics and Coherent Systems* (Moscow University Press, pp. 27-41). Moscow.

Lipkind, M. (2003). Definition of consciousness: Impossible and unnecessary? In F.-A. Popp and L. Beloussov (Eds.), *Integrative Biophysics* (Kluwer Academic Publishers, pp. 467-503). Dordrecht.

Lipkind, M. (2005). The field concept in current models of consciousness: A tool for solving the Hard Problem? *Mind and Matter*, 3, 29-85.

Lipkind, M. (2006). Free will and violation of physical laws: A new concept of volition based on A. Gurwitsch's field theory. In L. V. Beloussov, V. Voeikov, and V. N. Martynyuk (Eds.), *Biophotonics and Coherent Systems in Biology* (Springer US). New York. (In Press).

Lipkind, M. (2006). The hard problem and naturalistic meaning of the extra ingredient. *Mind and Matter*. (Submitted).

Livingstone, M. S. and Hubel, D. H. (1987). Psychophysical evidence for separate channels for the perception of form, color, movement, and depth. *The Journal of Neuroscience*, 7, 3416-3468.

Loeb, J. (1906). *The Dynamics of Living Matter*. New York: Columbia University Press.

Loeb, J. (1912). *The Mechanistic Conception of Life*. Chicago: University Chicago Press.

Lotka, A. (1925). *Elements of Physical Biology*. Baltimore: Williams and Wilkins; Republished in 1956 as *Elements of Mathematical Biology*. New York: Dover.

Mahan, B. M. and Myers, R .J. (1987). *University Chemistry*, 4th edition. Menlo Park, CA, Reading, MA, Don Mills, Ont., Workingham, Amsterdam, Sydney, Singapore, Tokyo, Madrid, Bogota, Santiago, San Juan: The Benjamin/Cummings Publishing House.

Mayr, E. (1961): Cause and effect in biology. *Science,* 134, 1501-1506.

McDougall, W. (1938). *The Riddle of Life: A Survey of Theories*. London: Methuen.

McFadden, J. (2000). *Quantum evolution*. London: Harper Collins.

McFadden, J. (2002a). Synchronous firing and its influence on the brain's electromagnetic field: Evidence for an electromagnetic theory of consciousness. *Journal of Consciousness Studies*, 9, 23-50.

McFadden, J. (2002b). The conscious electromagnetic information (cemi) field theory: The hard problem made easy? *Journal of Consciousness Studies*, 9, 45-60.

Monod, J. (1971). *Chance and Necessity: An Essay on the Natural Philosophy of Modern Biology*. New York: Knopf.

Montero, B. (2003). Varieties of causal closure. In S. Walter and H.-D. Heckmann (Eds.), *Physicalism and Mental Causation: The Metaphysics of Mind and Action* (Imprint Academic, pp. 173-187). Exeter, UK.

Moore, G.,E. (1922). *Philosophical Studies*. London: Routledge and Kegan Paul.

Nagel, E. and Newman, J. (1958). *Gödel's Proof*. London, Boston, Henley UK: Routledge and Kegan Paul.

Nagel, T. (1974). What is it like to be a bat? *Philosophical Review*, 83, 435-450.

Obeso, J. A., Rothwell, J. C. and Marsden, C. D. (1981). Simple tics in Gilles de la Tourette syndrome are not prefaced by a normal premovement EEG potential. *Journal of Neurology, Neurosurgery and Psychiatry*, 44, 735-738.

Pagels, H.,R. (1985). *Perfect Symmetry*. New York: Simon and Schuster.

Penrose, R. (1989). *The Emperor's New Mind*. Oxford: Oxford University Press.

Penrose, R. (1994). *Shadows of the Mind*. Oxford: Oxford University Press.

Pockett, S. (1999). Anaesthesia and the electrophysiology of auditory consciousness. *Consciousness and Cognition*, 8: 45-61.

Pockett, S. (2000). *The nature of consciousness: A hypothesis*. Lincoln NE: Universe Ltd.

Pockett, S. (2002a). Difficulties with the electromagnetic field theory of consciousness. *Journal of Consciousness Studies*, 9, 51-56.

Prigogine, I and Stengers, I. (1984). *Order out of Chaos*. New York: Bantam.

Ramachandran, V. S. (1990). Visual perception in people and machines. In A. Balke and T. Troscziankopp (Eds.), *AI and the Eye* (John Wiley and Sons Ltd., pp. 21-77). New York.

Ramachandran, V. S. and Anstis, S. M. (1986). The perception of apparent motion. *Scientific American*, 254, 101-109.

Revonsuo, A. (2000). Prospects for a scientific research program on consciousness. In T. Metzinger (Ed.), *Neural Correlates of Consciousness* (Bradford Book, MIT Press, pp. 57-75). Cambridge MA, London.

Romijn, H. (2002). Are virtual photons the elementary carriers of consciousness? *Journal of Consciousness Studies*, 9, 61-81.

Rosenberg, G. H. (1996). Rethinking nature: hard problem within the hard problem. *Journal of Consciousness Studies*, 3, 76-88.

Searle, J. (2000a). Consciousness and free action. In *Toward a Science of Consciousness*, Tucson 2000, Consciousness Research Abstracts, Tucson AZ, April 10-15, 2000, p. 70, Abstract 123, PL9.

Searle, J. (2000b). Consciousness. *Annual Revue of Neuroscience*, 23, 557-578.

Searle, J. (2000c). Consciousness, free action, and the brain. *Journal of Consciousness Studies*, 7, 3-22.

Sheldrake R. (1986): Morphogenic fields: Nature's habits. In R. Weber (Ed.), *Dialogues with scientists and sages:Tthe search for unity* (Penguin Group, Arkana, pp. 71-88). London.

Sheldrake, R. (1981). *A New Science of Life: The Hypothesis of Formative Causation*. Los Angeles: Tarcher.

Sheldrake, R. (1993). Morphic resonance and collective memory. *Proceedings of the 2nd Symposium on Consciousness*, pp. 93-98. Athens (January 1992).

Sheldrake, R. (1994a). *Seven experiments that could change the world: A do-it-yourself guide to revolutionary science*. London: Fourth Estate.

Sheldrake, R. (1994b). Experiments that could change the world. *Network*, 54, 8-10.

Sirag, S.-P. (1993). *Consciousness: A hyperspace view*. Appendix in J. Mishlove (Ed.), *Roots of Consciousness* (Council Oak, pp. 327-365). Tulsa.

Sirag, S.-P. (1996). A mathematical strategy for a theory of consciousness. In S. R. Hameroff, A. W. Kaczniak, and A. C. Scott (Eds.), *Toward a Science of Consciousness* (MIT Press, pp. 579-588). Cambridge MA.

Sutherland, N. S. (1989). Consciousness. In: N.S. Sutherland (Ed.), *The Macmillan Dictionary of Psychology* (Macmillan, p. 90). London.

Szent-Gyorgi, A. (1957). *Bioenergetics*. New York: Academic Press.

Treisman. A. (1986). Features and objects in visual processing. *Scientific American*, 254, 114-125.

Wächterhauser, G. (1988). Before enzymes and templates: theory of surface metabolism. *Microbiological Reviews*, 52, 452-484.

Waddington, C. H. (1966). Fields and Gradients. In M. Locke (Ed.), *Major Problems in Developmental Biology* (Academic Press, pp. 105-124). New York, London.

Waddington, C. H. (1968). The basic ideas in biology. In C. H. Waddington (Ed.), *Towards a Theoretical Biology: Prolegomena* (Aldine Publishing Co., pp. 1-31). Birmingham.

Wegner, D. M. (2002). *The Illusion of Conscious Will*. Cambridge, MA, London: The MIT Press.

Weiss, P. (1939). *Principles of Development*. New York: Holt, Rinehart and Winston.

Welch, G. R. (1992). An analogical 'field' construct in cellular biophysics: history and present status. *Progress in Biophysics and Molecular Biology*, 57, 71-128.

Wilkes, K. V. (1984). Is consciousness important? *British Journal of the Philosophy of Science*, 35, 223-243.

Wilkes, K. V. (1988). – , yishi, duh, um, and consciousness. In A. Marcel and E. Bisiach (Eds.), *Consciousness in Contemporary Science* (Oxford University Press, pp. 17-41). Oxford.

Wilson, D. L. (1999). Mind-brain interaction and violation of physical laws. *Journal of Consciousness Studies*, 6, 185-200.

Zeki, S. (1992). The visual image in mind and brain. *Scientific American*, 254, 68-77.

Zeki, S. (2000). The disunity of consciousness. *Consciousness and Cognition* 9(2), S30.

In: Consciousness and Learning Research
Editor: Susan K. Turrini, pp. 47-61

ISBN 1-60021-333-2
© 2007 Nova Science Publishers, Inc.

Chapter 2

RECONSIDERING AN INDEPENDENCE ASSUMPTION IN DISSOCIATING CONSCIOUS AND UNCONSCIOUS MEMORIES

Leonard D. Stern

Eastern Washington University, Cheney, WA 99004, USA

ABSTRACT

A fundamental issue in memory research is whether performance based on conscious and unconscious mental processes can be experimentally distinguished in unimpaired individuals. Although Jacoby's (1991) process dissociation procedure (PDP) appears to be successful in assessing the separate contributions to memory performance of these two processes, the procedure is controversial because of evidence that requisite assumptions of independence between the processes may not hold. Studies by Curren and Hintzman (1995) have demonstrated that violating a particular independence assumption can cause the PDP to yield invalid estimates of unconscious processes. The studies described here question the generality of Curren and Hintzman's conclusions. It is suggested that their results may have been due to a minority of their stimuli having unusually low probabilities of being produced in a word stem completion task by conscious and unconscious processes. Using existing data of Stern, McNaught-Davis, and Barker (2003) that utilized the PDP to estimate conscious and unconscious contributions to a memory task, the effects of including items with low probabilities of being output through these two processes are examined. As the proportion of the low probability items is increased, outcomes similar to those described by Curren and Hintzman are obtained that characterize violations of the crucial independence assumption. A model is introduced to help explain these outcomes. It is concluded that violating an underlying assumption of independence is not an inevitable consequence of applying the PDP but, rather, may represent a special circumstance that can be avoided or corrected.

INTRODUCTION

Jacoby's (1991) process-dissociation procedure (PDP) is intended to assess the separate contributions of conscious and unconscious processes to performance of a memory task. The PDP is consistent with the idea that conscious experiences are verbally describable, a view that Schooler and Fiore (1997) characterize as "the standard criterion for determining whether an event/process was consciously experienced" (p. 241). The PDP is implemented using inclusion and exclusion test instructions. For example, if participants have processed a list of words, exclusion test instructions request that a word stem (e.g., sli_ _) be completed to form a word other than one from the study list. Stems completed to form studied words under these circumstances can be attributed to unconscious processes because the completions occur in spite of attempts to exclude words based on information that would allow their prior study to be described. Inclusion test instructions request that each stem be completed to form a studied word, or, if one cannot be provided, the first suitable word that comes to mind. Studied words provided·under these instructions can be attributed to a combination of conscious and unconscious processes.

What might be the relation between conscious and unconscious processes? There are good theoretical reasons to expect dependencies between the two. Reder and Gordon (1997), for example, suggest that the distinction between conscious and unconscious processes is a function of the activation level of a concept's representation in memory whereby concepts enter consciousness when their activation energy exceeds threshold; otherwise, a concept may be cognitively available at a subliminal level to the extent it has become activated through, for example, repetition or exposure duration. Reber's (1992) evolutionary view that posits brain structures responsible for consciousness evolved from more primitive systems operating unconsciously also suggests possible bases for their interdependence. However, in both views, if different tasks tap different representational systems (e.g., the perceptual and semantic system in Reder and Gordon's view) then conscious and unconscious processes can appear to operate independently. The idea that memory consists of separable subsystems responsible for processing different forms of information is embodied in Johnson's MEM framework which is comprised of 16 components whose domains of operations most broadly distinguish between perceptual and reflective operations. In Johnson and Reeder's (1997) words "although most tasks are unlikely to tap into one subsystem only, dissociations among memory measures are nevertheless likely because different measures draw disproportionately on different memory subsystems" (p. 274).

Jacoby's PDP is based on the assumption that conscious and unconscious processes are independent. The independence assumption has not gone unquestioned (e.g., Bodner, Masson and Caldwell, 2000; Joordens and Merikle, 1993) but has been held as tenable until contrary evidence is available (Jones, 1987; Jacoby, Yonelinas, and Jennings, 1996). The independence assumption is advantageous in that it allows calculation of a conscious (C) and an unconscious (U) component to a memory task from performance based on inclusion and exclusion test instructions. For participants who have processed a list of words and are tested with a word stem completion task, the probability of completing a stem with an old word under exclusion test instructions is the probability that the word is not consciously remembered (1–C) but comes automatically to mind based on unconscious processes (U) as depicted in the following formula:

$$P_{old|exclusion} = (1-C)U \tag{1}$$

Under inclusion test instructions, the probability of completing a stem is the probability the word is consciously remembered (C) plus the probability that it is not consciously remembered but is provided on the basis of unconscious processes as depicted in the formula shown below:

$$P_{old|inclusion} = C + (1-C)U \tag{2}$$

These formulas allow the value of C to be obtained after $P_{old|exclusion}$ and $P_{old|inclusion}$ have been determined in an experiment:

$$C = P_{old|inclusion} - P_{old|exclusion} \tag{3}$$

Having solved for C, it is possible to obtain the value of U:

$$U = P_{old|exclusion} / (1-C) \tag{4}$$

Although the PDP has been usefully applied to a number of memory phenomena (Bergerbest and Goshen-Gottstein, 2002; Hertel and Milan, 1994; LeCompte, 1995; Payne, 2001) data presented by Curren and Hintzman (1995) have called into question the validity of its estimates of U. According to Curren and Hintzman, when a word's susceptibility to processes underlying C and U are correlated, a circumstance Curren and Hintzman term violation of stochastic indepencence, estimates of U derived from the PDP will be biased low. Stochastic independence will not hold, for example, if high frequency words are both consciously more retrievable and more readily come to mind due to unconscious processes. Because the PDP determines the value of U only after retrieval on the basis of C fails, then, when stochastic independence does not hold, estimates of U are based on words whose U values are relatively low.

To demonstrate their claim, Curren and Hintzman varied the presentation duration of words in a study list, a manipulation expected to affect C but not U (Greene, 1986; Neill, Beck, Bottalico, and Molloy, 1990). In several studies, Curren and Hintzman found the PDP yielded predicted increases in C as study duration increased, but, paradoxically, lowered estimates of U. The left panel of Figure 1 illustrates Curren and Hintzman's account of these findings. It shows that when estimates of U are based only on words not produced by processes underlying C, U estimates will be lowered as a result of a positive association between a word's susceptibility to being provided by processes underlying C and U.

In addition to demonstrating artifactual dissociation of C and U based on means pooled over words and participants, Curren and Hintzman supported their account with correlations obtained by pooling data over words or over participants. From estimates of C and U obtained by pooling over words, it was found that participants with high C estimates tended to have low U estimates; pooled over participants, estimates of C and U were found to be positively associated for old words (i.e., C_{old} and U_{old}), as were C_{old} and U_{new} and U_{new} and U_{old}.

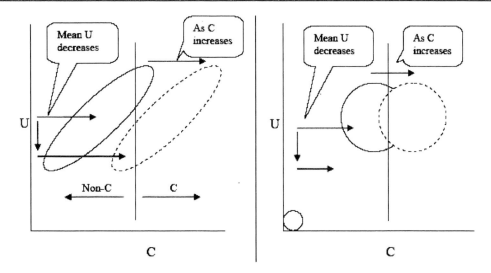

Figure 1. Theoretical distributions of C and U values of words used in the PDP. The left panel depicts
Curren and Hintzman's (1995) view; the right panel depicts the proposed view.

Curren and Hintzman were initially cautious about implications of their findings to the
PDP in general as well as to word stem completion tasks in particular saying that their results
"do not necessarily impugn the independence and strategy assumptions beyond the particulars
of the present experiments, but they do suggest that these assumptions need to be more
thoroughly evaluated in any application of the process-dissociation procedure" (1995, p. 546).
In a subsequent response to Jacoby, Begg, and Toth (1997), Curren and Hintzman (1997)
were more forceful in their criticism of the PDP applied to word stem completion tasks saying
the procedure "is founded on assumptions that can be difficult to understand, even more
difficult to empirically evaluate, and unlikely to be entirely correct. . . . We maintain that
independence is not a good assumption when process dissociation is applied to word-stem
completion." (p. 503).

To help assess the impact of Curren and Hintzman's criticisms of the PDP, the search
phrase "process dissociation procedure" was entered into *PsychInfo*. Figure 2 shows the
number of articles returned as a function of year of publication. Considering the lag between
planning and publishing research, the data are consistent with the possibility that Curren and
Hintzman's (1995) article has contributed to a decline in the perceived usefulness of the PDP.

Although Curren and Hintzman presented important evidence that has evidently raised
serious concerns about the validity of estimates of U obtained with the PDP in word stem
completion tasks, a number of findings are not readily reconcilable with their view. One is
that other manipulations that theoretically should increase C but not affect U do not
consistently reveal artifactual dissociation of C and U. For example, Toth, Reingold, and
Jacoby (1994) manipulated level of processing (participants either rated a word's pleasantness
or detected whether the current word shared vowels with the previous word) and found that
type of processing had a significant effect on C but not U. Stern et al. (2003) obtained similar
results in their Experiments 1a and 1b. Jacoby, Begg, and Toth (1997) list a number of studies
in their Table 1 that employed a divided attention manipulation and used the PDP to derive C
and U estimates from word stem or word fragment completion tasks. There was no consistent
evidence in these studies that U decreased when C increased. According to Curren and

Hintzman, such inconsistencies may result from lack of statistical power and/or impure effects of the manipulation on C and U. An example of the latter possibility would be divided attention decreasing both C and U. Under these circumstances U could fall because of the attention manipulation and rise because of correlational effects (see bottom panel of Curren and Hintzman's (1994) Figure 1).

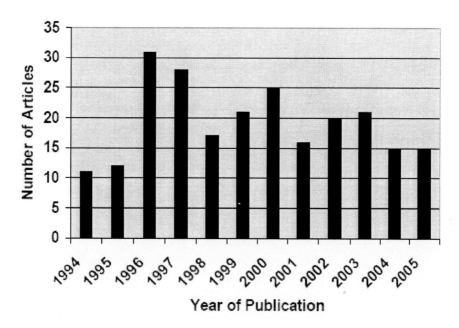

Figure 2. Number of Published Articles on the PDP as a Function of Year of Publication.

A second problem with Curren and Hintzman's interpretation of their findings is that patterns of outcomes they use to support violations of the assumption of stochastic independence appear to occur when subjects adopt a generate-recognize but not a direct retrieval strategy in word stem completion (Jacoby, 1998). Jacoby suggests that, as in the case of statistical procedures that are valid when underlying assumptions hold, the C and U estimates produced by the PDP are valid only when participants adopt a direct retrieval and not a generate-recognize strategy in word stem completion.

An important issue, then, is whether PDP-derived estimates of U from word stem completion tasks are fundamentally flawed because stochastic independence can never be assumed or whether violations of this assumption can be avoided. The possibility explored here is that the effects of violating stochastic independence demonstrated by Curren and Hintzman were due, at least in part, to a minority of their stimuli having very low probabilities of being consciously retrieved or coming automatically to mind during testing. The suggested situation may be conceived of as a polarized version of Curren and Hintzman's view, and is pictured in the right panel of Figure 1. It is suggested here that excluding most of these stimuli, referred to here as non-performing words, can reduce the chances of finding outcomes characteristic of violations of the assumption of stochastic independence.

SIMULATIONS

The effects on PDP-derived estimates of U due to words with unusually low C and U values in a word stem completion task will be examined using data obtained in study 1 of Stern, McNaught-Davis, and Barker (2003). The intent of the Stern et al. study was to examine the effectiveness of a Guided PDP (GPDP) that tested memory with a sequence of two questions. The first asked whether the participant recognized a test stem as corresponding to a previously rated word and the second depended on the participant's recognition decision and the test instruction condition (inclusion, exclusion). In the inclusion test instruction condition, participants who recognized the test stem were asked to provide the remembered completion; participants who did not were asked to provide the first suitable word that came, to mind. In the exclusion test condition, participants who recognized the test stem were asked to provide a different word as the completion; participants who did not recognize the stem were asked to provide the first suitable completion that came to mind. As can be seen in Table 1, the pattern of GPDP-derived estimates of C and U were similar to that obtained by Toth, Reingold, and Jacoby (1994) who used a study task that had participants process list words semantically or nonsemantically and obtained C and U estimates with conventional PDP instructions. The procedures used in Stern et al.'s studies 1a and 1b were closely matched to those of Toth et al. with the exception of the method for achieving process dissociation.

Table 1. Mean C and U Estimates as a Function of Study List Processing and PDP Method Obtained by Stern et al. (2003) and Toth et al. (1994)

Experiment	PDP Method	Memory Component	Type of Processing	
			Nonsemantic	Semantic
Stern et al. Exp. 1a	Standard (N=60)	C	.00	.27
		U	.48	.44
	Guided (N=60)	C	.06	.23
		U	.47	.50
Stern et al. Exp. 1b	Standard (N=27)	C	-.04	.29
		U	.45	.34
	Guided (N=26)	C	.04	.23
		U	.46	.51
Toth et al.	Standard	C	.03	.27
		U	.45	.42

If the presence of nonperforming words was important in producing evidence Curren and Hintzman used to demonstrate violation of the assumption of stochastic independence, then including words with zero values of C and U in Stern et al.'s Experiment 1 data should produce similar outcomes. Specifically, as nonperforming words are added to the Stern et al. data, evidence should become increasingly apparent of a paradoxical dissociation of C and U when data are collapsed over participants and words, of a negative correlation between estimates of C_{old} and U_{old} when data are collapsed over words, and of a positive correlation between C_{old} and U_{old} when data are collapsed over participants.

Paradoxical Dissociation

Data from Stern et al.'s Experiment 1a were used to examine the effect of nonperforming words on paradoxical dissociation of C and U estimates. To simulate successive increments of 10% nonperforming words on mean C and U values, each participant's C value and the probability of providing an old word in the exclusion test condition (i.e., $P_{old|exclusion}$) were divided by 1.0 plus and increment of 0.1 for each successive 10% nonperforming word increment. Using these new values, each participant's U value was then calculated. An example of these adjustments and an explanation of the underlying reasoning for them are presented later in this chapter.

Table 2 shows the effect of successive 10% increments of nonperforming words on mean C and U estimates of participants in the combined standard and guided PDP instructions conditions of Stern et al.'s Experiment 1a. The data indicate that as the percent of nonperforming words is increased by units of 10, a paradoxical dissociation of C and U appears and that the difference between the U values in the semantic and nonsemantic processing conditions becomes statistically significant ($t(119) = -2.13$, $p < .05$) when 40% of the test items are nonperforming.

Table 2. Effects of Nonperforming Words on Mean C and U Values Based on Participant Means of Stern et al.'s Experiment 1a

% Increment of Nonperforming Words	Mean C		Mean U		$\overline{U}_{semantic} - \overline{U}_{nonsemantic}$	
	Semantic	Non-semantic	Semantic	Non-semantic	$t(119)$	Significance level
0	.25	.03	.47	.47	-0.29	.78
10	.23	.03	.40	.43	-1.03	.30
20	.21	.03	.36	.39	-1.53	.13
30	.19	.03	.32	.36	-1.87	.06
40	.18	.02	.30	.33	-2.13	.04

Correlations

Calculated from participant means. Data from Experiment 1a of Stern et al. were used to examine the effect of nonperforming words on correlations between C_{old} and U_{old} obtained from participant means. To reduce biasing effects due to exclusion = 0 data (see later discussion) any participant with an exclusion score of zero in the semantic or nonsemantic processing condition of the control or guided instruction condition was eliminated from the analysis (N = 14). Table 3 shows correlations between C_{old} and U_{old} as a function of % nonperforming words included in the data set. It can be seen that with successive 10%

increments of nonperforming words, the correlation becomes increasingly negative and statistically significant.

Table 3. Effects of Nonperforming Words on Correlation between C_{old} and U_{old} Based on Participant Means of Stern et al.'s Experiment 1s

% Increment of Nonperforming Words		
	r	2-Tail Significance level
0	-.12	.22
10	-.22	.03
20	-.29	.01

Calculated from word means. Data from Stern et al.'s Experiment 1b were used to investigate the effect of nonperforming words on correlations between C_{old} and U_{old} based on word means. Experiment 1b, a replication of Experiment 1a was utilized because not all data of participants' responses to individual words were available from Experiment 1a. To perform the analysis, for each of the 80 test words, the proportion of participants completing a stem to form a semantically or nonsemantically processed item was calculated and these proportions converted to form C and U values for each word. Table 4 shows that the correlation between C_{old} and U_{old} for the 80 test words was close to zero ($r = .02$) before any nonperforming words were added, and that with successive increments of eight words with zero C and U values, the correlation became increasingly positive and reached statistical significance when 24 nonperforming words had been added ($r(102) = .19, p < .05$). Table 4 also shows correlations between C_{old} and U_{new} as a function of 10% increments of nonperforming words. That the pattern of correlations between C_{old} and U_{new} and C_{old} and U_{old} is similar is not surprising given the correlation between U_{old} and U_{new} for the original set of 80 words was highly significant ($r(78) = .55, p < .01$).

Table 4. Effects of Nonperforming Words on Correlation between C_{old} and U_{old} and C_{old} and U_{new} Based on Word Means of Stern et al.'s Experiment 1b

% Increment of Nonperforming Words	C_{old} and U_{old}		C_{old} and U_{new}	
	r	2-Tail Significance level	r	2-Tail Significance level
0	.02	.84	.06	.61
10	.11	.33	.12	.25
20	.16	.13	.17	.10
30	.19	.05	.20	.04
40	.22	.02	.23	.02

DISCUSSION

One important implication of these analyses is that progressive underestimation of U with increases in C may not be an inevitable consequence of application of the PDP but, instead, represent a special circumstance. That is, Curren and Hintzman's results may partly have been due to inclusion of a number of nonperforming words in study lists. Their Experiment 1, for example, utilized words that ranged in length from 5-9 letters and had stems that could be completed to form between 5-29 words. As reflected in the low baseline completion rate (M = .12), participants, even in the 10-sec study duration condition, may have failed to complete a number of stems to form target words. Curren and Hintzman's Experiment 5, which provided the best evidence of artifactual dissociation, utilized 5-letter words, as did all experiments of Stern et al. However, unlike the words used by Stern et al. (as well as others, e.g., Jacoby, 1998) which had baseline completion rates of .20-.67 (M = .39) those of Curren and Hintzman included some with zero baseline completion rates (range = 0-.88) and thus may have produced effects shown here to arise from the presence of nonperforming words.

Models

Two models will be presented to help clarify proposed mechanisms underlying data produced in a PDP. One model, termed the fast-food model, will take a narrative form; the other, termed the 2-coin model, will be more abstract.

Fast-food model. Consider a fast-food restaurant that offers its customers a game with monetary awards. Customers using a drive-through window or those ordering at a counter can be instant winners if a ticket attached to a food purchase so indicates. Customers whose ticket does not signal a win can follow instructions to mail in their losing ticket together with identifying information for an alternate chance to win.

Imagine, now, a complication in the process. Managers of the restaurant chain, wishing to reduce the chance there will be disgruntled customers who don't win instantly and then fail to attend to instructions to mail losing tickets, require those who win by mail to not disclose details of their award. Thus, two classes of winners will exist: those who win instantly and can talk about the experience and those who win by mail and are not able to describe the experience.

Figure 3 gives illustrative details. The left panel shows the path of customers who have a 40% chance of being an instant winner and a 30% chance of winning by mail. The right panel differs only in that the chance of being an instant winner is 80%. Note that the probability of winning instantly and the probability of winning by mail are being treated as independent: changes in the probability of one, do not affect the probability of the other.

What if a suspicious outside observer wished to determine the probabilities of winning instantly or by mail. The observer could, by questioning customers, determine the probability of winning an award regardless of the mechanism, a probability we can call the inclusion rate. The observer could also, by interviewing people, exclude anyone who readily gave details of how the award was arrived at, a resulting probability we can call the exclusion rate. For the probabilities shown in the left panel of Figure 3, $P_{win|inclusion} = .40 + .18 = .58$ and $P_{win|exclusion} = .18$. Using equations 5 and 6 shown below, which are similar to equations 3 and 4, produces the values of .40 and .30 as the probabilities of winning instantly or by mail, respectively. For data shown in the left panel of Figure 3, $P_{win|inclusion} = .86$ and $P_{win|exclusion} = .06$; application of the formulas 5 and 6 yield probabilities of winning instantly and by mail of .80 and .30, respectively.

$$P_{win|instant} = P_{win|inclusion} - P_{win|inclusion} \tag{5}$$

$$P_{win|mail} = P_{win|exclusion} / (1 - P_{win|instant}) \tag{6}$$

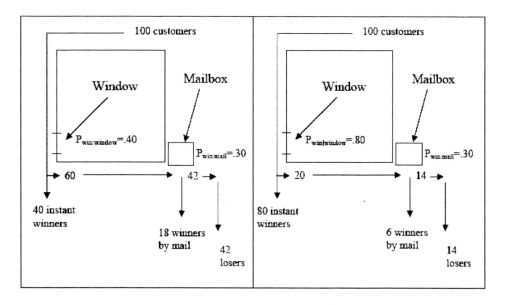

Figure 3. A representation of the fast-food model of process dissociation. 100 customers enter at the top and have either a 40% (left panel) or 80% (right panel) chance of being instant winners, and a 30% chance of subsequently winning by mail.

Consider, now, a further complication. Let some customers be diligent in following the rules of the game (referred to here as lucky customers) and others be careless (unlucky). Figure 4 shows outcomes of the game when 50% of the customers are lucky and 50% are unlucky (i.e., have a 0% chance of winning). From the left panel of Figure 4 it can be seen that the inclusion rate is .29 and the exclusion rate is .09. Inclusion and exclusion rates for the right panel are .43 and .03, respectively. Application of equations 5 and 6 yield the following probabilities of winning for situations depicted in the left and right panels of Figure 4:

$P_{win|instant} = .29 - .09 = .20$ $P_{win|instant} = .43 - .03 = .40$

$P_{win|mail} = .09 / (1 - .20) = .11$ $P_{win|mail} = .03 / (1 - .40) = .05$

One important outcome to note is that as the probability of winning instantly increases (left vs. right panel of Figure 4), the calculated probability of winning instantly also increases; however, the calculated probability of winning by mail decreases even though its actual probability does not change. This outcome is analogous to artifactual dissociation. The model also can be used to explain the correlations between probabilities of the two processes that may occur when data are collapsed in different ways. First, understand that in the fast-food model, customers are analogous to words in a process dissociation study and that each restaurant is analogous to an individual participant. On the basis of the two cases depicted in Figure 4 it can be seen that if data are combined over customers (words), restaurants (participants) with probabilities of instant wins (C) that are higher than the mean would tend to have lower probabilities of wins by mail (U), producing a negative correlation between the two probabilities.

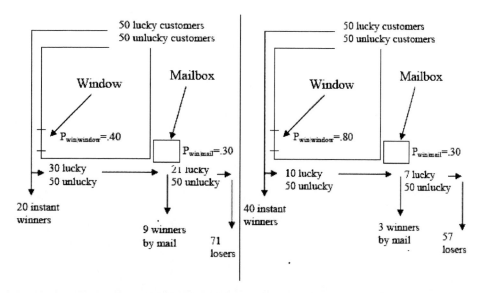

Figure 4. A representation of the fast-food model of process dissociation in which 50 lucky and 50 unlucky customers have either a 40% (left panel) or 80% (right panel) chance of being instant winners, and a 30% chance of subsequently winning by mail.

Furthermore, if, in the fast-food analogy, lucky and unlucky customers visit multiple restaurants offering the game, then, when data are combined over restaurants (participants) customers (words) who have high chances of winning instantly (C) will, because they are lucky, also have high chances of winning by mail (U), yielding a positive correlation between the variables.

An exclusion score of zero in the model corresponds to no one winning by mail. If the probability of winning by mail is greater than zero an exclusion score of zero can be due to chance or it can occur because the probability of winning instantly is sufficiently high to eliminate the possibility of a win by mail (or because of a combination of these circumstances). When the probability of winning by mail is greater than zero, these mechanisms contribute to underestimating the probability of winning this way, a consequence that, in the context of PDP studies, has been remedied by eliminating from analysis data of participants with exclusion scores of zero (Jacoby, Toth and Yonelinas, 1993). This same procedure was implemented here earlier in analyzing the correlation of C_{old} and U_{old} based on participant means.

Two-coin model. The 2-coin model, like the fast-food model, incorporates the idea that C is assessed before U. Imagine that 2 coins are available to be tossed and that the toss of coin 2, which represents U, occurs only when that of coin 1, which represents C, results in a failure. If the probability of a success in the toss of coin 1 is .40 and the probability of a success in the toss of coin 2 is .30, then, out of 100 plays the number of successes that can be expected is 40 from the toss of coin 1 and an additional 18 from coin 2 for a total of 58. If the probability of a success from the toss of coin 1 is raised to .80, then the total number of successes from tosses of both coins out of 100 plays will be 86. These outcomes are depicted in the top panel of Figure 5. Note that in Figure 5, the expected number of successes (i.e., number of words in the PDP) is shown at each node of a branch and the probability of a success (i.e., the probability of producing a target word in the PDP) is shown above or below each branch. Also note that in the 2-coin model, the total number of successes corresponds to an inclusion score and the number of successes from the toss of coin 2 corresponds to an exclusion score.

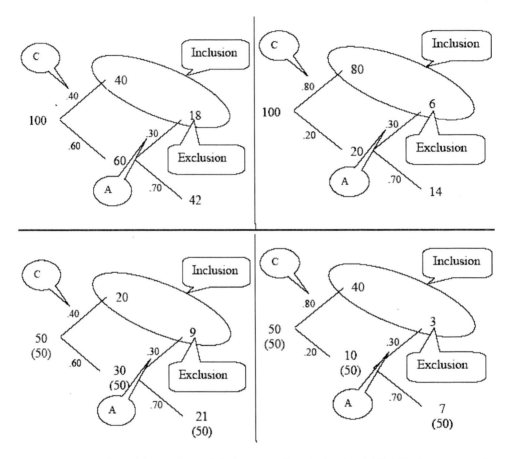

Figure 5. A representation of the 2-coin model of process dissociation in which 100 plays can result in a success in the toss of coin 1 at either a rate of 40% (left panel) or 80% (right panel) and a success in the toss of coin 2 at a rate of 30%. The bottom panel shows expected outcomes from these same probabilities when 50% of the plays are guaranteed failures.

If one were given inclusion and exclusion probabilities (.58 and .18, respectively for data shown in the left panel of Figure 5, and .80 and .06, respectively for data shown in the right panel of Figure 5) one could apply equations 3 and 4 to calculate the probabilities of successful outcomes of the tosses of coins 1 and 2.

Consider now the results if, in half the plays, the outcome was a failure in the toss of both coin1 and coin 2. These outcomes, which in the PDP represent the effects of nonperforming words, are depicted in the lower panels of Figure 5. Application of Equations 3 and 4 to the inclusion and exclusion probabilities would produce C and U estimates characteristic of paradoxical dissociation.

The adjustments made previously to simulate the effect of adding nonperforming words to a data set will be illustrated using the 2-coin model. As described earlier, these adjustments had mean C and mean probability of producing an old word in the exclusion test conditions of each participant divided by 1 plus an increment of .10 for each additional 10% of nonperforming words added to the data set. Figure 6 shows the effects on inclusion and exclusion scores resulting from adding 10 nonperforming words to a set of 100 test words with arbitrarily selected C and U values of .20 and .50, respectively. Note that number of nonperforming words in Figure 6 are shown in parentheses at the node of branches and that C and U values calculated when nonperforming words are present are shown in parentheses above branches. For the data shown in the left panel where an additional 10% of the words are nonperforming, C obtained from equation 3 is .1818 (i.e., 20/110) and the exclusion score is .3636 (i.e., 40/110), so, using equation 4, U = .3636/(1-.1818) = .44. The right panel of Figure 6 show C and U probabilities obtained when the data set contains an extra 20% nonperforming words.

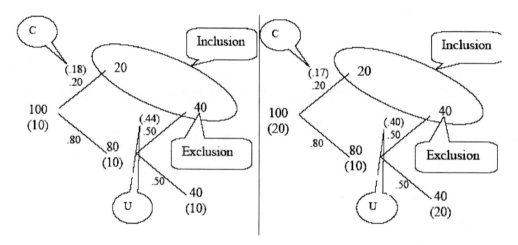

Figure 6. Effects of 10 % (left panel) and 20% (right panel) nonperforming words on arbitrarily selected values of C and U.

CONCLUSION

Curren and Hintzman (1995) underscored an important assumption underlying use of the PDP in producing valid estimates of the separate contributions of conscious and unconscious processes to a memory task. They demonstrated that violating the assumption of stochastic independence can lead to artifactual dissociation of C and U estimates whereby manipulations that do not affect processes contributing to U but do affect those contributing to C yield estimates of these components that change in opposite directions; that is, as estimates of C increase, estimates of U decrease. Violating the assumption of stochastic independence also was shown to produce correlations between estimates of C and U that are negative when data are collapsed over words and positive when data are collapsed over participants.

Simulations presented here indicate that in a stem completion task, words that are unlikely to be produced on the basis of processes underlying C and U can make important contributions to effects that characterize violations of stochastic independence. Data of Stern et al. (2003) that exhibited no significant effects characteristic of violation of stochastic independence increasingly displayed these effects as nonperforming words were incorporated into the data set.

Although these demonstrations do not establish that nonperforming words were responsible for Curren and Hintzman's results, they do suggest that when using the PDP, care be given to choosing stimuli for a word stem completion task. Perhaps the approach used by Stolz and Merikle (2000) is advisable. They selected as stimuli completions that were second most frequently provided for each stem. Through careful choice of stimuli the effects of violating the assumption of stochastic independence appear to be avoidable.

As made apparent in the fast-food model, the stochastic independence assumption is separable from the assumption of process independence. Thus, if, by careful selection of stimuli, one minimizes the effects otherwise brought on by stochastic dependence, one still needs to consider possible violations of process independence in interpreting the values of C and U. It is worth noting that Curren and Hintzman's demonstration of the effects of violating the assumption of stochastic independence is most convincing if one assumes process independence. That is, Curren and Hintzman increased study time to raise C without affecting U.

The approach taken here and in the article by Stern et al. (2003) has been to address possible shortcomings in the PDP by finding methods to avoid or reduce their effects. Because the PDP offers a way to unobtrusively separate conscious and unconscious components of a memory task, finding ways to fine-tune the procedure may be worth the effort.

REFERENCES

Bergerbest, D., and Goshen-Gottstein, Y. (2002). The origins of levels-of-processing effects in conceptual test: Evidence for automatic influences of memory from the process-dissociation procedure. *Memory and Cognition, 30,* 1252-1262.

Bodner, G. E., Masson, M. E. J., and Caldwell, J. I. (2000). Evidence for a generate-recognize model of episodic influences on word-stem completion. *Journal of Experimental Psychology: Learning, Memory, and Cognition, 26,* 267-293.

Curran, T., and Hintzman, D. L. (1995). Violations of the independence assumption in process dissociation. *Journal of Experimental Psychology: Learning, Memory, and Cognition, 21,* 531-547.

Curren, T., and Hintzman, D. L. (1997) consequences and causes of correlations in process dissociation. *Journal of Experimental Psychology: Learning, Memory, and Cognition, 23,* 496-504.

Greene, R. L. (1986). Word stems as cues in recall and completion tasks. *Quarterly Journal of Experimental* Psychology, *38A,* 663-673.

Hertel, P. T., and Milan, S. (1994). Depressive deficits in recognition: Dissociation of recollection and familiarity. *Journal of Abnormal Psychology, 103,* 736-742.

Jacoby, L. L. (1991). A process dissociation framework: Separating automatic from intentional uses of memory. *Journal of Memory and Language, 30,* 513-541.

Jacoby, L. L. (1998). Invariance in automatic influences of memory: Toward a user's guide for the process-dissociation procedure. *Journal of Experimental Psychology: Learning, Memory, and Cognition, 24,* 3-26.

Jacoby, L. L., Begg, I. M., and toth, J. P. (1997). In defense of functional independence: Violations of assumptions underlying the process-dissociation procedure? *Journal of Experimental Psychology: Learning, Memory, and Cognition, 23,* 484-495.

Jacoby, L. L., Toth, J. P., and Yonelinas, A. P. (1993). Separating conscious and unconscious influences of memory: Measuring recollection. *Journal of Experimental Psychology: Learning, Memory, and Cognition, 22,* 139-154.

Jacoby, L. L., Yonelinas, A. P., and Jennings, J. M. (1997). The relation between conscious and unconscious (automatic) influences: A declaration of independence. In J. D. Cohen and J. W. Schooler (Eds.), *Scientific approaches consciousness* (pp. 13-47). Mahwah, NJ, Erlbaum.

Johnson, J. K., and Reeder, J. A. (1997). Consciousness as meta-processing. In J. D. Cohen and J. W. Schooler (Eds.), *Scientific approaches consciousness* (pp. 261-293). Mahwah, NJ, Erlbaum.

Joordens, S., and Merikle, P. M. (1993). Independence or redundancy? Two models of conscious and unconscious influences. *Journal of Experimental Psychology: General, 122,* 462-467.

LeCompte, D. C. (1995). Recollective experience in the revelation effect: Separating the contributions of recollection and familiarity. *Memory and Cognition, 23,* 324-334.

Neill, W. T., Beck, J. L., Bottalico, K. S., and Molloy, R. D. (1990). Effects of intentional versus incidental learning on explicit and implicit tests of memory. *Journal of Experimental Psychology: Learning, Memory, and Cognition, 16,* 457-463.

Payne, K. B. (2001). Prejudice and perception: the role of automatic and controlled processes in misperceiving a weapon. *Journal of Personality and Social Psychology, 81,* 181-192.

Reber, A. S. (1992). An evolutionary context for the cognitive unconscious. *Philosophical Psychology, 5,* 33-52.

Reder, L. M., and Gordon, J. S. (1997). Subliminal perception: Nothing special, cognitively speaking. In J. D. Cohen and J. W. Schooler (Eds.), *Scientific approaches consciousness* (pp. 125-134). Mahwah, NJ, Erlbaum.

Schooler, J. W., and Fiore, S. M. (1997) Consciousness and the limits of language: You can't always say what you think or think what you say. In J. D. Cohen and J. W. Schooler (Eds.), *Scientific approaches consciousness* (pp. 241-257). Mahwah, NJ, Erlbaum.

Stern, L. D., McNaught-Davis, A., and Barker, T. (2003). Process Dissociation Using a Guided Procedure. *Memory and Cognition, 31,* 641-655.

Stolz, J. A., and Merikle, P. M. (2000). Conscious and unconscious influences on memory: Temporal dynamics. *Memory, 8,* 333-343.

Toth, J. P., Reingold, E. M., and Jacoby, L. L. (1994). Toward a redefinition of implicit memory: Process dissociations following elaborative processing and self-generation. *Journal of Experimental Psychology: Learning, Memory, and Cognition, 20,* 290-303.

In: Consciousness and Learning Research
Editor: Susan K. Turrini, pp. 63-77

ISBN 1-60021-333-2
© 2007 Nova Science Publishers, Inc.

Chapter 3

FEAR AND LEARNING

Jacklin Fisher[1] and Jan Horsfall[2]

[1]Faculty of Health Science, Australian Catholic University, Sydney, Australia,
[2]Mental Health Nurse Consultant, Sydney, Australia

ABSTRACT

This chapter explores the consequence of fear and anxiety on student learning in clinical settings. Student identified clinical incidents and their emotional corollary, particularly the emotions of fear and anxiety, provide the focus of the study. Mental health settings were selected because community attitudes towards the mentally ill frequently equate mental illness with the potential for violence, criminality and even homicide. It can be anticipated therefore that health care students undertaking clinical education in mental health settings are likely to be apprehensive and fearful and may confront considerable difficulty attempting to assimilate theory into practice in these learning environments. Data were gathered from one hundred and thirty students undertaking clinical experience in mental health settings. Two hundred and sixty critical incident reports were read and their content analyzed within three broad categories: description of incident, affect produced and effect on student learning. Immediate emotional and cognitive responses and perceived levels of fear and anxiety triggered in the students by the critical incident are reported. The impact of these emotions and cognitions was ascertained through small group debriefing and reflection exercises with the students. The findings from the study demonstrate the need for educators to integrate into the clinical curriculum learning activities aimed at assisting students manage fear and anxiety.

INTRODUCTION

Community attitudes towards the mentally ill remain negative and many people are fearful of mental illness (Bell et al, 1998; Bradshaw and Fisher, 1996; Davies, 1995; Human Rights and Equal Opportunity Commission, 1993; Perese, 1996). It is not the purpose of this chapter to explore the reasons for these negative attitudes except to say that historical notions about the causes of mental illness, and negative portrayals of the mentally ill in movies and other media images have contributed to a powerful negative stereotype that labels all mentally ill people as different and potentially dangerous. Health care students (medical, occupational therapy, social work, nursing) may also hold these negative community attitudes and their first clinical placement in a mental health setting is frequently fraught with apprehension and fear. Additionally, there are many situations in mental health settings where students may observe or become involved in incidents that challenge existing values, attitudes, and ethics. Witnessing a display of aggressive behavior in a client, the use of voluntary and involuntary treatments such as seclusion rooms, medications and electro-convulsive therapy, are likely to be confronting. Bizarre and psychotic behaviors can cause increased anxiety in the students as well as reinforce existing negative attitudes.

Assimilating, transforming and applying theoretical knowledge to professional clinical practice is the focus of student learning in clinical environments. Whilst much research acknowledges the variable nature of the clinical learning environment, and emphasizes reflection on practice to make sense of positive and negative experiences, studies that identify incidents that trigger anxiety and fear and the consequences of these on student learning are scarce. The present research addresses these issues and elucidates the reality of student learning experience in environments where fear and anxiety are high. This chapter examines the relationship between fear and learning arising from research into 130 second-year student nurses' clinical learning experiences in urban Australian mental health settings.

LITERATURE REVIEW

Anxiety is defined as a feeling of apprehension, uneasiness, uncertainty, or dread, the source of which is often unknown or vague (Varcarolis, 2002). In contrast to the less specific precipitants of anxiety, fear is a reaction to a specific known danger. The physiological correlates of anxiety and fear are similar. Pervasive anxiety can undermine self-esteem and impact negatively on a person's daily life, whereas fear is more situation-specific and therefore transitory (Varcarolis, 2002). The term stressor pertains to environmental changes that individuals experience or perceive as challenging, threatening, or damaging to their well being (Varcarolis, 2002). Some people call stressors "stress", but technically stressors are events, experiences, or even thoughts that result in individuals stating that they "feel stressed". Hence, feeling stressed overlaps with feelings of anxiety, which is the most common response to stressors. Anxiety is commonly considered to be the most basic human emotion (Horsfall and Stuhlmiller, 2001).

Stress, anxiety and fear induce physiological, perceptual, cognitive and behavioural responses in the individual. Physiological responses are caused by excessive sympathetic nervous systems arousal and include increased heart rate, elevated blood pressure and increased rate and depth of respirations. Other immediate physiological effects include excessive perspiration and increased muscle tension. Perceptual effects range from heightened sensory awareness in mild anxiety to gross perceptual distortions in severe anxiety. Similarly, when only mildly anxious, positive cognitive changes occur including increased concentration and problem solving abilities. By contrast, difficulties in concentration and thought blocking occur when a person is extremely fearful. Behavioral changes include impaired verbal communication, such as, frequent changes of topic, rapid or loud speech, repetitive questioning, joking and wordiness in moderate anxiety, to ineffective communication arising from fear-based perceptual and cognitive distortion. Nonverbal behavioural changes include tremor, pacing and hand wringing in moderate anxiety, to panic and complete behavior disorganization such as screaming, running wildly or clinging to something or a person in extreme fear (Antai-0tong, 2003; Holmes, 2001). Clearly if anxiety or fearfulness is triggered in students these physiologic, perceptual, cognitive and behavioural responses will impact on their ability to assimilate, transform and apply theoretical knowledge to direct patient care.

Holoday-Worret (1996) considers that student fear and anxiety in mental health settings have two primary sources. These are: negative preconceptions or stereotypes about those who live with a mental illness, and self-doubt or performance inadequacy. Fears focusing on client anger or aggression commonly arise from ongoing stereotypical negative images of mentally ill people portrayed by news and entertainment media.

Other student apprehensions about clinical learning in mental health settings focus on patients and include the following: concerns about having nothing to offer distressed people; not knowing what to talk about; worry about saying the wrong thing and harming patients; and fears that clients may reject them or their attempts to help (Fontaine, 2003). Even though these concerns are couched in patient-focused language, they could equally be understood as student doubts about their skills or themselves in relation to interacting and conversing with clients in mental health facilities. These apprehensions may be realistic for many students who cannot assume they will be able to readily interact with a constructive attitude and approach, or be able to easily find the "right words". On the other hand, many patients are appreciative of a good listener and pick up cues about the students' interest in them as people (Horsfall and Stuhlmiller, 2001).

In mental health settings the apprehensions, concerns and fears of students and novice health professionals commonly correspond with those of recently diagnosed or newly admitted psychiatric clientele. Such patients may have reasonable fears about: the thoughts and feelings intrinsic to a psychotic episode; the hospital, loss of liberty and incarceration; violence at the hands of other patients; and health professionals' skills and behaviors. Furthermore, people who speak English as a second language may worry about not being understood or being prejudiced against, as well as cultural or family attributions of stigma or shame (Horsfall and Stuhlmiller, 2001). These concerns are similar to those of students new to mental health settings. Students may hold fears about: madness in general; their own coping abilities or mental health; their disapproval of psychiatric hospitals whilst having no choice about having to learn about patients with mental illness; patient violence; nurse or doctor criticism or unhelpfulness; and not being understood by clients or staff.

Perese (1996) interviewed 38 baccalaureate-nursing students to identify factors contributing to positive or negative undergraduate experiences in the clinical setting. She found the most commonly cited positive factors included staff professionalism, enthusiasm and acceptance of students, diversity of learning opportunities and direct involvement with patients. The most frequently cited negative factors or environmental stressors were related to student perceptions of staff performance. Similarly Slimmer and colleagues (1990) in a survey of 45 students found significant associations between the clinical learning site and effects on students' attitudes towards mental illness and psychiatric nursing. They found that the most important criterion to evaluate the appropriateness of a clinical learning site was the professional competency of the staff and their active support of student participation in therapeutic activities.

Stevens and Dulhunty (1992) found nursing students at the commencement of their studies held negative attitudes towards mental illness similar to those held in society. However, once in the clinical environment, active support and encouragement by staff, particularly during threatening events, positively changed their attitudes towards mental health nursing (O'Brien 1995). Similarly, greater knowledge and contact with psychiatric patients increased positive attitudes, and student confidence, and reduced fear of people with mental health problems (Ferguson and Hope, 1999; Olade,1979; Napoletano,1981; McLoughlin and Chalmers, 1991; Lam et al. 1994). Furthermore Pye and White (1996) found that placement experience in a mental health facility positively influenced undergraduate students decisions regarding a career in mental health nursing.

A number of authors suggest promoting student reflection on both positive and negative experiences in mental health settings is critical to learning, to increasing self awareness in the students, and to the successful resolution of sometimes confronting events. Pierson's (1998) literature review notes the theoretical underpinnings of reflective practice. She cites Heidegger's notion that reflection involves two modes of thought; calculative thinking defined as "a superficial level of thinking that suggests a superficial looking back at experience that is not unlike looking in a mirror" (Pierson 1998:2), and contemplative thinking involving a "spontaneous and fundamental process of exploration" (Pierson 1998:3) that requires time and cannot be forced or commanded. Heidegger believed that the integration of these two modes of thinking facilitated the development of meaning from experience. Pierson (1998:3) surmises " ...it is the integration of calculative and contemplative thinking that allows the scientist and the artist to create theories and forms that transcend present ways of thinking, doing and being". Severinsson (1998) considers that reflection increases the capacity to understand problems, for example, by reducing the theory practice gap through reflecting on the difference between how things should be done and how they are actually done in the clinical setting. Horsfall (1990) and Johns (1995) noted that it was through students reflecting on practice issues that research findings and theoretical knowledge are assimilated into nursing practice. Johns (1995:4) drew on Carper's (1978) four patterns of learning in clinical settings; "the empirical"; "the personal" involving understanding of the self in the clinical context; "the ethical" concerning the management of conflicting values and "the aesthetic" involving a synthesis of the above into the "skill of knowing, envisioning and responding to clinical situations with appropriate and skilled action". Of these four patterns, the personal, ethical, and aesthetic provide the foci most relevant to student learning in conditions where fear and anxiety in the students are triggered by environmental stressors.

METHOD

Students from a large metropolitan University in Australia participated in the study. The students undertook their mental health clinical practicum over a three-week period in a variety of settings including community mental health centres, psychiatric units attached to general hospitals and designated psychiatric hospitals. For the purposes of evaluating the clinical teaching and learning environment, the clinical teacher obtained permission from the students to collect and collate their written responses to a reflective exercise on critical clinical incidents they observed or participated in. Data was collected from a convenience sample of 130 students from a possible cohort of 248-second year students undertaking their mental health clinical. The sample was selected on the basis that they had completed their clinical experience when the project commenced.

As part of their learning activities each student was requested to outline in writing two critical incidents that they perceived were important to them in some way. The students were asked to explore each incident using the following format adapted from the work of Minghella and Benson (1995).

(1) What actually happened? (the facts)
(2) What did I think/feel about it at the time?
(3) What do I think/feel about it now? (on reflection)
(4) What did I do that I feel I could have done better/differently.
(5) What did I do well?
(6) Thoughts following peer reflection and debriefing.

Hour long peer reflection and debriefing sessions with small groups (eight students to one facilitator) were conducted daily or second daily during the three-week clinical placement. These sessions were aimed at developing deeper "contemplative thinking" in the student (Pierson 1998:3). During these sessions critical incidents identified by the students were discussed in a supportive environment following the format above. The impact of fear and anxiety on the learning process was determined from student written responses to this reflective exercise based on the critical clinical incidents.

Two hundred and sixty written critical incident reports were collated and analyzed to determine the environmental stressors that triggered fear and anxiety and the impact of fear and anxiety on student learning. The complexity of many of the incidents described meant it was common for each incident to evoke a range of concepts and themes. The desire to make a detailed analysis of the content meant that one incident could produce more than one theme or concept. For example a student may say she was "scared and angry" and these emotions were coded separately. Any recurring content that cast light on the questions: "What are the environmental stressors on clinical placement?" "To what degree is fear and anxiety a response to these stressors?" and "How fear and learning interact on a clinical placement" were coded.

To ensure the meanings intended by the students remained, only manifest level of content was accepted and no attempt was made to identify the latent meaning of each student response (Thomas, 1990). The original phrasing was retained as far as possible when sorting the data into thematic groups. To validate the content analysis a mental health nursing academic and the two researchers, independently analysed the thematic groupings. Minor changes were made to the groupings to accommodate variations resulting from this independent analysis. Only major findings are reported, all thematic groups with a frequency of less than 10 have been removed from the data. Thus the frequency of items in each of the three broad categories may not necessarily equate to the total number of critical incidents analyzed.

RESULTS

The analyzed data were allocated one of the following three categories: incidents identified by students; emotional responses triggered in the student by the critical incident; and feelings or thoughts after the group debriefing and reflective exercise.

Incidents Identified by Students

Three major themes were identified from student responses to the question "*What actually happened? (The facts).*" These included two hundred and ten described incidents involving an interaction with a patient; 37 described incidents involving staff members; and 37 described incidents involving treatment.

There were seven sub themes identified in incidents involving interactions with patients. These were witnessing psychotic behavior, witnessing verbal abuse by patients and threatened violence by patients. Other sub themes included: whether students felt they were therapeutic, witnessing strong emotions from the patient, invasion of student professional boundaries and witnessing actual violence by patients. The two sub themes involving staff were: witnessing uncaring/unprofessional behavior towards patients by staff and student impressed by staff competence. Incidents involving therapy treatment included three sub themes, namely administration of medication, incidents involving group therapy and incidents involving the administration of electro-convulsant therapy (ECT).

Patient focused incidents included observing psychotic behaviour or actual and threatened violence and verbal abuse by patients. Issues around violence featured in 27% of the incidents and students described psychotic behaviour in patients in 25%.

Invasion of student professional and personal boundaries, which included the patient asking personal questions, the patient attempting to become intimate with the student and sexual and racial harassment by patients, was mentioned in 7% of the critical incidents. Witnessing strong emotions from patients such as grief and fear were also mentioned in 7% of the incidents. Positive incidents such as the students being therapeutic for a client were selected in 8% of the critical incidents.

Incidents involving staff were described in 13% of the student identified critical incidents. Incidents involving staff most commonly involved the student witnessing what they stated as uncaring and unprofessional behaviour towards the patient in manner, speech and lack of attention. Seven per cent of critical incidents described witnessing uncaring/unprofessional behaviour of staff towards patients. However, in 6% of critical incidents, students described how impressed they were with staff, their attitudes of caring, and their effectiveness.

Treatment-focused incidents included giving medication 5%, group therapy 4%, and the administration of ECT 3.5%. Students noted that they wished they had more information before witnessing the administration of ECT.

Some edited common examples recorded by students in their critical incident reports are included below to illustrate the intensity of emotions, and range of environmental stressors and interpersonal experiences nursing students face when in mental health settings.

The following example was rated under the sub themes 'witnessing psychotic behavior' and 'witnessing actual violence by patient'.

> A new admission was brought in by the police, very psychotic and experiencing mania. She was jumping on tables, pacing up and down, spitting, laughing to herself, trying to abscond and showing physical aggression towards staff. The staff tried to medicate her with Valium and Serenace but she threw it in their faces. Security was brought in and she was medicated through injection.

Common experiences described by students in the critical incidents were observing threatened violence, and witnessing verbal abuse. The following example encapsulates these two sub themes identified as well as the sub theme "student was impressed by staff competence".

> I was sitting outside amongst the patients, when two patients started with a verbal argument. The situation quickly changed to both standing in front of each other screaming abuse at each other, raising hands as if to hit, but not actually going through with it. I felt absolutely terrified and I was shaking with fear. I thought I was going to burst into tears and at the same time helpless at not knowing how to deal with the situation. I didn't become involved; a staff member came and defused the situation. This showed me what I could have done - easy to see someone else do it!

Table 1. Critical incidents described by students

	Frequency identified	Percentage of incidents
Witnessing psychotic behaviour	72	25.4%
Witnessing verbal abuse by patients	34	11.9%
Threatened violence by patients	30	10.6%
Student felt they were therapeutic for a client	24	8.5%
Witnessing uncaring/unprofessional behavior towards patients by staff	21	7.4%
Witness strong emotions from patient eg. Grief and fear	19	6.7%
Invasion of student professional/privacy boundaries	19	6.7%
Student was impressed by staff competence	16	5.6%
Incidents involving administration of medications	15	5.3%
Witnessing actual violence by patients	12	4.2%
Incidents involving group therapy	12	4.2%
Incidents involving administration of ECT	10	3.3.5%

Emotional Response Triggered in the Student from the Critical Incident

Nine themes were identified from student responses to the question *"What did I think/feel about it at the time?"* These themes were: fear; uncomfortable/upset/concerned; shocked/surprised/amazed; pity/sadness; confused/didn't know what to do; positive feelings; anger; no feelings; embarrassment. The most common feeling described by the students was that of fear (20%), which included being, scared, frightened, anxious or nervous. Feelings of discomfort/upset/concern were also frequently mentioned (19%). Shock, surprise and amazement were mentioned by 16% of the students. The next most frequently described feelings were pity and sadness for the patient, and confusion and not knowing what to do, both comprising 10% of the student responses each. Positive feelings such as enjoyment, happiness, excitement, and pleasure made up only 8.4% of the feelings aroused in the students. Angry feelings were aroused in 6.2% of students and embarrassment was mentioned by 4.5%. Five per cent of students did not identify any feelings following the incident.

The following quotation demonstrates the intensity of emotional responses the students felt after a critical incident. In keeping with the method of identifying only manifest level of content this response was sorted into the confused/didn't know what to do thematic grouping.

> I was walking down the hall and saw X sitting down by himself. I asked him how his sleep was and he said good. I didn't quite hear him so I said "pardon".
>
> He then said "enough".
>
> I thought he meant enough sleep, but he then said "enough I don't want to talk to you anymore."
>
> I said "alright" and stood up to leave and walk away.
>
> He said after me "I don't want to talk to you about how I feel, you could be my f----- daughter .... I don't like how they let young people in here to talk about that stuff".
>
> Then I said "that's alright you don't have to talk to me if you don't want to".
>
> I felt very very small and stupid and confused, and mumbled something about being sorry before slinking off.

For some students simply entering a psychiatric institution triggered intense feelings as demonstrated in the following quote, which was, categorize in the theme of 'fear'.

Upon arrival at the psychiatric hospital I felt overwhelmed with fear and trepidation as I entered the acute psychiatric ward...

Many incidents described by students occurred on the first day or in the first week of their clinical placement. The critical incident described below was categorized as triggering the emotions 'fear' and 'embarrassment' in the student.

> I was watching one of the patients in the TV room whilst the activities were on. The nurse had asked me to keep her quiet and take her to the toilet if she needed to go. She asked to go to the toilet so I took her hand and started to walk out of the TV room with her. I felt her grip on my hand get tighter, and then she squeezed my shoulder and tried to stop me walking. She then turned me around grabbing my jumper and twisting it up. She did this roughly and became quite aggressive accusing me of robbery and murder. Whilst holding my jumper at the neck I thought she was going to hit me on the head with the tape recorder she was trying to pick up. I was extremely scared and a little embarrassed as there were quite a few people in the room doing activities at the time. Some of the nurses came up and calmed the patient down and took her to the toilet...

Table 2. Emotional response triggered in the student from critical incidents

	Frequency identified	Percentage of responses
Fear	70	19.7%
Uncomfortable/upset/concerned	66	18.6%
Shocked/surprised/amazed	57	16.1%
Pity/sadness	38	10.7%
Confused/didn't know what to do	37	10.5%
Positive feelings	30	8.5%
Anger	22	6.2%
No feelings identified by student	18	5%
Embarrassment	16	4.5%

Interaction between Fear and Learning in Clinical Settings

The majority of student responses (85%) noted that the selected incident and its emotional corollary had a negative impact on their learning experiences but that participating in small group discussions that facilitated reflection on the critical incidents assisted them to feel better and make meaning from their experiences. However there were many students for whom the reflective exercise had no effect (15%) or who felt only somewhat better; some students had quite strong, distressing reactions which were only partially resolved through educational input via the reflective exercise.

There were six thematic groupings identified from student responses to educational input via the reflective exercise. These themes were: reflective exercise helped/feels better; thinks differently about the incident/new point of view; learned something about how others might respond; reflective exercise had no effect/thinks feels the same, good to hear the experiences/feelings of peers; reflective exercise increased self awareness.

Twenty-eight per cent of the student responses included statements indicating that they 'felt better' emotionally after the reflective exercise. Twenty-seven per cent of the responses revealed that reflection and debriefing enabled them to view the incident, from different perspectives. Seventeen per cent of the student responses indicated that the reflective exercise and debriefing sessions provided opportunities to learn how other people respond to similar incidents. Fifteen per cent of students stated there was no change in their thoughts or feelings following the debriefing/reflective exercise. Others (9%) indicated it was valuable to hear the experiences and feelings of their peers, and that the reflective exercise helped to raise their self-awareness.

Two of the students' responses grouped into the 'helping/feels better' theme are presented below.

Discussing the incident made a great difference, especially getting other people's point of view on the procedure (ECT). It made me realise that there was nothing wrong with the way I reacted. In the discussion everybody told me I made the right decision and it was my way of coping. Some of the people in the group said they felt the same way I did, but attended the procedure anyway, even though they didn't want to. The discussion helped to give me closure.

After discussing it with my group I feel better as some agreed that they would have behaved in a similar way. It helped to discuss my feelings and to work through them.

The following student response was grouped into both 'helping/feels better' and 'increased self awareness'.

...As one of the clients spoke about their own issues I found myself overwhelmed and actually had to combat my emotions in an effort not to breakdown. ...after debriefing and speaking about what I had heard, I felt better and more capable of coping with my emotions. ...I felt more reassured and learned how to detach myself emotionally without losing empathy.

Table 3. Feelings/thoughts in student after educational intervention

	Frequency identified	Percentage of responses
Reflective exercise helped/feels better	83	27.9%
Thinks differently about the incident/new point of view	81	27.3%
Learned something about how others might respond	51	17.2%
Reflective exercise had no effect/ thinks feels the same	45	15.2%
Good to hear the experiences/feelings of peers	26	8.8%
Reflective exercise increased self awareness	11	3.7%

DISCUSSION

The primary goal of this study was to obtain information from students about the critical incidents they experience whilst on mental health clinical practicum, their emotional responses to these incidents and how their thoughts and feelings about the incidents interact with student learning. The findings from the data analysis of the critical incidents identified a wide range of predominantly negative environmental stressors. Significantly these stressors triggered feelings of fear, upset, and shock in the majority of students.

Twenty- seven per cent of the critical incidents involved threatened and actual violence, and verbal abuse. These descriptions included both patient assaults on staff and patient assaults on other patients. The dominance of these extreme environmental stressors in the critical incidents suggests that nursing students on mental health clinical placement fear for their personal safety and face considerable personal and professional conflict arising from their experiences in the clinical setting. It was not rare for students to be exposed to risky situations which arose from breaches of policy, for example students being asked to restrain a patient while they were being forcibly drugged; or the student being left alone with a patient whilst on walks in public places. The authors view this finding as potentially serious both in regard to the personal safety of the students and the duty of care of both the clinical setting and the students' academic institution. Violence in the workplace represents a fundamental violation of human rights. Employers and academic institutions have a responsibility for the occupational health and safety of students and employees as well as patients. Mental health settings are not exempted from occupational health and safety legislation to provide a safe and secure environment nor from criminal jurisdiction.

It is well known that both witnessing and/or experiencing episodes of violence can result in significant emotional and/or physical distress (Engel and Marsh 1986; Janoff-Bulman 1985; Holden 1985). The consequences for the students experiencing fear-inducing situations were reflected in the intensity of emotions triggered. Witnessing actual and threatened violence whilst on mental health clinical placement is likely to be the first time the student confronts the possibility of violence in their practice. The fact that a patient may respond aggressively and violently in a nursing context challenges idealistic notions that caring on the part of a nurse should be accepted and appreciated by the patient (Fisher 1998). Recent evidence suggests that violence against nurses in Australia is increasing (Poster 1996; Jackson 1998).

Over 25% of the critical incidents involved witnessing psychotic behavior in patients. This included escape attempts, catatonia, and behavioral responses to delusions, hallucinations such as shouting at visions, cowering in the corner in fear, and pacing the corridors muttering and grimacing. Deviant behavior that challenges social norms can be personally threatening through confronting strongly held values and beliefs in the student. Attempting to understand the client's perspective of reality can trigger frustration, fear and doubts about the validity of these long held values and beliefs. As a result the students' personal identity and self-esteem may be challenged triggering anxiety and confusion in the student and further affecting the ability for student learning to occur.

Unfortunately, these negative environmental stressors were not confined to incidents involving patients, but also extended to incidents involving clinical staff. There were more critical incidents that identified uncaring/unprofessional behaviour towards patients by staff than incidents complimenting staff competence. The authors believe that a number of interpretations can be taken from this finding. First, there is a possibility that the students may have misinterpreted the therapeutic role of staff in 'limit setting' and controlling problematic behaviour in patients as evidence of uncaring behaviour. Second, clinical staff working in stressful situations may, under pressure, use 'black humor' or express negative sentiments as a means of coping with that stress. The students may have interpreted these comments as indicative of negative attitudes towards patients. Third, it is possible that mental health staff have negative attitudes towards mentally ill people in some mental health clinical settings. Students who overhear negative comments or witness uncaring/unprofessional behaviour towards patients have interpreted this as unacceptable or distressing. The authors believe that it should be of serious concern to clinical staff, to consumers of mental health services, and to educators, that students so frequently identified problematic attitudes towards patients by staff.

Although not the focus of this study, these findings also provide insights into the treatment experiences of consumers and the therapeutic milieu of the clinical mental health setting. Horsfall and Stuhlmiller (2001) found the anxieties and fears of students and novice health professionals commonly paralleled those of recently diagnosed or newly admitted patients.

Given the dominance of environmental stressors identified by the students in their critical incident analysis, it is not surprising to note that the students also identified predominantly negative feelings arising from these critical incidents. Moreover a substantial majority of students described intense feelings of fear, shock or anger. Powerful feelings such as anxiety and fear will not only interfere with effective learning but also impede the ability to establish a therapeutic relationship with the client, and affect attitudes towards people with mental illness. Fear and extreme anxiety causes increased heart rate, respirations and muscle tension, perceptual distortions, difficulties in concentration, thought blocking, and impaired verbal communication skills such as repetitive questioning. Clearly if anxiety or fearfulness is triggered in students the physiologic, perceptual, cognitive, and behavioral responses identified in the literature review will impact on their learning and their ability to assimilate, transform and apply theoretical knowledge. In many instances the students felt immobilized, not knowing what they should do to resolve the situation.

Students who themselves have experienced abuse or have personal experiences with mental illness may have particular difficulty in a mental health setting (Sutherland, 1995). Unresolved fears and anxiety are likely to interfere with the learning process, preventing students from applying their theoretical knowledge to the clinical setting. They may also impact on the future career choices of these students, reducing the likelihood of a career choice in mental health nursing.

Professional learning in mental health is focused on the development of a therapeutic relationship with the mentally ill client. Knowledge that underpins the therapeutic relationship includes interpersonal and communication skills, positive attitudes and 'the humanistic approach of unconditional positive regard for the client, along with self-awareness in the student (Landeen et al.1992). Negative attitudes and feelings of fear and anxiety not only diminish effective student learning, but also the development of rapport, empathy and a therapeutic relationship with a client (Bower, Webb and Stevens, 1994; Purdon, 1992; Tierney, 1995). With the experience of such strong emotions in the student it is likely that anxiety will increase unless these feelings are directly addressed in the clinical environment. Educators therefore face considerable challenges in facilitating appropriate and rewarding learning experiences for health care students in clinical mental health settings. Teaching strategies in these settings must not only foster the integration of theory with clinical practice and the development of high level interpersonal skills, but must also focus on diminishing environmental stressors so that fear and anxiety in the student is reduced and therapeutic attitudes towards patients can develop.

The importance of the reflective exercise in reducing fear and anxiety and facilitating learning was very clearly demonstrated in this study. Eighty five per cent of students stated they had gained something out of the reflective exercise, including finding a new perspective, learning how others might respond, feeling 'better', increasing self awareness and valuing hearing the experiences and feelings of their peers. Proponents of reflective practice support this sense of gaining a new point of view from the reflective exercise (Horsfall 1990; Minghella and Benson 1995; Pierson 1998; Reynolds and Murphy, 1996; Severinsson 1998). The emergence of these positive emotions and thoughts represents a significant shift from predominantly negative emotions arising from the critical incident. This study found that daily or second daily, supervised reflection on the critical incidents in a safe environment within the clinical setting, assisted the student to resolve some of his or her own personal conflicts that arose from the critical incident thereby reducing levels of fear and anxiety, and promoting student learning and the development of positive attitudes.

LIMITATIONS

There are a number of reasons why it is necessary to be cautious in generalising too broadly from this study. Firstly, despite the written instructions to students that a critical incident need not necessarily be a negative incident, the very process of identifying something that the student considers to be critical tends to bias the student to selecting incidents that have impacted negatively. Secondly, although the authors believe the students sampled were a representative cohort of students from their particular year, not all the students were sampled, and those that were, were selected on the basis of convenience. It is possible but unlikely, that if all of the students had been sampled the findings may have been different.

CONCLUSION

This study examined the actual experience of students on mental health clinical practicum. Student descriptions of critical clinical incidents were used to identify these experiences. The content analysis of these critical incidents found that students tended to describe disturbing incidents, most commonly involving both real and threatened violence, and psychotic behaviour. The critical incidents outlined a range of very challenging situations, including ones that would be hard for anyone (e.g. walking into a patient's room and finding them in the middle of a suicide attempt) and ones which are harder for young inexperienced students than their teachers may realize. These incidents typically aroused strong, often painful emotional responses such as fear, discomfort and shock in the student. In turn these emotional responses made it difficult for the student to maintain focus on their learning tasks and hindered the ability for students to develop therapeutic relationships with clients. This study supported previous research promoting reflection and debriefing on clinical experiences as critical to the positive resolution of the critical incidents and to enhancing student learning. However, it is clear that further research is needed to explore both the relationship between fear and learning, and the impact of fear on learning in clinical settings.

The findings from this study reinforce the need for clinical staff and educators to assist the student to become aware of, process, and resolve fear, anxiety and personal conflict arising from the clinical setting. Leaving the student to resolve these feelings alone and unsupported can impede the capacity for students to achieve learning outcomes aimed towards translating theory into practice and challenge stereotypical attitudes. Successful resolution of these conflicts assists both the students and their teacher to decrease negative stereotypes of people with a mental illness, foster an understanding of themselves and the client as people with both human rights and human needs, and develop a positive outlook towards a career as a mental health professional.

REFERENCES

Antai-Otong, D. (2003). *Psychiatric Nursing Biological And Behavioral Concepts*. Thomson Delmar Learning. New York. USA.

Bell, A., Horsfall, J. and Goodin, W. (1998). The mental health nursing clinical confidence scale: a tool for measuring undergraduate learning on mental health clinical placements. *Australian and New Zealand Journal of Mental Health Nursing, 7*, 184-190.

Bower, D., Webb, A. and Stevens, D. (1994). Nursing students knowledge and anxiety about AIDS: An experiential workshop. *Journal of Nursing Education, 33*, 6, 272-276.

Bradshaw, J., and Fisher, J. (1996). My stories. An experiential learning activity for mental health settings. In *Proceedings of the first International Nursing Education Conference* p.251). Hamilton, Canada: McMaster University.

Clinton, M., and Hazelton M. (2000). Scoping mental health nursing education. *Australian and New Zealand Journal of Mental Health Nursing, 9*, 2-10.

Davies, J. (1995). Fear Busters. *Nursing Times*, 91, n.21, 46-47.

Engel, F., and Marsh, S. (1986). Helping the employee victim of violence in hospitals. *Hospital and Community Psychiatry, 37*, 2, 159-162.

Ferguson, K., and Hope, K. (1999). From novice to competent practitioner: tracking the progress of undergraduate mental health nursing students. *Journal of Advanced Nursing, 29* (3), 630-638.

Fisher, J. (1998) Violence against nurses. In Horsfall J (Ed) *Violence and Nursing.* Royal College of Nursing Australia. Canberra.

Fontaine, K.L. (2003). Introduction to mental health nursing. In Fontaine, K.L (Ed.) *Mental health nursing.* 5th edn. (pp.3-48). Upper Saddle River New Jersey: Prentice Hall.

Holden, R. (1985). Aggression against nurses'. *The Australian Nurses Journal,* 15,3,44-48.

Holmes, D. (2001). *Abnormal Psychology 4th Edition.* Allyn and Bacon. Needham Heights, MA, USA.

Holoday-Worret, P. A. (1996). Student issues regarding client and environment. In K. M. Fortinash and P. A. Holiday-Worret (Eds.) *Psychiatric-Mental Health Nursing.* (pp. 27-36). St Louis Missouri: Mosby-Year Book.

Horsfall, J. (1990). Clinical placement: prebriefing and debriefing as teaching strategies. *Australian Journal of Advanced Nursing, 8, 1, 3 - 7.*

Horsfall, J., and Stuhlmiller, C., with Champ, S. (2001). *Interpersonal Nursing For Mental Health.* New York: Springer.

Human Rights and Equal Opportunity Commission. (1993). *Human Rights and Mental Illness. Report of the National Inquiry into the Human Rights of People with Mental Illness.* Australian Government Publishing Service. Canberra.

Jackson, J (1998). Violence in the workplace. (In Horsfall J (Ed) *Violence and Nursing).* Royal College of Nursing Australia. Canberra.

Janoff-Bulman, R. (1988). The aftermath of victimisation: Rebuilding shattered assumptions. (In *Trauma and Its Wake,* ed, Figley C). Bruner/Mazel, New York.

Johns, C. (1995). The value of reflective practice for nursing. *Journal of Clinical Nursing,* 4(1) 23-30.

Lam, A., McMaster, R., and Troup, C. (1993). A pilot study: nursing students' attitudes, interest, and concerns in the mental health field. *The Australian Journal of Mental Health Nursing, 2*(6), 281-286.

Landeen, J., Byrne, C. and Brown, B. (1992). Journal keeping as an educational strategy in teaching psychiatric nursing. *Journal of Advanced Nursing.* 17, 347-355.

McLoughlin, J., and Chalmers, J. (1991). Student nurses' attitudes toward mental illness: impacr of education and exposure. *Australian Journal of Mental Health Nursing, 1* (4), 12-16.

Minghella, E., and Benson, A. (1995). Developing reflective practice in mental health nursing through critical incident analysis. *Journal of Advanced Nursing*, 21, 205-213.

Napoletano, M. (1981). Correlates of change in attitudes toward mental illness among vocational nursing students. *Psychological Reports,* 49, 147-150.

O'Brien, A. (1994). Measuring graduate attitudes to educational preparation for practice in mental health nursing. *Australian and New Zealand Journal of Mental Health Nursing,* 4, 132-142.

Olade, R. (1979). Attitudes towards mental illness: a comparison of post-basic nursing students with science students. *Journal of Advanced Nursing,* 4, 39-46.

Parkinson, F. (1997). *Critical Incident Debriefing - Understanding And Dealing With Trauma,* London, Souvenir Press.

Perese, E. (1996). Undergraduates' perceptions of their psychiatric practicum: Positive and negative factors in inpatient and community experience. *Journal of Nursing Education,* 35, 6, 281-285.

Pierson, W. (1998). Reflection and nursing education. *Journal of Advanced Nursing,* 27, 1, 165-170.

Poster, E. (1996). A multinational study of psychiatric nursing staffs' beliefs and concerns about work safety and patient assault. *Archives of Psychiatric Nursing,* 6, 365-373.

Pye, S. and Whyte, L., (1996). Factors influencing the branch choice of students in a nursing undergraduate program. *Nurse Education Today,* 16, 432-436.

Reynolds, P. and Murphy, B. (1996). Culture shock, sink or swim? The use of critical incidents to overcome barriers to deep learning. *Proceedings First International Nursing Education Conference of the Nursing Education Research Unit.* McMaster Univesity. Hamilton. Canada. p.25.

Severinsson, E. (1998). Bridging the gap between theory and practice: a supervision program for nursing students. *Journal of Advanced Nursing,* 27, 6, 1269-1277.

Slimmer, L., Wendt, A. and Martinkus, D. (1990). Effect of psychiatric clinical learning site on nursing students' attitudes toward mental illness and psychiatric nursing. *Journal of Nursing Education,* 29, 3, 127-133.

Stevens,J. and Dulhunty,G. (1992). New South Wales nursing students' attitudes towards a career in mental health, *Proceedings of the 18th National Convention of the Australian College of Mental Health Nurses, Inc,* Ballarat Victoria, 108-112.

Sutherland, J. (1995). Educational Innovations. The mental health consultation model: A conceptual framework for structuring the psychiatric nursing practicum. *Journal of Nursing Education,* 34, 3, 131 -133.

Thomas, B. (1990). *Nursing Research An Experiential Approach.* Toronto. C. V. Mosby Co.

Tierney, N. (1995). HIV/AIDS - Knowledge, attitudes, education of nurses: A review of the research. *Journal of Clinical Nursing,* 4, 1, 13-21.

Varcarolis, E. M. (2002). Understanding anxiety and anxiety defenses. In E. M. Varcarolis (Ed.) *Foundations Of Psychiatric Mental Health Nursing. A Clinical Approach.* (4th edn.), pp.282-299. Philadelphia: Saunders.

Wong, J. (1987). Towards effective clinical teaching in nursing. *Journal of Advanced Nursing,* 12, 505 - 513.

In: Consciousness and Learning Research
Editor: Susan K. Turrini, pp. 79-95

ISBN 1-60021-333-2
© 2007 Nova Science Publishers, Inc.

Chapter 4

SEXUAL EFFECTS AND DRUGS OF ABUSE: POSSIBLE LINKS THROUGH LEARNING

Chana K. Akins[a] and *Neil Levens[b]*

[a]Department of Psychology, University of Kentucky,
Lexington, KY 40506-0044, USA
[b]Department of Psychology, University of South Carolina,
Columbia, SC 29208, USA

ABSTRACT

Clinical research points out that there is a comorbid relationship between drug addiction and high-risk sexual behavior. Much of this relationship has been explained as the use of sexual behavior as a way to exchange for drugs of abuse. However, studies using animal models have implicated neural and psychological mechanisms that may link drug abuse and risky sexual behavior. Both drug taking and sexual behavior involve overlapping neural circuitry, and both events also evoke dopamine efflux in the nucleus accumbens. This neural overlap appears to be sufficient to induce cross-sensitization. However, this cross-sensitization appears to be unilateral with chronic drug exposure resulting in the enhancement of sexual motivation and sexual behavior, but not the reverse. In contrast to the cross-sensitization literature, the findings of reinstatement studies have suggested that the neural overlap and involvement of dopamine may not be sufficient for the reinstatement of drug-seeking behavior following a sexual event that presumably primes the system. The purpose of the present chapter is to review this empirical literature and to discuss the possible role of learning as a link between the two, with particular emphasis on the incentive sensitization view of drug addiction.

---

[*] Address correspondence to: Chana K. Akins, Department of Psychology, University of Kentucky, Lexington, KY 40506-0044. e-mail: ckakin1@uky.edu; phone: (859) 257-1103; fax: (859) 323-1979

INTRODUCTION

There is increasing clinical evidence for a comorbidity between psychostimulant abuse and compulsive sexual behavior (e.g., Kall, 1992; Kall and Nilsonne, 1995; Washton, 1989). For example, psychostimulant use has been linked to increased sexual activity, multiple sex partners (Ross, Hwang, Zack, Bull, and Williams, 2002; Weatherby, Shultz, Chitwood, McCoy, McCoy, Ludwig, and Edlin, 1992) and unprotected sex (Booth, Kwiatkowski, and Chitwood, 2000). Moreover, psychostimulant abusers have a higher than normal incidence of sexually transmitted diseases (Washton, 1989).

One contributing factor to this comorbid relationship between drug abuse and risky is clearly that drug addicts are exchanging sexual favors for drugs and/or money to support their drug habit. Another possible contributing factor for the drug abuse-sex relationship may be based on the incentive sensitization view of addiction (Robinson and Berridge, 2000, 2003). This view proposes that potentially addictive drugs may induce neural adaptations in the brain – e.g., in the neural reward circuitry (i.e., nucleus accumbens) and as a result, the brain systems involved in motivation and reward become hypersensitized to drugs. This sensitization induced by repeated psychostimulant administration may also be manifest as enhanced motivation toward natural rewards such as sex since the same brain systems involved in drug-induced adaptations are also known to be involved in sexual motivation and sexual behavior (Fiorino and Phillips, 1999a; Fiorino, Coury, and Phillips, 1997; Levens and Akins, 2004). The role of Pavlovian conditioning in incentive sensitization is becoming more evident. As a result of a hypersensitized reward-related brain system, cues that have become associated with drug-taking, via Pavlovian conditioning, may thereby activate the incentive-salience process (Robinson and Berridge, 2003). That is, the cues that are now conditioned stimuli (CSs) may increase in value and evoke approach responses or "wanting" (Berridge and Robinson, 2003). These physiological and psychological processes could contribute to our understanding of why some drug addicts also engage in risky sexual behavior.

EFFECTS OF DRUGS OF ABUSE ON SEXUAL MOTIVATION AND SEXUAL BEHAVIOR

Behavioral sensitization is defined as enhanced responding to a drug after repeated administration of the drug. The incentive-sensitization theory (Robinson and Berridge, 2000, 2003) proposes that prolonged use of certain drugs creates neural adaptations in the limbic-motor circuitry, specifically the mesolimbic dopamine system, and that these adaptations are expressed as behavioral sensitization. The same circuitry involved in the expression of behavioral sensitization is also known to play a role in natural motivated behaviors such as sexual behavior (Phillips, Pfaus, and Blaha, 1991). Thus, repeated psychostimulant administration that leads to behavioral sensitization may be manifest as enhanced sexual motivation. Indeed, the incentive sensitization theory predicts that drug sensitization should facilitate responding to classes of naturally rewarding stimuli, a phenomenon referred to as cross-sensitization.

Evidence for cross-sensitization of drugs of abuse on sexual behavior has been investigated in a limited number of experiments. Fiorino and Phillips (1999a) investigated the effects of behavioral sensitization induced by amphetamine on sexual arousal in sexually naive male rats. Rats were placed in bilevel chambers that contained a set of ramps that allowed movement from one platform to the other. After 30 minutes, they were injected with either amphetamine (1.5 mg/kg i.p.) or saline and placed back into the bilevel test chambers. Two hours after the injection, they were returned to their home cages. Injections were given every other day for a total of 10 injections. Twenty-one days after the 10th injection, male rats were tested for sexual behavior in the bilevel test chambers. Activity counts, as measured by level changes, were recorded for 5 minutes before a receptive female rat was introduced for 30 min. Various measures of sexual interaction were recorded during the 30 min test. Ten sexual behavior tests were conducted, one every 4 days.

Results showed that rats that were given amphetamine every other day displayed enhanced activity on the 10th injection compared to the first one. In addition, they had progressively greater activity across injections compared to saline controls, confirming that sensitization had occurred. When tested for sexual behavior, sensitized rats made significantly more level changes than the control group on the 10th test during the first 5 minutes before the female was introduced. In addition, amphetamine-sensitized rats demonstrated shorter latencies to mount and a greater number of mounts, intromissions, and ejaculations compared with saline control rats. The findings demonstrate that prior chronic exposure to amphetamine facilitated sexual responding.

In a similar experiment, Levens and Akins (2004) investigated the effect of cocaine-induced behavioral sensitization on male sexual learning using a Pavlovian sexual conditioning paradigm. In this paradigm, an initially neutral object, a conditioned stimulus (CS), is presented to a male for several seconds followed by an opportunity to copulate with a receptive female, the unconditioned stimulus (US). After several pairings of the CS and US, the CS comes to elicit approach behavior. This conditioned approach behavior is indicative of learning and of the establishment of an association between the CS and the US.

Levens and Akins (2004) also tested for a drug-sex cross sensitization using an alternative species, Japanese quail. We wanted to test for the generality of the phenomenon across species with the assumption that if this phenomenon occurs similarly in birds as in mammals, it may also be more likely to also occur in humans. Additionally, sexual conditioning in male Japanese quail is a well-studied phenomenon (see Domjan, Cusato, and Krause, 2004 for review).

To test whether cocaine-induced behavioral sensitization would influence conditioned approach behavior and other aspects of learned sexual behavior, male quail were randomly assigned to one of four groups: Paired Cocaine ($n = 6$), Unpaired Cocaine ($n = 6$), Paired Saline ($n = 6$), or Unpaired Saline ($n = 6$). During sensitization training, both paired and unpaired cocaine groups received a daily injection of cocaine (10 mg/kg intraperitoneally or ip) and were immediately placed into a locomotor chamber for 30 min. This occurred once a day for 6 consecutive days. Saline groups received the same treatment except they were given an injection of saline (ip) once a day for 6 days. Following a 10-day withdrawal period, 10 sexual conditioning trials were conducted. During conditioning, paired subjects were presented with the CS object (a small wooden block lowered from the ceiling of the test cage) and the amount of time subjects spent in an area marked off that contained the CS (the CS zone) was recorded. After 30 sec, the CS was raised and a door that led to a small chamber adjacent to the test cage and that contained a receptive female quail was opened. During the last 5 conditioning trials, a taxidermically-prepared model of a female bird was presented behind the door rather than the live female. This was done to reduce the variability of male sexual responding that might occur as a result of the female's behavior. Once males entered the cage, the door was closed, and they were given 5 min to interact with the female or model (US). During the 5 min interaction period, latency to copulate (beginning when the door was opened) and the frequency of cloacal contacts made toward the female was recorded.

Unpaired subjects received the same treatment as paired subjects except that they were given 5 min to interact with the female bird (first 5 trials) or a taxidermic model of a female (last 5 trials) 3 hr prior to the CS presentation and in their home cages, in an unpaired fashion.

Figure 1 represents mean photobeam breaks during the 30 min locomotor activity trials. Cocaine administration resulted in significantly greater locomotor activity than saline on each trial and across trials. Thus, providing evidence that behavioral sensitization had occurred.

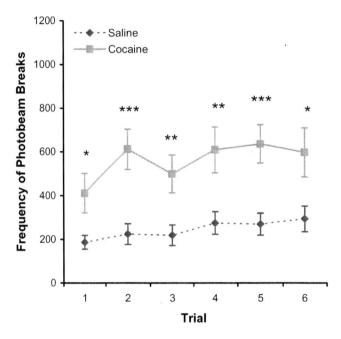

Figure 1. Mean frequency of photobeam breaks across 6 locomotor activity trials, each for 30 min.* = significantly different from saline, p<0.05; ** = p<0.01; *** = p<0.001. (Reprinted with permission).

The mean time birds spent in the CS zone during the 30 sec CS presentation across sexual conditioning trials is represented in Figure 2. The paired cocaine and paired saline groups both increased the amount of time they spent near the CS, an indication of conditioned approach behavior. However, group Paired Cocaine had enhanced conditioned approach responding compared to the paired saline group across trials and overall.

Because of differences in how paired and unpaired groups received the female US (i.e., for paired groups, a door was opened allowing paired males to interact with the female, whereas, for unpaired groups, the female was placed in the cage with the male), comparisons for latency to copulate were only measured in paired subjects. Figure 3 represents mean latency to first copulation with a female for the paired groups.

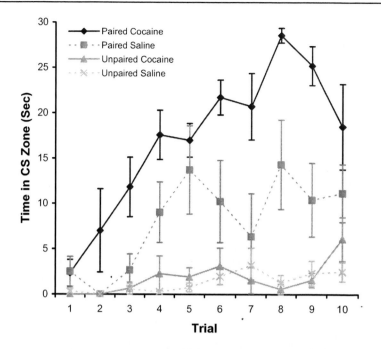

Figure 2. Time (sec) spent in the CS zone (+SEM) during the 30 sec presentation of the CS across 10 sexual conditioning trials. (Reprinted with permission).

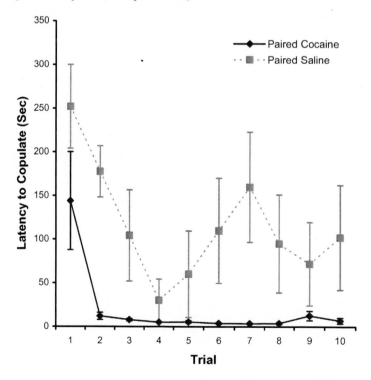

Figure 3. Latency to copulate (±SEM) during a 5 min test for paired subjects that received a CS foll followed by Copulatory opportunity across sexual conditioning trials (Reprinted with permission).

Latency to copulate decreased across trials for both paired groups, however group Paired Cocaine had a shorter overall latency than group Paired Saline. Mean frequency of cloacal contacts with the female during the 5 min US period is presented in Figure 4. Although, these data appear to be highly variable at each trial, overall, Group Paired Cocaine made more cloacal contacts than Groups Paired Saline.

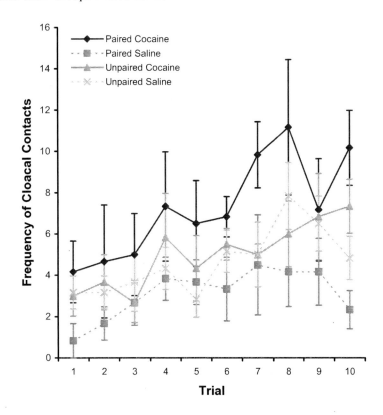

Figure 4. Frequency of cloacal contacts (±SEM) made toward a live female or model of a female during 5 min of each sexual conditionin trial (Reprinted with permission).

In summary, Levens and Akins (2004) found that cocaine-induced behavioral sensitization facilitated conditioned approach behavior, latency to copulate with a female, and increased the frequency of copulation. These findings concur with other studies on the effect of drug-induced sensitization on naturally-rewarding stimuli (Fiorino and Phillips, 1999a; Nocjar and Panksepp, 2002), and they suggest that learning may play an important role in the enhancement of naturally rewarding stimuli by psychostimulants. Harmer and Phillips (1999) reported evidence for the role of learning in a food conditioning paradigm. Using a conditioned inhibition paradigm, rats that were sensitized to amphetamine were given excitatory conditioning in which a stimulus signaled the presentation of sucrose. Then they were presented with a compound stimulus that contained the excitatory stimulus and a new one in the absence of sucrose presentation (inhibitory conditioning). Harmer and Phillips (1999) found that prior repeated exposure to amphetamine facilitated both excitatory and inhibitory conditioning. Together, these results suggest that chronic psychostimulant exposure may enhance future Pavlovian learning.

CONTEXT-SPECIFICITY OF DRUG EFFECTS ON SEXUAL MOTIVATION AND SEXUAL BEHAVIOR

In the previously discussed experiments (Fiorino and Phillips, 1999a; Levens and Akins, 2004), drug administration and sensitization occurred in a context that was distinct from the context in which sexual responding was allowed to occur. However, Fiorino and Phillips (1999a) also proposed that not only did chronic exposure to amphetamine enhance later sexual responding but that it may have increased the incentive value of the test chamber cues once these cues became associated with the female through learning.

To determine whether their findings were the result of a conditioned association formed between the drug and the test environment, Fiorino and Phillips (1999a) conducted a second experiment in which rats were sensitized with amphetamine in unilevel chambers that were the same size as the bilevel chamber but received a sexual behavior test in the bilevel chambers. The results of this experiment were similar to those in the first experiment. Amphetamine-sensitized males demonstrated shorter mount latencies and a greater number of intromissions and ejaculations than saline controls. Therefore the sexual behavior that was facilitated by behavioral sensitization occurred independently of the environment in which drug had been administered. Rather, behavioral sensitization may have enhanced the incentive qualities of the receptive female, such as the female's pheromones, sounds, earwiggling, and darting behaviors.

This supports the notion that motor sensitization that later enhances sexual responding is context-independent.

In another experiment designed to explore context-specificity of drug conditioning effects, Mitchell and Stewart (1990) injected male rats with morphine (10 mg/kg ip) immediately before placement into a mating arena, with no female present, for 1 hour. On alternate days, they were given saline injections in the animal colony. An unpaired group received the opposite; morphine injections in the animal colony and saline injections in the mating arena. A third group, the control group, received saline injections in both environments. All groups received 4 injections in the arena and 4 in the animal colony. Two days after the last injection of morphine, all rats were injected with saline and given a 30 minute copulation test while in the mating arena.

Results showed that the paired group demonstrated significantly more female-directed behavior (including anogenital exploration, pursuing, sniffing, grooming, and climbing over the female) than either the unpaired group or the control group. Similar results occurred when the rats were tested again for sexual behavior one week later. In addition, latencies to initiate copulation in the environment previously paired with morphine decreased. Thus, rats that were tested for sexual behavior in the same environment where they previously received cocaine showed more sexual motivation than male rats that were tested for sexual behavior in a place other than where they received morphine. This suggests that the context that became associated with the drug state may have later facilitated or modulated behaviors toward the naturally rewarding stimuli of the female such as ear wiggling, etc. It also suggests that under some conditions, cross sensitization may be context specific.

EFFECTS OF SEXUAL EXPERIENCE ON DRUG RESPONDING

The literature on the effects of psychostimulant exposure and sexual motivation and behavior supports the notion that the overlapping dopaminergic circuitry and reward-related structures may be sufficient to result in enhancement of drug effects on sexual responding. A related question of interest is whether sexual experience or multiple sexual events enhances later responding to drugs of abuse, also referred to as cross-sensitization. There is evidence that similar to repeated drug administration, sexual experience or multiple sexual events sensitize neurons in the dopamine pathway (Kohlert and Meisel, 1999; Bradley and Meisel, 2001). Bradley and Meisel (2001) investigated whether sexual experience would facilitate drug-induced sensitization. They found that when sexually experienced female hamsters were given an amphetamine challenge (1.0 mg/kg) and tested for locomotor activity, they showed an increase in locomotor activity within the first 10 min after injection whereas sexually naïve female hamsters responded to amphetamine 20 min after injection. These findings support the incentive sensitization theory in that there may be converging neural mechanisms mediating responses to drugs and sexual behavior (Robinson and Berridge, 1993).

To date, no experiments have replicated Bradley and Meisel (2001). Levens (2003) attempted to replicate this experiment in using the same procedure in which they previously found that chronic cocaine enhanced sexual conditioning (Levens and Akins, 2004), except presenting cocaine and sexual conditioning trials in reverse order. Male quail were given 10 sexual conditioning trials, one per day. Sexual conditioning trials consisted of presentation of a CS object for 30 sec followed by 5 minutes to interact with a receptive female quail (Group Sex-Paired) or 5 minutes of visual exposure to a receptive female quail (Group No Sex-Paired). Comparable unpaired groups (Groups Sex-Unpaired and No Sex-Unpaired) received similar treatment as their paired counterpart, however, they were given copulatory opportunity or visual access to a female bird for 5 minutes, 3 hours prior to the presentation of the CS object. After the 10 conditioning trials, all birds were given a 10 day withdrawal period, followed by an injection of cocaine and placement into a locomotor activity chamber, once a day for 6 days.

There was virtually no evidence for sexual conditioning in this experiment. All groups showed similar approach behavior toward the CS object, and there were no differences in the frequency of cloacal contact movements made toward the female. Perhaps the only evidence for a conditioned effect is that the sex-paired group had a decrease in latency to copulate with the female.

Figure 5 shows the frequency of photobeam breaks across locomotor activity trials. Although activity increased across trials, there were no significant group differences either overall or across trials. One apparent explanation for this lack of finding is that, although all of the groups copulated with the female, the paired groups may not have been sexually conditioned. This might suggest the importance of learning for the occurrence of this phenomenon.

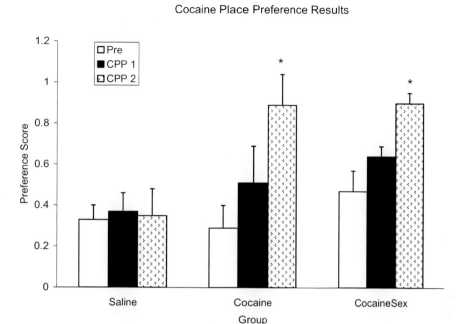

Figure 5. The preference score for groups saline, cocaine, and cocaine-sex during pre-exposure, and CPP tests 1 and 2. * = significantly different from saline, $p < 0.05$.

Another possibility is that males may be less respondent to psychostimulants than females. For example, female rats demonstrate greater levels of psychostimulant-induced locomotor activity (Camp and Robinson, 1988) and demonstrate a more robust behavioral sensitization to cocaine than male rats (van Haaren and Meyer, 1991). Bradley and Meisel (2001) found enhancement of psychostimulant-induced locomotor activity in female hamsters that were sexually experienced. It is possible that if we had used females as subjects, we may have demonstrated this effect.

Finally, it is possible is that the amount of sexual experience male quail were given in our experiment may not have been sufficient to sensitize neurons in the dopamine pathway and therefore not sufficient to induce a cross sensitization. Bradley and Meisel (2001) gave female hamsters 6 weeks of copulatory experience with a male hamster. Male quail in our experiment only received 10 days of experience.

REINSTATEMENT OF DRUG-SEEKING BY A SEXUAL EVENT

Another learning paradigm that has been used to study drug and sex interactions is the reinstatement procedure. The reinstatement procedure has typically been used to investigate events that induce drug relapse or drug-seeking behavior in animals that have been chronically exposed to drugs. In one variation of this procedure, male rats are trained to press a lever to self-administer drugs intravenously. The rats are then subjected to extinction in which lever pressing no longer results in drug administration. Subsequently, when these rats are re-exposed to the previously self-administered drug, reinstatement of drug-reinforced behavior occurs (deWit and Stewart, 1983). Previous research with drugs of abuse has demonstrated reinstatement of heroin-reinforced behavior following prolonged drug free periods (deWit and Stewart, 1983; Shaham, Rodaras, and Stewart, 1994). It has also been demonstrated that exposure to intermittent footshock stress reinstates heroin and cocaine-seeking behavior using this procedure (see Shaham, Erb, and Stewart, 2000 for review).

Shaham and colleagues (Shaham, Puddicome, and Stewart, 1997) used this reinstatement procedure to investigate whether sexual arousal could reinstate heroin-taking behavior in male rats. Rats were trained to self-administer heroin by pressing an active lever. They were then given extinction during which saline was substituted for heroin when the active lever was pressed. Following extinction, male rats were given exposure to a receptive female rat in the self-administration chamber. Under these conditions, male rats failed to reinstate heroin-taking behavior, thus indicating that sexual arousal may not be sufficient to reinstate drug-taking behavior.

Akins and Harris (unpublished) recently conducted a similar study using a variation of the reinstatement procedure that relies more heavily on Pavlovian conditioning rather than operant conditioning. In their experiment, male quail were trained to demonstrate a cocaine-induced conditioned place preference (CPP). They were then given 21 extinction trials that consisted of access to the entire chamber without cocaine or saline injections, similar to prior CPP tests. The day after the last extinction trial, a reinstatement test was conducted in which subjects were given 1 of 3 treatments: subjects that previously received saline received a saline injection (group saline), and those that received cocaine were either given a cocaine injection (group cocaine) or copulatory opportunity with a female bird in the home cage for 5 min (group cocaine-sex). Each treatment was followed immediately by placement into the center chamber with access to the entire chamber for 15 min.

A preference score was calculated for each group to assess whether subjects increased the amount of time in their initially their trained context or their initially nonpreferred context. For both cocaine groups, the calculation was time in drug-paired chamber divided by time in drug paired chamber plus time in saline-paired chamber. For the saline group, this was time in initially least preferred chamber divided by least preferred plus preferred chamber. The greater the preference score, the more time the subjects spent in the drug paired chamber or for saline controls, the more time they spent in the initially least preferred side.

Figure 6 illustrates the preference score for each group during pre-exposure and the two CPP tests. Cocaine and cocaine-sex groups had significantly greater preference scores than the saline group during the last CPP test, suggesting a shift in preference for the compartment in which they had been placed after receiving an injection of cocaine.

The preference score for each group during the last CPP test and for extinction trials 1, 7, 14, and 21 is represented in Figure 7. Cocaine and cocaine-sex groups demonstrate a decrease in preference score across trials, meaning they were spending decreasing the amount of time they spent in the drug-paired chamber across extinction trials. The asterisks on this figure represents a significant difference for groups during each trial. Cocaine and cocaine-sex groups had a higher preference score on the last CPP test, and on extinction trial 1 but not by the 7th extinction trial.

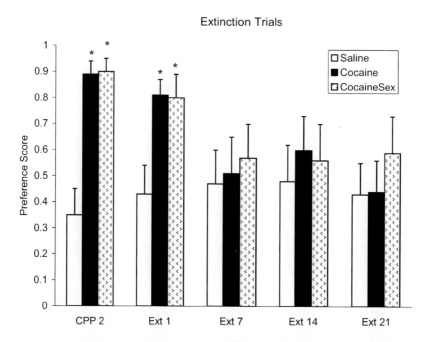

Figure 6. Preference score for groups saline, cocaine, and cocaine-sex for the last CPP trial and extinction trials 1, 7, 14, and 21. * = significantly different from saline, $p < 0.05$.

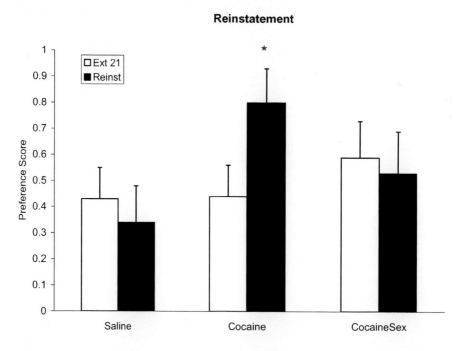

Figure 7. Preference score for groups saline, cocaine, and cocaine-sex during the reinstatement test in which subjects were given an injection of saline, and injection of cocaine, and copulatory opportunity in their home cage, respectively. * = significantly different extinction trial 21.

To determine whether the preference for the drug-paired chamber was reinstated, we compared preference scores for the last extinction trial with the reinstatement test. The results as shown in Figure 8 indicate a significant increase in time spent in the cocaine-paired chamber relative to time spent in the chamber after extinction for the group that received a priming dose of cocaine. However, there was no significant increase in preference score from the last extinction trial to the reinstatement trial when subjects were given copulatory opportunity with a receptive female quail.

Together, the findings of the reinstatement studies with rodents and quail suggest that sexual arousal and sexual conditioning may not be sufficient to elicit a drug reinstatement. Alternatively, one might argue that the experimental manipulations in Akins and Harris (unpublished) were not adequate to alter the dopaminergic system. Although we did not measure dopamine efflux to determine this, Shaham et al. (1997) used a similar procedure as that used by Pfaus and colleagues (Pfaus, Damsma, Nomikos, Wenstern, Blaha, Phillips, and Fibiger, 1990) who found a reliable increase in dopamine output in the nucleus accumbens. Another possibility is that although a sexual event and a drug-taking event activate similar brain systems, there are other significant differences that contribute to their differences in functionality. For example, the opioid system as well as areas of the brain that are not involved in drug reward, such as the mPOA, may mediate sexual motivation and behavior.

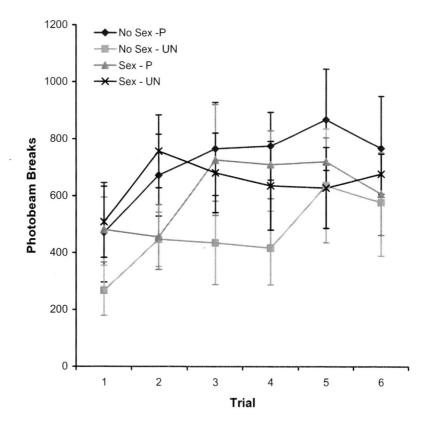

Figure 8. Mean frequency of photobeam breaks for groups No Sex-Paired, No Sex-Unpaired, Sex-Paired, and Sex-Unpaired, axross trials.

Finally, as suggested by Shaham et al. (1997), it is possible that although copulation with a female activates brain systems involved in both sexual behavior and reinstatement of cocaine-seeking behavior, the activation of these systems by sexual stimuli may result in behaviors directed toward sexual stimuli not toward drug-related stimuli. In other words, there might be an increase in interest in sexual-related cues rather drug cues as a result of priming the reward system with sexual behavior. Further research is needed to explore this possibility.

DISCUSSION

It is well accepted that there is a link between drug abuse and compulsive and high-risk sexual behavior. Clinical studies have consistently found correlations and indicators between drug-related activities and risky sexual behaviors, as well as their relationship to sexually transmitted diseases (e.g., Brooks, Adams, Balka, Whiteman, Zhang, and Sugarman, 2004; Tapert, Aarons, Sedler, and Brown, 2001). Controlled studies using animal models have provided valuable information about the neural and psychological mechanisms that might link drug abuse and high-risk sexual behavior.

The neurochemical events that underlie drug taking behavior and sexual behavior are similar. Both behaviors typically induce increases in extracellular dopamine in the nucleus accumbens. Repeated administration of psychotimulants and discontinuation of drug exposure elicits augmented efflux of dopamine in the NA (Robinson and Becker, 1986; Pierce and Kalivas, 1997). Increases in dopamine efflux have also been associated with sexual interactions in male and female rats (Fiorino et al., 1997; Pfaus, et al., 1990; Mermelstein and Becker, 1995; Pfaus, Damsa, Wenkstern, and Fibiger, 1995) and female hamsters (Meisel, Camp, and Robinson, 1993). In addition, there is augmented dopamine efflux in the NA of amphetamine-sensitized male rats during sexual behavior compared to nonsensitized male rats (Fiorino and Phillips, 1999b).

Repeated administration of psychostimulants results in long-term neural adaptations in the limbic-motor circuitry that are manifest as behavioral sensitization (Robinson and Becker, 1986; Kalivas and Stewart, 1991; Robinson and Berridge, 1993; Pierce and Kalivas, 1997). This same limbic-motor circuitry is believed to be involved in other motivated behaviors such as sexual behavior (e.g., Phillips, et al., 1991). Current research on drug-induced behavioral sensitization and sexual behavior corroborates the data from neurochemical studies. Several studies have demonstrated the enhancing effects of chronic drug exposure on later sexual motivation and sexual behavior (Fiorino and Phillips, 1999a; Levens and Akins, 2004; Nocjar and Panksepp, 2002; Mitchell and Stewart, 1990). This literature supports the incentive sensitization view of addiction which suggests that neural adaptations occur in reward-related brain areas and become sensitized, and that this sensitization appears to increase the incentive value of natural rewards.

Learning has also been proposed to play a role in the psychological process of cross-sensitization (Berridge and Robinson, 2003; Robinson and Berridge, 2003). Stimuli acquire increased incentive salience as a result of Pavlovian associations formed between the stimuli and drug taking. These stimuli may then drive individuals to "want" or have cravings for the drug or, perhaps, other natural rewards. Indeed, the dopaminergic circuitry involved in reward has been thought to play an important role in Pavlovian associations and incentive salience of cues (Berridge and Robinson, 1998; Dickinson, Smith, and Mirenowicz, 2000). Therefore, it may be, at least in part, the sensitization of incentive salience to the drug cues that results in drug-seeking behavior and perhaps, even sex-seeking behavior.

Not all of the literature supports the notion of overlapping systems or of a link of sex and drug-taking behavior though learning. The findings of studies investigating the reverse of drug-sex cross sensitization, that is, whether sexual experience alters subsequent responding to drugs are not in agreement. One study, to date, has demonstrated that sexual experience sensitizes amphetamine-induced locomotor activity in female hamsters (Bradley and Meisel, 2001). The findings of two other studies (Levens, 2003; Shaham et al., 1997) failed to demonstrate that multiple sexual events were sufficient to sensitize later responding to drugs. However, these studies are difficult to compare because the former used female hamsters and the latter two used male quail and male rodents, respectively. In addition, the three studies used different behavioral paradigms (see above). It could also be argued that the findings of Bradley and Meisel (2001) were not very robust since they only found an augmentation of locomotor activity in amphetamine-sensitized female hamsters during the first 10 min, after which difference in locomotor activity was not evident.

Reinstatement studies also do not suggest a simple overlap between sexual behavior and drugs. Exposure to a receptive female and copulation do not appear to be sufficient to reinstatement of drug-seeking behavior (Shaham et al., 1997; Akins and Harris, unpublished). This appears to be the case even though exposure to an estrus female has been shown to provoke activity in both the dopamine (Hull, Lorraine, and Matuszewich, 1995) and opioid systems (Agmo and Berenfeld, 1990). It is possible that the surge in dopamine that occurs as a result of a sexual event is not sufficient to evoke a reinstatement. Another possibility as described by Shaham et al. (1997) is that the lack of finding might that stimuli associated with a sexual event may result in behaviors directed toward those stimuli but not drug-related stimuli. In this case, a sexual event is not likely to increase interest in drug-related cues. Alternatively, perhaps in order to observe evidence of reinstatement of drugs on sexual behavior and vice versa, exposure to the drug and to the sexual event need to occur in the same context. There is some evidence that cross-sensitization of sex and drugs is context-specific (Mitchell and Stewart, 1990). Further studies are needed to investigate the latter two possibilities.

In conclusion, in spite of some disparity in findings about the complementary nature of drugs and abuse and sexual behavior, growing evidence suggests that learning may be involved. Pavlovian associations can occur between stimuli related to drug taking, a sexual event, and/or other environmental cues. These associations can alter conditioned responding to drug-taking and/or sexual cues to induce "drug-seeking" or "sex-seeking" (referred to by Berridge and Robinson, 2003, as "wanting"). These behaviors may lead to relapse, or in the case of drugs and risky sexual behavior, a reciprocal relapse pattern in which drug addicts experience a drug binge episode, followed by risky sexual behavior, and another binge.

REFERENCES

Agmo, A., and Berenfeld, R. (1990). Reinforcing properties of ejaculation in the male rat: Role of opioids and dopamine. *Behavioral Neuroscience*, 104, 177-182.

Akins, C. K., and Harris, E. (unpublished). Reactivation of cocaine conditioned place preference by cocaine and sexual reinforcement.

Berridge, K. C., and Robinson, T. E. (1998). What is the role of dopamine in reward: Hedonic impact, reward learning, or incentive salience? *Brain Research Review*, 28, 309-369.

Berridge, K. C., and Robinson, T. E. (2003). Parsing reward. *TRENDS in Neurosciences*, 26(9), 507-513.

Booth, R. E, Kwiatkowski, C. F., and Chitwood, D. D. (2000). Sex related HIV risk behaviors: differential risks among injection drug users, crack smokers, and injection drug users who smoke crack. *Drug and Alcohol Dependence*, 58, 219-26.

Bradley, K. C., and Meisel, R. L. (2001). Sexual behavior induction of c-Fos in the nucleus accumbens and amphetamine-stimulated lomocotor activity are sensitized by previous sexual experience in female Syrian hamsters. *Journal of Neuroscience*, 21(6), 2123-2130.

Brooks, J. S., Adams, R. E., Balka, E. B., Whiteman, M., Zhang, C., and Sugarman, R. (2004). Illicit drug use and risky sexual behavior among African American and Puerto Rican urban adolescents: the longitudinal links. *Journal of Genetic Psychology*, 165(2), 203-220.

Camp, D. M., and Robinson, T. E. (1988). Susceptibility to sensitization. I. Sex differences in the enduring effects of chronic d-amphetamine treatment on locomotion, stereotyped behavior, and brain monoamines. *Behavioural Brain Research*, 30, 55-68.

De Wit, H., and Stewart, J. (1983). Drug reinstatement of heroin-reinforced responding in the rat. *Psychopharmacology*, 79, 29-31.

Dickinson, A., Smith, J., and Mirenowicz, J. (2000). Dissociation of Pavlovian and instrumental incentive learning under dopamine antagonists. *Behavioral Neuroscience*, 114, 468-483.

Domjan, M., Cusato, B., and Krause, M. (2004). Learning with arbitrary versus ecological conditioned stimuli: Evidence from sexual conditioning. *Psychonomic Bulletin and Review*, 11,(2), 232-246.

Fiorino, D. F., Coury, A., and Phillips, A. G. (1997). Dynamic changes in nucleus accumbens dopamine efflux during the Coolidge effect in male rats. *Journal of Neuroscience*, 17, 4849-4855.

Fiorino, D. F., and Phillips, A. G. (1999a). Facilitation of sexual behavior in male rats following *d*-amphetamine-induced behavioral sensitization. *Psychopharmacology*, 142, 200-208.

Fiorino, D. F., and Phillips, A. G. (1999b). Facilitation of sexual behavior and enhanced dopamine efflux in the nucleus accumbens of male rats after D-amphetamine-induced behavioral sensitization. *Journal of Neuroscience*, 19(1), 456-463.

Harmer, C. J. , and Phillips, G. D. (1999). Enhanced conditioned inhibition following repeated pretreatment with *d*-amphetamine. *Psychopharmacology*, 142, 120-131.

Hull, E. M., Lorrain, D. S., and Matuszewich, L. (1995). Extracellular dopamine in the medial preoptic area: Implications for sexual motivation and hormonal control of copulation. *Journal of Neuroscience*, 15(11), 7465-7471.

Kalivas, P. W., and Stewart, J. (1991). Dopamine transmission in the initiation and expression of drug- and stress-induced sensitization of motor activity. *Brain Research Reviews*, 16, 223-244.

Kall, K. I. (1992). Effects of amphetamine on sexual behavior of male i.v. drug users in Stockholm—a pilot study. *AIDS Education and Prevention*, 1, 6-17.

Kall, K. I., and Nilsonne, A. (1995). Preference for sex on amphetamine: a marker for HIV risk behaviour among male intravenous amphetamine users in Stockholm. *AIDS Care*, 7, 171-188.

Kohlbert, J. G., and Meisel, R. L. (1999). Sexual experience sensitizes mating-related nucleus accumbens dopamine responses in female Syrian hamsters. *Behavioral Brain Rsearch*, 99, 45-52.

Levens, N. (2003). *Sex and drug interactions in male Japanese quail: Incentive sensitization and dopamine.* Unpublished dissertation.

Levens, N., and Akins, C. K. (2004) Cocaine induces conditioned place preference and increases locomotor activity in male Japanese quail. *Pharmacology, Biochemistry, and Behavior*, 68, 71-80.

Mermelstein, P. G., and Becker, J. B. (1995). Increased extracellular dopamine in the nucleus accumbens and striatum of the female rat during paced copulatory behavior. *Behavioral Neuroscience*, 109, 354-365.

Miesel, R. L., Camp, D. M., and Robinson, T. E. (1993). A microdialysis study of ventral striatal dopamine during sexual behavior in female Syrian hamsters. *Behavioral Brain Research*, 55, 151-157.

Mitchell, J. B., and Stewart, J. (1990). Facilitation of sexual behavior in the male rat in the presence of stimuli previously paired with systemic injections of morphine. *Pharmacology, Biochemistry, and Behavior*, 35, 367-372.

Nocjar, C., and Panksepp, J. (2002). Chronic intermittent amphetamine pretreatment enhances future appetitive behavior for drug- and natural-reward: Interaction with environmental variables. *Behavioral Brain Research*, 128, 189-203.

Pfaus, J. G., Damsma, G., Nomikos, G. G., Wenkstern, D., Blaha, C. D., Phillips, A. G., and Fibiger, H. C. (1990). Sexual behavior enhances central dopamine transmission in the male rat. *Brain Research*, 530, 345-348.

Pfaus, J. G., Damsma, G., Wenkstern, D., Fibiger, H. C. (1995). Sexual activity increases dopamine transmission in the nucleus accumbens and striatum of female rats. *Brain Research*, 693, 21-30.

Phillips, A. G., Pfaus, J. G., and Blaha, C. D. (1991). Dopamine and motivated behavior: Insights provided by in vivo analysis. In: Willner, P., and Scheel-Kruger, J. (Eds.). *The mesocorticolimbic dopamine system: From action to motivation.* Wiley, London, pp. 199-224.

Pierce, R. C. and Kalivas, P. W. (1997). A circuitry model of the expression of behavioral sensitization to amphetamine-like stimulants. *Brain Research Reviews*, 25, 192-216.

Robinson, T. E., and Becker, J. B. (1986). Enduring changes in brain and behavior produced by chronic amphetamine administration: A review and evaluation of animal models of amphetamine psychosis. *Brain Research Reviews*, 11, 157-198.

Robinson, T. E., and Berridge, K. C. (1993). The neural basis of drug craving: An incentive-sensitization theory of addiction. *Brain Research Reviews*, 18, 247-291.

Robinson, T. E., Berridge, K. C. (2000). The psychology and neurobiology of addiction: An incentive-sensitization view. *Addiction*, 95(Supl 2), S91-S117.

Robinson, T. E., Berridge, K. C. (2003). Addiction. *Annual Review of Psychology*, 54, 25-53.

Ross, M. W., Hwang, L. Y., Zack, L., Bull, L., and Williams, M. L. (2002). Sexual risk behaviours and STIs in drug abuse treatment populations whose drug of choice is crack cocaine. *International Journal of STD and AIDS*, 13, 769-774.

Shaham, Y., Erb, S., and Stewart, J. (2000). Stress-induced relapse to heroin and cocaine seeking in rats: A review. *Brain Research Reviews*, 33, 13-33.

Shaham, Y., Rodaros, D., and Stewart, J. (1994). Reinstatement of heroin-reinstated behavior following long-term extinction: Implications for the treatment of relapse to drug-taking. *Behavioral Pharmacology*, 5, 360-364.

Shaham, Y., Puddicombe, J., and Stewart, J. (1997). Sexually arousing events and relapse to heroin-seeking in sexually experienced male rats. *Physiology and Behavior*, 61(2), 337-341.

Tapert, S. F., Aarons, G. A., Sedlar, G. R., and Brown. S. A. (2001). Adolscent substance use and sexual risk-taking behavior. *Journal of Adolescent Health*, 28(3), 181-189.

Van Haaren, F., Meyer, M. E. (1991). Sex differences in locomotor activity after acute and chronic cocaine administration. *Pharmacology, Biochemistry, and Behavior*, 39 (4), 923-927.

Washton, A. M. (1989). Cocaine abuse and compulsive sexuality. *Medical Aspects of Human Sexuality, December,* 32-40..

Weatherby, N. L., Shultz, J. M., Chitwood, D. D., McCoy, H. V., McCoy, C. B., Ludwig, D. D., and Edlin, B. R. (1992). Crack cocaine use and sexual activity in Miami, Florida. *Journal of Psychoactive Drugs, 24,* 373–380.

In: Consciousness and Learning Research
Editor: Susan K. Turrini, pp. 97-117

ISBN 1-60021-333-2
© 2007 Nova Science Publishers, Inc.

Chapter 5

MOLECULAR CORRELATE OF CONSCIOUSNESS

Leonardo R. Lareo and *Carlos Corredor*

Pontificia Universidad Javeriana, School of Sciences
Department of Nutrition and Biochemistry,
Computational and Structural Biochemistry and Bioinformatics,
Bogotá, D. C., Colombia, S. A.

ABSTRACT

Consciousness will be understood for the purpose of this chapter as the capacity to discriminate between the self and the environment. In this sense, it is an attribute that mammals, including man, share. But, just as in a play of collective creation the message is both constructed and conveyed through actors and scenic props, consciousness is a process that is built in successive stages in response to stimuli that come from inside and from the environment through the recruitment of certain neurons to construct neuron circuits glued together by proteins. The circuits are constructed in stages in response to external stimuli and are built upon to construct new and ever expanding circuits that will fire in step when the same stimulus is registered by the brain. In this way, different circuits involving different neurons will be built and will respond to different stimuli allowing for discrimination between stimuli. This is the first of a series of similar processes that will successively be accrued by the brain and that will allow in man for the more complex mental processes that differentiate *Homo sapiens* from other species. We will argue that the main protein involved in the construction of these circuits is the ionotropic glutamate receptor activated by N-Methyl-D-Aspartate (iGluR-NMDA). iGluR-NMDA is a three to five subunit membrane spanning voltage gated Ca^{++} channel. The actual number of subunits is not known, but from theoretical and preliminary electron microscopy considerations we believe the five unit ensemble is preferred in most brain regions. There are three different types of subunits from which one, NR1, must always be present for the channel to operate. NR2 and NR3 come in four and two types respectively, thus allowing for a very large number of potential five member receptor combinations. While not all combinations are possible, this potentiality, combined with differential neuron to neuron distribution, would explain the individual build up of neuronal circuits that make the response to similar stimuli unique to each individual. This

---

* Telephone 57-1-3208320 Ext. 4137/4071; FAX 57-1-3208320-2-4059; l.lareo@javeriana.edu.co

is further compounded by the observation that the response to glutamate can be modulated by several agonists and antagonists, making the response to the neurotransmitter different in different neuronal molecular ambient occurring in a given area of the brain. The molecular events that lead to circuit build-up would start by the voltage gated opening of the iGluR-NMDA Ca^{++} channel in a postsynaptic neuron in the presence of glutamate and certain agonists such as glycine. Ca^{++} influx would result in expression of certain proteins such as ligins and cadhesins and their mobilization to the synapse where they would build protein bridges that will make permanent links between the participating neurons. Apart from these considerations, there are several lines of evidence supporting this proposal: The number of iGluR-NMDA's is different in different parts of the brain, the number of iGluR-NMDA's in cerebellum is large at birth and diminishes with age, hypocampal iGluR-NMDA's seem to be important in memory construction and, under anesthesia, there is inactivation of iGluR-NMDA.

INTRODUCTION

A very large amount of work has been done in the past few years, which is starting to identify neural networks involved in recognition and development of the Self. The involvement of certain regions of the brain such as the medial prefrontal cortex has been documented. Brain scans have shown how certain neural circuits become activated when people are confronted with stimuli that try to differentiate self from non-self However, how these neural circuits are built up and what are the molecular events involved, is still unclear [1]. In this chapter, we will argue that creating self-awareness and consciousness involves protein synthesis at the synapses of participating neurons triggered by the opening of voltage-gated specifically designed heteromultimeric iGluR-NMDA.

Consciousness can be defined for the purpose of this chapter as the capacity of any given individual to differentiate the self from the surroundings [1]. In this sense, consciousness is a characteristic probably shared by both humans and animals whose brain has a neo-cortex [2] The acquisition of consciousness probably involves a process in which memory of a given external stimulus is first obtained and new stimuli can then be compared with the "memorized" stimulus. Same stimuli can be recognized as similar while different stimuli can be discriminated from the first one and create a new memory. In this manner, sort of a tree of similar and of divergent memories will be acquired throughout life that will somehow, step by step, provide the individual in the awake state with the capacity to recognize external stimuli and react to them in a way that will ensure its very survival. This stage of development we can call the conscious state.

Biochemical studies have shown that RNA and protein synthesis are involved in the process of the building up and consolidation of memory [3]. Initially it was thought that short-term memory involved mRNA synthesis [4] while long-term memory consolidation involved protein synthesis as shown by the fact that it can be inhibited in rats by protein synthesis inhibitors [5]. We now know that both RNA and protein synthesis are involved in short and long term consolidation [6]. However, short and long-term memory can be thought of as steps in a process that under certain conditions may lead to structural changes at the molecular and morphological levels, as it seems to occur in long-term memory consolidation. We pose that acquisition of memory of, for instance, an external visual stimulus could involve a process such as follows: a ray of white light hits rhodopsin receptors in a particular set of retinal cells. The cis-trans transition of the opsin-associated retinal on the surface of the photoreceptor cells causes a conformational change in the protein that is somehow transmitted through G-protein signaling pathway and triggers depolarization in the surface of dipolar retinal cells, which, in turn, activate the synaptic terminal of fibers of the optic nerve [7]. The generated impulse would travel through the axons to the soma of their respective cells in the occipital cortex. The following molecular steps are a matter of speculation. Let us suppose, in a very simplistic way, that the depolarization reaches the soma of neuron A whose membrane has synapses to some 50 plus dendrites and axons belonging to a similar number of other neurons. Let us further suppose that even though there is a possibility of transmitting the impulse to all dendrites and axons in contact with A, only a synapse with neuron B will be somehow activated and the impulse will travel to only B and no to any other neuron. Neuron B will also have potential connections to a large number of other cells, but only that connecting to neuron C will be somehow activated. Through this process, the impulse will go to neurons D, E, F, G and H. Now, H will also establish connections to cells in other parts of the brain. There is no reason, whatsoever, to propose a linear circuit. Instead, we can think that neuron B will also establish a connection to neuron J, which in turn will establish connection with two or three different neurons and so forth, branching out at every certain neuron. In this manner, a circuit similar to a tree will have been built. We will not worry at this point about the type of molecular connection established, except to introduce the idea that it has to be mediated by newly synthesized proteins with a given half-life. If no new stimulus reaches the retinal cell, the proteins involved in the connection will be degraded. However, let us now suppose that exactly the same stimulus reaches the same retinal cell before the involved proteins have been hydrolyzed. In this case, the stimulus will cause the same cells to respond in the same sequence. If a further stimulus is received, the neuronal circuit will again fire sequentially as a unit and may even recruit new cells at the end of some branches in the circuit in different parts of the brain. But at this point, the circuit will have been established and will thereafter fire in the same way every time the same stimulus hits the receptor cell.

Let us now suppose that a different stimulus, perhaps of a different wavelength and therefore frequency, hits the same receptor cell. The nerve impulse will travel to the same occipital cortex neuron but once there, it will not follow the same path. It will now establish a new connection with neuron L which in turn, and following the same sequence, will establish connections first with M, then with M', N, N', N'', O, O', O'', O''', P, etc.. and then, with other cortical neurons. If no further stimulus of the kind is received, the proteins will be degraded and the circuit will not respond if the stimulus is received later on. On the other hand, if further stimuli are again received before protein degradation, then a new branched circuit will be established that will respond sequentially as a unit every time that very same stimulus hits the retinal cell. Thus, by this mechanism, two independent branched circuits will be established responding to different stimuli. Discrimination between the two pathways, and therefore, recognition of the stimuli as different, will depend on higher areas of the cortex.

Let us now address the question of how are the interneuronal connections established. For the purpose of this argument, we assume a developed brain where all basic neuronal growth has stopped and innervation processes have been completed. The depolarization would somehow signal the nucleus to express a gene that we will call gene A. Gene A will be expressed as mRNA A that will leave the nucleus and will randomly reach one or more of the synapses on the cell membrane. mRNA A will be translated into protein A that will somehow link the two synaptic membranes and would allow for depolarization of the post synaptic membrane transmitting a nerve impulse to the linked neuron. This protein link will somehow allow impulses to flow from Neuron A to neuron B where a similar process will be triggered to link neuron B to neuron C, and so forth. The protein link will have a short half-life and in absence of a repeated stimulus, both mRNA's and proteins will be degraded. However, if a new train of stimuli is received by the same circuit within a reasonable lapse of time, a protein or protein complex will be expressed both in the pre and, more importantly, in the postsynaptic membranes. The expression of these proteins will have a consequence: new stimuli to the same neuronal circuit will result in a neurotransmitter release from the presynaptic neuron and activation of the protein receptor in the postsynaptic neuron. For this activation to provide long-term circuit formation, a different type of protein must be expressed. These proteins must be adherence proteins whose expression would be the result of Ca^{++} influx, which will signal the expression of the adhering proteins. For Ca^{++} influx to occur, the protein receptor mentioned above must be sensitive to the neurotransmitter and be associated with a Ca^{++} channel.

The above is admittedly an oversimplification of a very complicated process. Several excellent reviews of circuitry formation in the hippocampus and other parts of the brain are available [8]. However, our purpose is not to review these higher functions. We will limit ourselves to propose that the receptor protein which actually participates in the formation of long term connections is the glutamate receptor and that it will not only participate in the building up of a permanent connection, but in fact, in the transmission of the nerve impulse between the neurons of the established branched circuits.

Since so many different neurons are involved in the brain process proposed above, the question arises as to how can a given type of macromolecule discriminate between different incoming stimuli in different neurons. Admittedly, a human brain may have some 10^{11} neurons and each one of them may have some 10^3 synapses. Therefore, in order to have point to point unique connections we would need to have some 10^{14} different types of proteins. This is a number that far exceeds known genomic determined protein types that might not surpass 10^5. Therefore, no single protein can be suited for such a task. In order to approach the number of different neuron-to-neuron connections, a heteromeric complex of polypeptide subunits must have developed through the evolutionary process. If we were to have 2 subunits to give a dimer, we could only have four possible combinations. If there were three subunits to form trimers, then we can have up to 27 combinations. If we continue with this train of thought, we can calculate that if there are 14 different subunits to make up pentamers, there is a possibility to have 5^{14}, i.e., about 10^{10} different possible arrangements. Now, if we can have pentamers, hexamers and heptamers, the possibilities become absolutely enormous: 5^{14} x 6^{14} x 7^{14} which could probabilistically take care of any neuron to neuron connection possible in a unique form. Therefore, we must look for a macromolecular ensemble of five to seven different subunits each one of which can be present in up to 14 different isomeric forms. On the basis of all published results related to memory formation and other brain functions, we believe that the only protein complex that satisfies these requirements is the iGluR-NMDA glutamate receptor.

The iGluR-NMDA

In order to understand how is the iGluR-NMDA receptor involved in all these processes, it is necessary to introduce the features that make the receptor ideally suited for this role. Authors [9] have shown that the iGluR-NMDA receptor is a heteromeric complex made up of three different kinds of polypeptide subunits. The peptide subunits have been assigned to three different groups called NR1, NR2 and NR3 [10]. It has been shown that there are four types of NR2 [11] and two types of NR3 [12], each type being the expression product of different genes called GRIN2 and GRIN 3. There are up to eight different polypeptide NR1 chains, which are the products of gene splicing of the GRIN1 gene [13]. Of course, all these genes are present in every cell in the organism, but we hold that there is differential expression in any particular cell [14, 15]. In this way, it is possible to imagine that if all subunits were expressed in one single cell, there would be an equal probability that any of the 10^{14} plus pentamers and hexamers could be assembled. Even though possible, such a random assemblage would not have any possible physiological meaning. Therefore, one can imagine that rather than an equal expression of all genes in a particular cell, only some of GRIN genes would be expressed in any given cell at any given time. What this means is that a particular set of the three subunits would be expressed in one cell in response to a given stimulus. From the product of the expression, a small number of pentamers could be assembled in any given cell.

In order to make this concept more easily understood, let us suppose that a neuron in the occipital cortex would express genes GRIN1, GRIN2A and GRIN3A, but would not express any other GRIN genes. In this case, the pentamer would be made up of one NR1 and two each NR2A and NR3A. Other arrangement could be one NR2A and two each NR1 and NR3A or one NR3A and two each NR1 and NR2A. Let us call the first arrangement pentamer A, and the other two, pentamers B and C. As can be realized, this particular neuron could form three different complexes, and with adequate sorting and directing from Golgi only one of the complexes could migrate to a particular dendrite. Other possible complexes would not migrate to the same dendrite, but they would do so to other dendrites. If this were the case, in this way only one particular protein arrangement would be possible at a particular synapse and this would ensure that a unique connection between two neurons is established. Let us further argue that it is arrangement A that migrates through the axon to another intermediate neuron in the pathway that eventually leads to the hippocampus. Moreover, let us further suppose that the intermediate neuron also express pentamer A and the next connecting neuron does the same until the last neuron in the path. In this way, we can say that a circuit has been established by the connections that would be product of pentamer A in all neurons involved. A similar argument could be advanced if it were pentamer B or pentamer C the ones that participate in establishing three different circuits. Each one of these circuits would fire if the initial neuron receives the particular stimulus that led to the establishment of circuit A, B or C, and thus, it would be recognized and differentiated from other stimulus that triggers firing of the other two circuits.

It will be noticed that this argument can be used to explain the building of any number of actual circuits with the simple expression of only three of the GRIN genes. Notice that we are proposing that a single cell would not express every single GRIN gene, but rather, that there is a differential expression of particular genes as a result of an external stimulus which would involve signaling pathways inside each of the cells involved. This could seem a mute argument were not for the fact that there are several lines of evidence that show differential expression of GRIN genes both in time and in different regions of the brain which will be reviewed below. Let us now turn our attention to the neurons and synapses.

Neurons

Neurons are cells of complex geometry and of great differences in size. Communication transactions between neurons occur at specific points in the plasma membrane. Most neurons are highly elongated and they are polarized in such way that one pole normally receives information and the opposite pole transmits information to other cell or cells. The receptive pole is called the dendritic zone where several connections can occur while the transmitting pole possesses terminal branches, the synaptic bulbs, often called boutons. The branched or unbranched process that connects the receptive pole with the transmitting pole is ordinarily an elongated process called axon.

Neurons may be divided into two general classes on the basis of type of input. Receptor neurons are those that receive and transduce environmental energy, such as light, heat, mechanical, electrical and chemical stimuli. In each case, the membrane is specialized to respond to the specific stimulus. Synaptic neurons are those that receive coded information from other neurons by means of synaptic contacts. The great complexity of the nervous tissue, compared to other tissues of the body, is probably the result of an evolutionary process through which the capacity of nerve cells to communicate with each other in a specific form became greater and greater.

Synapses

Synapses are specialized junctions through which neurons transmit signals to one another and to non-neuronal cells, such as muscle or gland cells. The word synapse comes from the Greek synaptein, where syn- means together, and haptein, to clasp.

At a typical synapse, such as a dendritic spine, a mushroom-shaped bud projects from each of two cells and the caps of these buds press flat against one another. At this interface, the membranes of the two cells flank each other across a slender gap, the synaptic cleft, the narrowness of which enables signaling molecules known as neurotransmitters to pass rapidly from one cell to the other by diffusion. Such synapses are asymmetric both in structure and in mechanism of operation. Only the so-called pre-synaptic neuron secretes the neurotransmitter, which binds to receptors facing into the synapse from the post-synaptic cell membrane. The part of the synapse where neurotransmitter is released is called the active zone. At active zones, the membranes of the two adjacent cells are held in close contact by cell adhesion proteins. There also exists a less elaborate form of junction called an electrical synapse. For the purpose of our arguments, we have only considered the so called chemical synapses, i.e. those which involve neurotransmitters.

Neurotransmitters

Neurotransmitters are usually small molecules such as acetylCoA, adrenaline, glutamate, or gamma amino butyric acid (GABA). The release of neurotransmitter is triggered by the arrival of a nerve impulse or action potential and occurs through an unusually rapid process of cellular secretion: Within the pre-synaptic nerve terminal, vesicles containing neurotransmitter sit "docked" and ready at the synaptic membrane. The arriving action potential produces an influx of calcium ions through voltage-dependent, calcium-selective ion channels, at which point the vesicles fuse with the membrane and release their contents to the outside. Receptors on the opposite side of the synaptic gap bind neurotransmitter molecules and respond by opening nearby ion channels in the post-synaptic cell membrane, causing ions to rush in or out and changing the local transmembrane potential of the cell. The result is excitatory, in the case of depolarizing currents, or inhibitory in the case of hyperpolarizing currents. Whether a synapse is excitatory or inhibitory depends on what type(s) of ion channel conduct the post-synaptic current, which in turn is a function of the type of receptors and neurotransmitter employed at the synapse.

Glutamergic Synapses

Glutamate is, perhaps, the most important neurotransmitter in the brain. It predominantly acts as an excitatory neurotransmitter and thus, glutamate receptors are of great importance in neural transmission. Glutamate acts at glutamatergic synapses where several glutamate receptors have been shown to exist. While there is no actual quantification, it is highly likely that more than 60% of the 10^{13}-10^{14} synapses in the human brain utilize glutamate as their neurotransmitter.

In figure 1 we present a diagram of a glutamergic synapse with the iGluR-NMDA postsynaptic location and some, of the more than 600 protein structures that interact with it, thus generating a multiplicity of differential signaling processes.

Glutamatergic synapses events trigger long-term changes in the biochemical state of postsynaptic cells [16]. The length of the synaptic current is a key element in determining the overall function of glutamatergic synapses. Transmission of the signal at these synapses is carried out by large, brief, excitatory synaptic currents (EPSC's). EPSC's mediated by iGluR-NMDA are quite slow and induce long trains of spikes enhancing the cell excitability.

Relatively high frequency afferent stimulation can evoke a long lasting increase in synaptic reactivity that has been called long-term potentiation (LTP). On the other hand, low frequency stimulation may induce either a decrease in synaptic transmission, the so-called long-term depression (LTD) or may cause a depression of LTP. The duration of the postsynaptic response is also of importance in determining the consequence of repetitive synaptic activity.

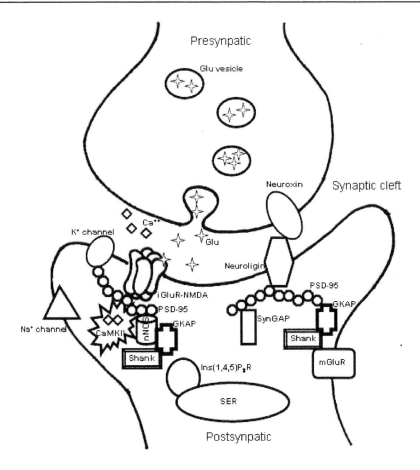

Figure 1. Glutamergic synapse.

Neural Circuits or Neural Networks

Intercommunicating sets of neurons appear as complex three-dimensional networks recognized as a neural network. According to Globus, [17] a neural network may be defined as one possessing the following characteristics: a) the transfer function depends on the ionic channels, modulated by neurotransmitters, neuromodulators and second messengers, b) the synaptic efficiency of the network is chemically tuned, c) the functional connectivity, or association of neurons, is dynamic, d) the network has the capacity of adaptability. Ben Best has expressed the same idea in this manner: "Our neurological hardware consists of plastic and non-plastic components. If the essence of our identities lies in the non-plastic components, then preservation of memory may be neither necessary nor sufficient to preserve our identities. There is some plasticity to the neurological circuits governing vision and walking, but the neurological wiring is predominantly not plastic. Moreover, hard-wiring of our nervous system may be reflected not only in our sensory and motor apparatus, but in our behavior and thought. It is essential that neurological control of heartbeat and respiration be hard-wired. Might the perception of self and the drive for self-preservation be equally essential -- and require hard-wiring?"

Hebbian Synapses

Hebbian learning is a hypothesis as to how neuronal connections are enforced in mammalian brains. This type of learning is named after Donald Hebb [18], who in 1949 proposed that the strength of a connection between two neurons is altered by the way they fire at a given time. Hebb's original principle is, in short, that when one neuron stimulates other neuron, which is also firing at the same time, the strength of the connection between the two neurons increases. On the other hand, if one is firing and the other one is not, then the connection strength is decreased. Hebbian theory thus explains the mechanism of synaptic plasticity in which an increase in synaptic effectiveness arises from the presynaptic cell's repeated and persistent stimulation of the postsynaptic cell. Wiesel and Hubel [19] extended the concept to explain experimentally demonstrated selective elimination of synapses proposing that actively used synapses survive while less actively used ones are removed.

Training and Learning Effects on Synapses

Work in the laboratory of Eric Kandel [20] has provided evidence for the involvement of Hebbian learning mechanisms at synapses in the marine invertebrate *Aplysia californica*. This marine snail presents an assorted repertoire of interesting behaviors and features for such a very simple creature. Its entire nervous system consists of only about 20,000 neurons. Gill withdrawal reflex exhibits nonassociative and associative learning behavior. In nonassociative learning, it is possible to generate habituation to repeated gentle touch to the siphon or dishabituation/sensitization to touch to the siphon by electric shocks to the tail. The effect may last for 24 hours or longer. This is long-term memory. In associative learning with classical conditioning, after gentle touch to siphon (condition stimulus: CS) paired with strong electric shock to tail (unconditioned stimulus: US) it is possible to detect that, prior to conditioning, the CS elicits a mild response while the US elicits a strong response. After conditioning, the CS alone elicits a powerful response that can last for days thus showing that temporal relationship of CS and US is critical for conditioning. These findings may be explained by neuron plasticity, i.e., the ability to change both the structure and chemistry of the brain in response to environmental stimuli. In fact, as a nerve cell is stimulated by new experiences and exposure to incoming information from the senses, it will actually grow new dendrites. Stimuli for plasticity may involve several possible mechanisms such as changes in sensitivity of sensory neurons to external stimuli, changes in sensory or motor neuron firing patterns, changes in spike amplitude or alterations in duration and/or efficiency of sensory-to-motor neuron or motor neuron-to-muscle synapses.

Thus, training and learning change the morphology and even the half-life of the connected neurons: networks with low level of use can be deleted eliminating previously formed connections and even involved dendrites. The human brain is, then, an active dynamic structure continuously affected reshaped by external and internal stimuli.

Impulse Transmission

While the above description suggests the manner in which permanent protein mediated circuits can be established, we have not explained how the electric impulse is transmitted in the circuit. Let us, then, turn our attention to the iGluR-NMDA.

As explained above, the iGluR-NMDA is composed of at least five subunits, one of which must be one of the eight possible NR1's. When glutamate binds at its site, there is a conformational change that allows the different subunits to change their relative positions and a channel will open [21]. We argued above that Ca^{++} entering the cell would activate the expression of certain genes to produce the proteins that maintain the connection. However, this channel is quite different from other ion channels in that it is not only a Ca^{++} channel, but in that, it is also a Na^+ and K^+ channel. We pose that once the permanent connection has been established, glutamate liberation will open the iGluR-NMDA channel and K^+ will flow out and Na^+ will flow in the postsynaptic membrane causing depolarization that will cause an action potential [22] that will, in turn, cause liberation of glutamate at the appropriate synapses, thus causing the neural impulse to be transmitted to all neurons involved in the circuit.

Notice that impulse spread has been associated with Na^+ and K^+ channels. Perry and Georgiev has proposed a different molecular approach to consciousness formation involving cholinergic channels [23, 24] and neuroligins [25]. Perry considers that the cholinergic system is one of the most important modulatory neurotransmitter systems in the brain and controls activities that depend on selective attention which are essential for conscious awareness and in consequence, he believes that this system is the basis of consciousness formation. Georgiev [26], on the other hand, purports that cytoskeleton organization is key in the control of total cerebral dynamics and that it may reorganize according to received electromagnetic stimuli. He has also suggested that β-neurexins [27] y neuroligins [28] participate in the process of neural "wiring".

Our proposal somehow put these proposals together in the sense that there is an iGluR-NMDA mediated $Na^+- K^+$ exchange that propagates the impulse at the synapse and adherence molecules at the involved synapses that hold them together to maintain the integrity of the circuit. There are several line of evidence to substantiate this proposal that we will now explore.

DIFFERENTIAL EXPRESSION OF NMDA WITH DEVELOPMENT

Consciousness, as a neuronal process, probably involves all brain structures. However, some areas are believed to be more important than others. Most frequently cited structures are the thalamo-cortical, prefrontal, parietotemporal and limbic areas and the somatosensory, visual and auditory association areas. However, the relevance of each one for each type of stimuli has been studied independently, even though it is clear that integration of all areas is essential for consciousness formation.

Reports of different distribution patterns of the iGluR-NMDA in the brain began to appear in the second half of the 1980's [29]. Abundant data about distribution heterogeneity of the different constitutive subunits of the receptor in mouse and rat brain are extant. However, few data is available for iGluR-NMDA distribution in the human brain.

Watanabe, *et al.*, using hybridization techniques to locate the receptor subunits in mouse brain, have reported in a series of papers a large variety in regional distribution [30, 31, 32, 33]. From their work it appears that, the NR1 subunit is found ubiquitously in the forebrain. This was to be expected because it is was previously recognized that the active channel associated to the iGluR-NMDA requires the presence of at least one NR1 subunit together with the other types of subunits [34, 35]. In contrast, the distribution of the four NR2 subunits mRNAs is highly variable from region to region. The NR2A and NR2B subunits mRNAs are selectively expressed in different areas of the telencephalon, such as the cerebral cortex and the hippocampus.

A broad range of combinations of the NR2A-D subunits mRNAs are found in different nuclei and subnuclei, the olfactory bulb, and the thalamus. In the hypothalamus, the suprachiasmatic nucleus, which receives a visual input from retina, expresses the NR2C subunit mRNA alone.

Besides, for different subunit distribution, there are also differences in the receptor concentration in different regions of the forebrain and even in subregions within a given region, such as the cerebral cortex, the hippocampal formation, and the thalamus.

Corresponding to the diverse distribution of the iGluR-NMNDA subunit mRNAs in the forebrain, pharmacological heterogeneity, i.e. the ability to respond to different pharmacological agents, of the receptor channel has been proposed based on ligand binding studies *in situ* [36, 37, 38].

Heterogeneity of electrophysiological properties of the iGluR-NMDA has also been reported for different subunit combinations [39, 40, 41] as well as during development, mainly during the first two weeks after birth [42, 43, 44].

The cerebellum contains a type of iGluR-NMDA different from the forebrain receptor, as shown by differences in affinity for agonists and antagonists [45]. The expression patterns found in the cerebellar granule cells and Purkinje cells are distinct from those seen in other brain regions. At mature stages, granule cells show strong expression of the NR2C subunit mRNA, whereas neurons in the telencephalon express NR2A and NR2B subunit mRNAs selectively. Purkinje cells show no significant expression of any of the NR2 subunit mRNAs, in striking contrast to most neurons in the brain that express all kind of subunit types.

Distribution of subunit mRNAs in brainstem and some nuclei and subnuclei has also been reported. In the anterior pretectal nucleus of the visual system NR1, NR2A and NR2D subunit mRNAs are mainly expressed. Differences in expression have been documented in the auditory system particularly in the inferior colliculus and in the cochlear nucleus complex and in the vestibular system, the general somatosensory and viscerosensory system, the somato motor, branchiomotor and visceromotor system, the precerebellar nuclei, red nucleus, raphe nuclei, reticular formation, tegmental nuclei, substantia nigra, ventral tegmental area and interpeduncular nucleus. It can be concluded that there are strong differential expressions of NR2 subunit mRNAs within the brainstem.

Of particular interest is the region-specific expression of the NR2B subunit mRNA observed in the lamina 2 of the spinal cord. This region contains sensory neurons that receive primary sensory afferents from nociceptors and thermoceptors [46]. iGluR-NMDA NR2B subunit antagonists derived from drugs such as ifenprodil, have proven beneficial in the treatment of neuropathic pain [47] and several other studies report the relevance of the NR2B subunit in pain process [48].

In non-human primates, iGluR-NMDA is expressed heterogeneously in the thalamus and the differential expression involves both subunit expression and nucleus specificity. Quantification of iGluR-NMDA expression in the thalamus of the macaque shows that the receptors are multimeric associations of NR1 and NR2A-NR2D subunits that form ligand-gated ion channels. Particular subunits are associated with modulatory binding sites that affect receptor activity. NR1 was the most abundant subunit, but NR2A, NR2B, and NR2D subunit mRNAs were also present but expressed in a very different pattern from that found in rodents [49].

DIFFERENTIAL EXPRESSION OF NMDA IN CONSCIOUSNESS RELATED PROCESSES

Attention

The amount of information that is potentially available through our sense organs is, apparently, far greater than our brains can handle. Much of this information must therefore be discarded, and the brain must select only those stimuli that are of greatest relevance for further processing. Attention is the means by which we actively process a limited amount of information from the enormous amount of information available through our senses, our stored memories, and our other cognitive processes. Thus, the word *attention* may be best applied to the selection and maintenance of conscious contents and it is, therefore, different from consciousness itself.

When monkey performance of operant tasks was used to model several brain functions and monitor the acute effects of MK-801, a relatively selective iGluR-NMDA antagonist, and phencyclidine (PCP), an iGluR-NMDA antagonist that is also active at sigma opiate receptors, was shown a selective disruption in learning, short-term memory and attention, time perception, and motivation tasks are all equally sensitive to disruption [50].

Using a modified open-field method, the effects of MK-801 on attention to a stimulus object located in a computer-generated central zone (CZ) were assessed. Results suggest that MK-801 blockade of attentional information processing from the external world can be located to the striatum [51].

The spontaneously hypertensive rat (SHR) is an accepted model for attention-deficit hyperactivity disorder (ADHD) since it displays the major symptoms of ADHD: hyperactivity, impulsivity, and poor performance in tasks that require sustained attention. In a study designed to determine whether iGluR-NMDA function is disturbed in the prefrontal cortex of SHR, it was found that impaired receptor function in the prefrontal cortex of SHR could give rise to impaired cognition and an inability to sustain attention [52].

Studies with neonatal mice that received iGluR-NMDA antagonists (D-amphetamine) showed a pattern of regional neuronal degeneration, disruptions of spontaneous motor activity, habituation deficits, and reversal of hyperactivity [53]. The role of the iGluR-NMDA in schizophrenia has been well documented. This condition is characterized by profound disturbance of attention [52]. Autism is perhaps the most extreme case of deficit of attention.

Neuroanatomical and neuroimaging studies suggest aberrations in brain regions rich in glutamatergic neurons. Furthermore, similarities in symptoms produced by iGluR-NMDA antagonists in healthy subjects and those seen in autism, imply that infantile autism might be a hypoglutaergic disorder [53]. *Post mortem* studies of brains of individuals with autism have identified anatomic and pathologic changes in cerebellum, hippocampus, caudate-putamen and prefrontal cortex including significantly increased mRNA levels of several iGluR-NMDA subunit genes [54].

Nootropic drugs such as Piracetam or Nootropyl ($C_6H_{10}N_2O_2$) are proven anti-aging drugs that are especially effective at enhancing memory, alertness, and attention in young and aged rats [55]. Data analysis indicates that this drug has effects on iGluR-NMDA densities in the hippocampus and has positive effects on cognitive performance and attention [56].

Learning and Memory

Several definitions of learning have been proposed. For Miller, it is a relatively permanent increase in response strength that is based on previous reinforcement and that can be made specific to one out of two or more arbitrarily selected stimulus situations. Relatively permanent means that the physical process involved in learning is transient, but the final effect of the entire sequence may last for days, months and even longer. Reinforcement is also associated with temporality and can be the result of two possible pathways: classical conditioning and instrumental learning. The last one is specific to an arbitrarily selected stimulus and it is the most important one [57]. For Thorpe, [58] it is 'a process which manifests itself by adaptive changes in individual behavior as a result of experience'. Maier and Schneirla [59] propse that learning is 'development of responses to limited aspects of the environment' and Tarpy [60] suggests that it is the 'relatively permanent change in behavior which occurs as a result of experience'

Knowledge could then be defined, as structured bodies of information possessed by the nervous system about the external and internal environment that condition the organism's reactions to external environment and internal stimuli [61]. The learning process implies generation of some kind of internal representations, which in a general sense, can be defined as neuronally encoded structured versions of the external environment and internal states, which could potentially guide the behavior [62]. Dudai [63] has defined learning as 'an experience-dependent generation of enduring internal representations, and/or experience-dependent lasting modification in such representations'. From these concepts, we can suggest that memory is the retention and retrieval over time of experience-dependent internal representations.

Helmholtz [64] and Freud [65], proposed that conscious perception is a product of inferences based on the previous knowledge of the world and the memoirs of past events. "Neurophylosophers" such as Terrence J. Sejnowski [66], expert in artificial intelligence, Daniel Dennett [67], psychologist; Patricia and Paul Churchland [68], David J. Chalmers [69] and Bernard J. Baars [70] have approached the subject from a psychological point of view. However, workers such as Francis Crick and Christoff Koch [71] recognize a common underlying process for learning, memory and consciousness formation that is to be found at neuronal and molecular level.

In the last decades a series of investigations have idenitfied iGluR-NMDA as the central molecule in learning and memory processes [72, 73, 74]. In 1999 Tsien, *et al.* [75] were able to generate a genetically modified mouse with a changed expression level and composition of the iGluR-NMDA and showed that there was a direct relationship between this receptor and learning and memory processes. Later studies on point mutations in four amino acid residues of the intracellular domains demonstrated that phosphorylation is essential for learning and memory. In fact, animals in which receptor phosphorylation was inhibited by point mutations were significantly inferior in their cognitive capacities as compared to the wild strain [76]. From this, the authors hypothesized that overactivation of the receiver is necessary for memory and learning enhancement.

ACTIVITY OF NMDA IN ALTERED STATES OF CONSCIOUSNESS

Altered states of consciousness (ASC) refer to those conditions that may be identified as differing from most normal, that is, more statistically frequent behavior and have no moral connotations. Several pathologies not induced by drugs or external stimuli have been recognized as ASC. Among them are the epileptic convulsive episodes, schizophrenia, neurodegenerative disorders such as Alzheimer's disease, etc. Not all altered states of consciousness are pathological. In fact, it is known that induction of some ASC can provide a wide range of beneficial effects such as relaxation to reduce "stress ", to improve the quality of sleep, to prolong periods of learning, etc.

In pathological ASC significant alterations have been reported both in the composition and in the expression of iGluR-NMDA. In schizophrenia, transcription of the receptor protein is altered in the thalamus and the hippocampus where reduced expression of the three ionotropic receptors (NMDA, AMPA and kainate) [77] has been reported in samples taken at autopsy. Other studies suggest that the NR1 subunit is significantly increased [78]. Striatum and limbic system iGluR-NMDA NR2B and NR2A subunits seem to interact with the haloperidol [79] a drug prescribed for schizophrenia.

In Alzheimer's disease, several works have demonstrated that the proportion of the NR1 subunit is significantly lower in susceptible regions of the brain [80]. Mishizen-Eberz, *et al.* have investigated the alterations of the iGluR-NMDA subunits occurring during the progression of the disease. They found that as the symptoms become more prominent, the levels of expression of the NR1 and NR2B subunits are significantly reduced, while the expression of the NR2A subunit was unaffected [81]. Other authors reported reductions of the NR2A subunit (41.4%, p <0.05) and NR2B (40.6%, p=0.058) in the hippocampus but no significant change in the levels of the NR2A subunit in the cerebellum of a patient with Alzheimer's disease [82].

The molecular mechanisms that are underlying the increased excitability of the temporary lobe and the hippocampal region in the epilepsy are not known. Interference with the balance between the excitatory and inhibitory neurotransmission pathways in the epileptic hippocampus can contribute substantially to reduce the threshold for the convulsions. Neder, *et al.*, have investigated the association of the changes in the expression of NR1 of the iGluR-NMDA in human epileptic hippocampus and found lightly reduced NR1 [83].

iGluR-NMDA involvement in other pathologies such as Creutzfeldt-Jakob and dementia associated with AIDS have been documented. In patients with Creutzfeldt-Jakob syndrome, the level of expression of the NR2A subunit was diminished in the jagged turn of the hippocampus [84]. In HIV infection there is iGluR-NMDA activation and increased intracellular calcium [85].

Finally, drugs that alter consciousness in experimental subjects have been shown to interact specifically with the iGluR-NMDA [86] in vitro.

CONCLUSION

Molecular Correlate of Consciousness. An Operational Definition

A molecular correlate of consciousness (MCC) will be defined as a minimal molecular state M_i, in a neural system, such that there is a correlation mapping from the states of M to states of consciousness, where a giving molecular state of M is sufficient under conditions S, for the corresponding state of consciousness, C. That is: If the involved molecular system is in state M_k the subject will have conscious state C_k.

MCC Main Features

It is important to realize that just as DNA is the key molecule in all living processes but it is not life itself not can it explain life, we propose that the iGluR-NMDA is the key molecule for consciousness formation without implying that the receptor is consciousness itself or that it can explain consciousness by itself.

We do maintain that the three-dimensional structure of the receptor is key to all circuit neuron interactions. In fact, geometrical and energetically considerations of the multimeric receptor immersed in a lipid bilayer and with both extracellular and intracellular domains allow one to predict that the particular conformation of a given complex will depend on the subunit composition and that that composition is unique to practically each neuron to neuron synapse. While these are theoretical considerations, we are still a far way from knowing the exact 3-D structure of the complex and, in fact, we do not even know the exact number of participating subunits. However, we can still consider the receptor as a multimeric unit in which the role and even the nature of each subunit is not completely elucidated, but the receptor role as a unit can be known.

We have argued that neural circuit establishment requires neuronal plasticity and the generation of new dendrites. This process implies associated changes in the cytoskeleton. In this respect, it has been demonstrated that there is an increase in the volume of F-actin that is dependent of the activation of the iGluR-NMDA [87]. A clear involvement of the receptor has been shown in tubulin and microtubule formation [88] as well as with synthesis of neuroligins and other proteins of adhesion [89]. This implies that for the quantum theories of memory that are based in changes in the cytoskeleton, the microtubules, and the proteins of adhesion, iGluR-NMDA is a common factor. Its participation in learning processes and memory, in factors that involve the visual processes, in the synaptic structures and even in anesthesia is also well documented. Other events exist in which there are changes of consciousness such as the trance and the dream state where, although not discussed in detail here, the iGluR-NMDA has a fundamental role [90].

Much work remains to be done in order to understand the way iGluR-NMDA is involved in the molecular processes discussed in this chapter. One main challenge is to elucidate the tertiary structure of all the subunits. This is a particularly difficult technical job due to the fact that the subunits are transmembrane proteins that are very difficult to crystallize. We are attempting to predict the structures of all the subunits using a computer assisted theoretical approaches that have given some interesting results. It is necessary to define the geometry of the complex and how it is altered when there is subunit substitution. Furthermore, it is important to understand the movements of each subunit relative to all others when glutamate binds to its site and a transmembrane channel is thus temporarily created. How can the same channel allows movement of such different ions as Ca^{++}, Na^+ and K^+ is a key question that has not been resolved. Deeper and deeper understanding of these molecular aspects will allow us to better understand the physical stage where consciousness is the real actor.

REFERENCES

[1]   Abeles, M. (1991) *Corticonics: neural circuits of the cerebral cortex.* Cambridge University, Cambridge, UK.

[2]   Sommerhoff, G. and K. MacDorman (1994) An account of consciousness in physical and functional terms: a target for research in the neurosciences. *Integr. Physiol. Behav. Sci.* 29, 151-181.

[3]   Lucas, C. (2005) Evolving an integral ecology of mind. *Cortex.* 41, 709-725.

[4]   Montag-Sallaz, M. and D. Montag (2003) Learning-induced arg 3.1/arc mRNA expression in the mouse brain. Learn. Mem. 10, 99-107.

[5]   Hydén, H. and Egyhazi, E. (1964) Changes in RNA content and base composition in cortical neurons of rats in a learning experiment involving transfer of handedness. *Proc. Natl. Acad. Sci. USA*, 52, 1030-1035.

[6]   Kraus, M., H. Schicknick, W. Wetzel, F. Ohl, S. Staak and W. Tischmeyer (2002) Memory consolidation for the discrimination of frequency-modulated tones in mongolian gerbils is sensitive to protein-synthesis inhibitors applied to the auditory cortex. *Learn. Mem.* 9, 293-303.

[7]   Gainutdinova, T. H., R. R. Tagirova, A. I. Ismailova, L. N. Muranova, E. I. Samarova, K. L. Gainutdinov, P. M. Balaban (2005) Reconsolidation of a context long-term memory in the terrestrial snail requires protein synthesis. *Learn. Mem.* 12, 620-625.

[8]   Schertler, G. F. X. (2005) Structure of rhodopsin and the metarhodopsin I photointermediate. *Curr. Op. Struc.Biol.* 15, 408-415.

[9]   Miyashita, Y. (2004) Cognitive memory: cellular and network machineries and their top-down control. *Science.* 306, 435-440.

[10]   Lee, K. Y., A. K. Chou, L. C. Yang and H. Buerkle (2003) NMDA receptors offer more than one functionality. *Anesth. Analg.* 96, 1533-1534.

[11] Hawkins, L. H., P. L. Chazot and F. A. Stephenson. (1999) Biochemical evidence for the co-association of three N-methyl-D-aspartate (NMDA) R2 subunits in recombinant NMDA receptors. *J. Biol. Chem.*, 274, 27211-27218.

[12] Monyer, H., R. Sprengel, R. Schoepfer, A. Herb, M. Higuchi, H. Lomeli, N. Burnashev, B. Sakmann and P. H. Seeburg (1992) Heteromeric NMDA receptors: molecular and functional distinction of subtypes. *Science* 256, 1217-1221.

[13] Andersson, O., A. Stenqvist, A. Attersand and G. von Euler (2001) Nucleotide Sequence, Genomic Organization, and Chromosomal Localization of Genes Encoding the Human NMDA Receptor Subunits NR3A and NR3B. *Genomics* 78, 178-184.

[14] Durand, G. M., P. Gregor, X. Zheng, M. V. Bennett, G. R. Uhl and R. S. Zukin (1992)Cloning of an apparent splice variant of the rat N-methyl-D-aspartate receptor NMDAR1 with altered sensitivity to polyamines and activators of protein kinase C. *Proc. Natl. Acad. Sci. U.S.A.* 89, 9359-9363.

[15] Sasner, M. and A. Buonanno (1996) Distinct N-methyl-D-aspartate receptor 2B subunit gene sequences confer neural and developmental specific expression. *J. Biol. Chem.* 271, 21316-21322.

[16] Monyer, H., N. Burnashev, D. J. Laurie, B. Sakmann, P. H. Seeburg (1994) Developmental and regional expression in the rat brain and functional properties of four NMDA receptors. *Neuron* 12, 529-540.

[17] Ottersn, O. P., I. A. Langmoen and L. Gjerstad (Eds.) (1998) The glutamate synapses as a therapeutical target: *Molecular organization and pathology of glutamate synapse.* Elsevier. Amsterdam.

[18] Globus, G. G. (1992) Towars a noncomputational cognitive neuroscience. *J. Cognit. Neurosci.* 4, 299-310.

[19] Hebb, D. O. (1949) *The organization of behavior.* Wiley, New York.

[20] Wiesel, T. N. and D. H. Hubel (1965) Comparison of the effects of unilateral and bilateral eye closure on cortical unit response in kittens. *J. Neurophysiol.* 28, 1029-1040.

[21] Kandel, E. R., J. H. Schwartz and T. M. Jessel (2000) *Principles of Neural Science.* McGraw-Hill. New York.

[22] Jin, R., M. Horning, M. L. Mayer and E. Gouaux (2002) Mechanism of Activation and Selectivity in a Ligand-Gated Ion Channel: Structural and Functional Studies of GluR2 and Quisqualate. *Biochemistry*, 41, 15635-15643.

[23] Hodking, A. L. and A. F. Huxley (1952) A quantitative description of membrane current and its application to conduction and excitation nerve. *J. Physiol.* 117, 500-554.

[24] Perry, E., M. Walker, J. Grace and R. Perry (1999) Acetylcholine in mind: a neurotransmitter correlate of consciousness. *TINS* 22, 273-280.

[25] Perry, E. K.,H. Ashton and A. H. Young (Eds.) (2002) *Neurochemistry of consciousness : neurotransmitters in mind.* John Benjamin's. Amsterdam.

[26] Georgiev, D. D. (2003) Conduction pathways in neuronal microtubules and cytoskeleton proteins: delocalized electrons, soliton propagation and conformational changes. http://cogprients.ecs.soton.ac.uk/archive/00002913.

[27] Georgiev, D. D. (2003) Conduction pathways in neuronal microtubules and citoskeletal proteins: delocalized electrons, soliton propagation and conformational changes. http://cogprients.ecs.soton.ac.uk/archive/00002913.

[28] Georgiev, D. D. (2002) The causal consciousness: β-neurexin promotes neuromediator release via vibrational multidimensional tunneling.

[29] http://cogprints.ecs.soton.ac.uk/archive/00002809.

[30] Georgiev, D. D. (2004) Interneuronal macroscopic quantum coherence in the brain cortex: The role of the intrasynaptic adhesive proteins β-neurexin and neuroligin-1. http://cogprients.ecs.soton.ac.uk/archive/00003008.

[31] Monaghan, D. T. and C. W. Cotman (1988) Distribution of N-methyl-D-aspartate-sensitive L-[H^3]glutamate-binding sites in rat brain. *J. Neurosci.* 5, 2909-2919.

[32] Watanabe, M., Y.Inoue, K. Sakimura and M. Mishina. (1993) Distinct distributions of five N-methyl-D-aspartate receptor channel subunit mRNA in the forebrain. *J. Comp. Neurology.* 338, 377-390.

[33] Watanabe, M., M.Mishina and Y.Inoue. (1994) Distinct distribution of five NMDA receptor channel subunit mRNAs in the brainstem. *J. Comp. Neurology.* 343, 520-531.

[34] Watanabe, M., M. Mishina and Y.Inoue. (1994) Distinct spatiotemporal distributions of the N-methyl-D-aspartate receptor channel subunit mRNA in the mouse cervical cord. *J. Comp. Neurology.* 345, 314-319.

[35] Watanabe, M., M.Mishina and Y. Inoue. (1994) Distinct spatiotemporal expressions of five NMDA receptor channel sununit mRNA in the cerebelum. *J. Comp. Neurology.* 343, 513-519.

[36] Ishii, T., K.Moriyoshi, H.Sugihara, K.Sakurada, H.Kadotani, M.Yokoi, C.Akazawa, R. Shigemoto, N. Mizuno, M. Masu and S. Nakanishi. (1993) Molecular characterization of the family of the N-methyl-D-aspartate receptor subunits. *J. Biol. Chem..* 268, 2836-2843.

[37] Meguro, H. , H.Mori, K.Araki, E.Kushiya, T.Kutsuwada, M.Yamazaki, T.Kumanishi, M. Arakawa, K.Sakimura and M.Mishina. (1992) Functional characterization of a heteromeric NMDA expressed from cloned cDNAs. *Nature.* 357, 70-74.

[38] Lynch, D. R. and R. P. Guttmann (2001) NMDA receptor pharmacology: perspectives from molecular biology. *Curr. Drug Targets.* 2, 215-231.

[39] Yamakura, T. and K. Shimoji (1999) Subunit- and site-specific pharmacology of the NMDA receptor channel. *Prog. Neurobiol.* 59, 279-298.

[40] Buller, A. L. and D. T. (1997) Monaghan Pharmacological heterogeneity of NMDA receptors: characterization of NR1a/NR2D heteromers expressed in Xenopus oocytes. *Eur. J. Pharmacol.* 5, 87-94.

[41] Hollmann, M., M., Hartley and S. Heinemann (1991) Ca2+ permeability of KA-AMPA--gated glutamate receptor channels depends on subunit composition. *Science* 252, 851-853.

[42] Brauneis, U., M., Oz, R.W. Peoples, F.F. Weight and L. Zhang (1996)Differential sensitivity of recombinant N-methyl-D-aspartate receptor subunits to inhibition by dynorphin. *J Pharmacol. Exp. Ther.* 279, 1063-1068.

[43] Smothers, C. T., J. J. Woodward (2003) Effect of the NR3 subunit on ethanol inhibition of recombinant NMDA receptors. *Brain Res.* 987, 117-121.

[44] King, M. S. and R. M. Bradley (2000) Biophysical properties and responses to glutamate receptor agonists of identified subpopulations of rat geniculate ganglion neurons. *Brain Res.* 866, 237-246.

[45] Liu Y. and J. Zhang (2000) Recent development in NMDA receptors. Chin. Med. J. 113, 948-956. Nabekura. J., I., Kawamoto and N. Akaike (1994) Change in voltage dependency of NMDA receptor-mediated response in nucleus tractus solitarii neurons. *Brain Res.* 648, 152-156.

[46] Chazot, P.L., S. K. ColemanM. Cik and F. A. Stephenson (1994) Molecular characterization of N-methyl-D-aspartate receptors expressed in mammalian cells yields evidence for the coexistence of three subunit types within a discrete receptor molecule. *J. Biol. Chem.* 269, 24403-2449.

[47] Sigiura, Y., C. L. Lee and E. R. Perl (1986) Central projections of identified, unmyelinated(C) afferent fibers in the innervating mammalian skin. *Science.* 234, 358-361.

[48] Smith, P. F. (2003) Therapeutic N-methyl-D-aspartate receptor antagonists: will reality meet expectation? *Curr. Opin. Investig. Drugs.* 4, 826-832.

[49] Chazot, P. L. (2004) The NMDA receptor NR2B subunit: a valid therapeutic target for multiple CNS pathologies. Curr. Med. Chem. 11, 389-396; Loftis, J. M. and A. Janowsky (2003) The N-methyl-D-aspartate receptor subunit NR2B: localization, functional properties, regulation, and clinical implications. *Pharmacol. Ther.* 97, 55-85.

[50] Ibrahim, H. M., D. .J Healy, A. J. Hogg, J. H. Meador-Woodruff (2000) Nucleus-specific expression of ionotropic glutamate receptor subunit mRNAs and binding sites in primate thalamus. *Brain Res. Mol. Brain Res.* 79, 1-17.

[51] Paule, M. G. (1994) Acute behavioral toxicity of MK-801 and phencyclidine: effects on rhesus monkey performance in an operant test battery. *Psychopharmacol Bull.* 30, 613-621.

[52] Dai, H. and R. J. Carey (1994) The NMDA antagonist MK-801 can impair attention to exteroceptive stimuli. *Behav. Brain Res.* 62, 149-156.

[53] Lehohla, M., L. Kellaway, V. A.Russell (2004) NMDA receptor function in the prefrontal cortex of a rat model for attention-deficit hyperactivity disorder. Metab. Brain Dis. 19, 35-42.[1] Fredriksson, A. and T. Archer (2003) Hyperactivity following postnatal NMDA antagonist treatment: reversal by D-amphetamine. *Neurotox. Res.* 5, 549-564.

[54] Dracheva, S., S. A. Marras, S. L. Elhakem, F. R. Kramer, K. L. Davis, V. Haroutunian (2001) N-methyl-D-aspartic acid receptor expression in the dorsolateral prefrontal cortex of elderly patients with schizophrenia. *Am. J. Psychiatry.* 158, 1400-1410.

[55] Carlsson, M. L. (1998) Hypothesis: is infantile autism a hypoglutamatergic disorder? Relevance of glutamate - serotonin interactions for pharmacotherapy. *J. Neural Transm.* 105, 525-535.

[56] Purcell, A. E., O. H. Jeon, A. W. Zimmerman, M. E. Blue and J. Pevsner (2001) Postmortem brain abnormalities of the glutamate neurotransmitter system in autism. *Neurology.* 57, 1618-1628.

[57] Giurgea, C. (1973) The 'Nootropic' Approach to the Pharmacology of the Integrative Activity of the Brain. *Cond. Reflex* 8, 108-115.

[58] Scheuer, K., A. Rostock, R. Bartsch, W. E. Muller (1999) Piracetam improves cognitive performance by restoring neurochemical deficits of the aged rat brain. *Pharmacopsychiatry.* 32 Suppl. 1, 10-16.

[59] Miller, N. E. (1951) Comments on multiple-process conceptions of learning. *Psychol Rev.* 58, 375-381.

[60] Thorpe,W. H. (1956) *Learning and instinct in animals*. Harvard University Press. Cambridge. Mass.

[61] Maier, N. R. F. and T. C. Schneirla (1964) *Principles of animal psychology*. Dover. New York.

[62] Tarpy, R. M. (1975) *Basic principles of learning. Scoot and Foresman*. Glenview. Ill.

[63] Burns, G. A. P. C., A. M. Arshad, S. Ghandeharizadeh, M. A. O'Neill and Y-S. Chen (2003) Tools and approaches for the construction of knowledge models from the neuroscientific literature. *Neuroinformatics* 1, 81-109.

[64] Dudai, Y. (1989) *The neurobiology of memory. Concepts, findings, trends*. Oxford University Press. New York.

[65] Helmholtz, H. von (1988) Concerning the perceptions in general. En: L. T. Benjamin (Ed.) *A History of Psychology: Original Sources and Contemporary Research*. McGraw-Hill Book Company. Nueva York, pp. 97-100.

[66] Ornstein, R. E. (1991) *Evolution of Consciousness: Of Darwin, Freud, and Cranial Fire: The Origins of the Way We Think*. Simon and Schuster. Nueva Cork.

[67] Churchland, P. S. and T. J. Sejnowski (1992) *The Computacional Brain*. MIT press. Cambridge. Mass.

[68] Dennett, D. C. (1991) *Consciousness Explained*. Little Brown and Company. Boston.

[69] Churchland, P. M. (1988) *Matter and Consciousness*. MIT Press. Cambridge. Mass.

[70] Chalmers, D. J. (1996) *The Conscious Mind: In Search of Fundamental Theory*. Oxford University Press. Nueva York.

[71] Baars, B. J. (1997) In the Theatre of Consciousness. Global Workspace Theory, A Rigorous Scientific Theory of Consciousness. *J. Consciousness Stud.* 4, 292-309.

[72] Crick, F. and C. Koch (1998) Consciousness and Neuroscience. *Cerebral Cortex* 8, 97-108.

[73] Tsien, J. Z. (2000) Building a brainier mouse. *Sci. Amer.* 400, 1-9.

[74] Tsien, J. Z. (2000) Linking Hebb's coincidence-detection to memory formation. *Current Opinion in Neurobiol.* 10, 266-273.

[75] Tang, Y-P., E. Shimizu, G. R.Dube, C. Rampon, G. A.Kerchner, M. Zhuo, G. Liu and J. Z.Tsien. (1999) Genetic enhacement of learning and memory in mice. *Nature* 401, 63-69.

[76] Lin, C. H., S. H. Yeh, H. Y. Lu and P. W. Gean (2003) The similarities and diversities of signal pathways leading to consolidation of conditioning and consolidation of extinction of fear memory. *J. Neurosci.* 10, 8310-8317.

[77] Harrison, P. J., A. J. Law and S. L. Eastwood (2003) Glutamate receptors and transporters in the hippocampus in schizophrenia. *Ann. N. Y. Acad. Sci.* 1003, 94-101.

[78] Mueller, H. T., V. Haroutunian, K. L. Davis, J. H. Meador-Woodruff (2004) Expression of the ionotropic glutamate receptor subunits and NMDA receptor-associated intracellular proteins in the substantia nigra in schizophrenia. *Brain Res. Mol. Brain Res.* 121, 60-69.

[79] Lee, J. and N. Rajakumar (2003) Role of NR2B-containing N-methyl-D-aspartate receptors in haloperidol-induced c-Fos expression in the striatum and nucleus accumbens. *Neurosci.* 122, 739-745

[80] Hynd, M. R., H. L. Scott and P. R. Dodd (2004) Selective loss of NMDA receptor NR1 subunit isoforms in Alzheimer's disease. *J. Neurochem.* 89, 240-247.

[81] Mishizen-Eberz, A. J., R. A. Rissman, T. L. Carter, M. D. Ikonomovic, B. B. Wolfe and D. M. Armstrong (2004)Biochemical and molecular studies of NMDA receptor subunits NR1/2A/2B in hippocampal subregions throughout progression of Alzheimer's disease pathology. *Neurobiol. Dis.* 15, 80-92.

[82] Bi, H. and C. I. Sze (2002) N-methyl-D-aspartate receptor subunit NR2A and NR2B messenger RNA levels are altered in the hippocampus and entorhinal cortex in Alzheimer's disease. *J. Neurol. Sci.* 200, 11-18.

[83] Neder, L., V. Valente, C. G. Carlotti, J. P. Leite, J. A. Assirati, M. L. Paco-Larson ML and J. E. Moreira (2002) Glutamate NMDA receptor subunit R1 and GAD mRNA expression in human temporal lobe epilepsy. *Cell Mol. Neurobiol.* 22, 689-698.

[84] Ferrer, I. and B. Puig (2003) GluR2/3, NMDAepsilon1 and GABAA receptors in Creutzfeldt-Jakob disease. *Acta Neuropathol.* 106, 311-318.

[85] Hayashi, T. and T. P. Su (2004) Sigma-1 receptor ligands: potential in the treatment of neuropsychiatric disorders. *CNS Drugs* 18, 269-284.

[86] Popescu, G., A. Robert J. R. Howe and A. Auerbach (2004) Reaction mechanism determines NMDA receptor response to repetitive stimulation. *Nature.* 430, 790-793.

[87] Fukazawa, Y., Y. Saitoh, F. Ozawa, Y. Ohta, K. Mizuno and K. Inokuchi (2003) Hippocampal LTP is accompanied by enhanced F-actin content within the dendritic spine that is essential for late LTP maintenance in vivo. *Neuron* 8, 447-460.

[88] Allison, D. W., A. S. Chervin, V. I. Gelfand andA. M. Craig (2000) Postsynaptic scaffolds of excitatory and inhibitory synapses in hippocampal neurons: maintenance of core components independent of actin filaments and microtubules. *J. Neurosci.* 20, 4545-4554.

[89] Song, J. Y., K. Ichtchenko, T. C. Sudhof and N. Brose (1999) Neuroligin 1 is a postsynaptic cell-adhesion molecule of excitatory synapses. *Proc. Natl. Acad. Sci. USA.* 96, 1100-1105.

[90] Eleazar, Z. and A. Berchanki (2001) Glutamatergic-cholinergic synergistic interaction in the pontine reticular formation. Effects on catalepsy. Naunyn-Schmiedeberg's Arch. *Pharmacol.* 363, 569-576.

[91] Manquillo, A., J. M. Martinez, F. Paradinas, J. Saez, P. Quintana, C. Revilla, P. Lopez-Esteban and J. M. Galan (1999) Behavior disorders during REM sleep. Two clinical cases. *Rev. Neurol.* 28, 1170-1174.

In: Consciousness and Learning Research
Editor: Susan K. Turrini, pp. 119-136

ISBN 1-60021-333-2
© 2007 Nova Science Publishers, Inc.

Chapter 6

INDIVIDUAL DIFFERENCES IN SECOND LANGUAGE LEARNING AMONG UNIVERSITY STUDENTS

Georgia Andreou[*], *Eleni Andreou*[**] *and Filippos Vlachos*[*]
[*]Department of Special Education, University of Thessaly, Greece
[**]Department of Primary School Education, University of Thessaly, Greece

ABSTRACT

In this chapter, we make an overview of the literature on the learning styles, approaches to studying and the role of gender and handedness on second language (L2) learning and we report our findings from a three-fold research we undertook at the university of Thessaly in a sample of 452 undergraduate students. In the first part of our research we investigated the influence of gender, handedness and Faculty choice on the performance of phonological, syntactical and semantic tasks in L2. In the second part we examined further how Greek students' approaches to studying in combination with gender, academic discipline and professional degree in English affect performance on verbal fluency tasks in English as a second language. In the third part of our research we investigated the relationship between Greek students' learning styles and performance in English phonological, syntactic and semantic tasks, in combination with their gender and discipline.

Our results showed that handedness alone did not influence the students' performance on L2 tasks. Gender was found to play an important role in our results with females performing better than males in both syntax and semantics. Approaches to studying alone or in combination with students' gender and professional degree in L2 influenced students' performance on syntactical L2 tasks, in which they used a deep or strategic approach, but not on phonological or semantic ones. Concerning learning styles, our study revealed that university students have a tendency to prefer a divergent learning style while performing phonological and semantic tasks and an accommodative learning style while performing syntactical tasks in L2.

In conclusion, our research findings suggest that individual differences influence the way people learn and succeed in language study. However, more research is needed in the field in order to make individual differences practical in the classroom and enable the most learners possible to learn a foreign language in their preferred styles using their own approaches to studying.

INTRODUCTION

Competence in more than one language can be approached at both individual and social levels. While many discussions about learning a second language focus on teaching methodologies, little emphasis is given to the contextual factors -individual, social, and societal- that affect students' learning. These contextual factors can be considered from the perspective of the language, the learner, and the learning process. This chapter discusses such perspectives as they relate to learning any second language, with a particular focus on how they affect adult learners of English as a second language.

Over the past several years there have been important changes in our understanding of the nature of effective second language (L2) learning. The study of individual differences in second language learning, such as gender, handedness, Faculty choice, learning styles and approaches to studying, has received considerable attention and has shown that there are a number of dimensions of learner differences which are generally acknowledged to affect the way people learn foreign languages, how they perform in actual language use and the eventual levels of success they achieve (Lujan-Ortega et al., 2000).

In addition, following the expansion in student numbers in higher education there has been a shift in emphasis in the approaches taken to teaching and learning (Sadler-Smith, 1996). Policy has moved towards student-centered methods and demands made on higher education students for greater autonomy and flexibility in their approaches to learning aimed at enabling them to achieve the maximum benefit from their time in higher education. Given the fact that a whole theory, the Linguistic Coding Deficiency Hypothesis (LCDH) (Sparks et al., 1989), was established after the observations of university second language (L2) educators that while some of their students learnt a FL quickly and easily, while others, given the same opportunities to learn, failed repeatedly, individual differences in second language learning among university students should be particularly taken into account.

FACTORS ASSOCIATED WITH L2 LANGUAGE LEARNING IN HIGHER EDUCATION LANGUAGE FACTORS

Several factors related to peoples' first and second languages shape their second language learning. These factors include the linguistic distance between the two languages, peoples' level of proficiency in the native language and their knowledge of the second language, the dialect of the native language spoken by the peoples (i.e., whether it is standard or nonstandard), the relative status of the peoples' language in the community, and societal attitudes toward the peoples' native language.

One of the factors we will discuss in this chapter is how peoples' level of proficiency in the native language (L1) may influence their L2 learning and more specifically how peoples' possible underlying linguistic coding deficits in L1 may interfere with their ability to learn a L2.

It is a common belief that university level L2 learners have acquired a certain competency in all of the linguistic codes, namely phonological, syntactic and semantic, in their L1. However, this is not always the case. The suggestion that L2 learning problems may occur in association with, or perhaps as a result of, L1 learning problems was first made in studies associated with students with learning disabilities (Carrol, 1973) and later confirmed in other studies (Cline, 2000; Downey et al., 2000; Ganschow et al., 2000; Sparks et al., 1999). Informal reports at several universities showed that substantial numbers of students were being referred for suspected learning disabilities after university entry. The referrals were made because of the students' inability to meet the L2 requirement at the university, giving rise to speculation that subtle native language problems became evident primarily because of the demands that the study of a new and unfamiliar symbol system placed on these students (Carrol, 1973). Prior to this, only one reference was made by Dinklage (1971) about Harvard university students, that addressed the possibility of language disabilities among students who had difficulties in L2 classes. Dinklage stated that these bright students who could not seem to learn a L2 exhibit three types of problems: 1) difficulty with the written (reading and writing) aspects of their native language 2) inability to distinguish the sounds of the L2 and, thus, difficulties with an oral communication approach to L2 learning and 3) memory problems for sounds and words. He supported the idea of an underlying language processing disability as the cause of L2 learning.

In other words, prior to 1980 the study of L2 learning for individuals who had found learning to read and write in their native language extremely problematic had been an under-researched area throughout the world (Ganschow et al., 2000). Since the 1980s, Ganschow and Sparks have conducted pioneering research into the nature of difficulties, why they are encountered and how they can be minimized. They suggested, in the form of the Linguistic Coding Dificiency Hypothesis (LCDH), that some individuals have difficulty in learning their native language in oral and/or written form and this difficulty is likely to affect ability to learn L2. The LCDH theory, with its emphasis on the specific components of language, i.e., phonological, syntactic and semantic, provides an explanation for why university students who appear to have learnt their native language adequately, in fact, have problems that have gone unnoticed but have been compensated for over the years. Generally, the problem areas are subtle, e.g., relatively weak spelling or a slow rate of reading. For the most part, the compensatory strategies used by these students mask their linguistic coding deficits in the native language and they often succeed well in academic settings. Most of the university students reported in studies by Lefebvre (1984), Pompian and Thun (1988) and Sparks, Ganschow and Pohlman (1989) were identified as learning disabled after university entry because of foreign language learning difficulties. What happens to these students is that their compensatory strategies become unworkable when they are placed in situations where they must learn a totally unfamiliar and new linguistic coding system. In the context of the LCDH it has been suggested that students who fail to reach a high level of proficiency in L2 might display a broad range of linguistic coding deficits. Studies have consistently shown that students who achieve higher scores on L2 tasks have significantly stronger native and second language aptitude skills than students who achieve lower L2 scores (Ganschow et al., 1998; Ganschow et al., 1994; Ganschow et al., 1991; Sparks et al., 1995). The most successful L2 learners are those who have strong skills in all of the linguistic codes, in particular the phonological code, which seems to have the most immediate impact on a student's performance in L2 tasks (Sparks et al., 1993).

Biological Factors

The neural substrates of L2 acquisition are largely unknown. It has been recently reported that L1 and L2 are represented differentially in cortical areas during discourse production or listening tasks (Dehaene et al., 1997; Kim et al., 1997). However, other imaging studies have reported common neural substrates of L1 and L2 during word generation tasks (Klein et al, 1995; Chee et al., 1999).

On the other hand, over the past 30 years evidence from a variety of sources supports the view that verbal behavior is a lateralized function (Springer et al., 1998). The two hemispheres of the brain seem to have somewhat different functions. The left hemisphere generally controls the majority of language function and the right hemisphere appears to be involved in maintaining focus of attention, and also possibly prosody. Right hemisphere lesions have been known to severely affect ability to analyze metaphors, summarize complex texts, as well as disrupt prosody in otherwise normal language.

In experimental neurolinguistics the role of the right hemisphere in language processing has been discussed extensively over the last decades. Especially such language-related aspects as intonation (emotional prosody), pragmatics, semantics and non-verbal communication (gesticulation and facial expressions) have been proposed to be primarily processed by the right hemisphere (Van Lancker, 1997). Moreover, the right hemisphere has been assumed to play a key role at the beginning of the language acquisition process, when someone is beginning to learn a second language. It has been assumed that the right (non language-dominant) hemisphere "helps" the left hemisphere in so far as it adopts a holistic strategy to make the language learning process easier in its initial stages. The initial stages are the first years of the acquisitional process, when a learner is not yet experienced enough to develop grammatical "automatisms" in the second language (left hemisphere) and thus resorts to imagery and holistic thinking to tackle the acquisitional problems.

According to Obler (1981) and Galloway and Krashen (1980), the initial stages of adult second language acquisition recapitulate children's right-to-left hemispheric shift in relative hemispheric dominance during L1 acquisition. This is in line with the assumption of Paradis (1994), who states that monolingual children have to rely on right hemisphere-based pragmatic processing during their first years of language acquisition, in order to derive an interpretation for utterances in that language for which the required automatic linguistic competence has not yet been fully internalized.

Two biological variables, gender and handedness are the main factors often associated with language lateralization and their influence will be discussed in this chapter. Many previous studies have shown gender differences in performance on a variety of cognitive tasks (Crow et al., 1998; Janowski et al., 1998). One of the differences reported is a female superiority on verbal fluency tasks. In general, females are reported to be more verbally fluent than men (Stumpf, 1995), although mixed results have also been obtained. For instance, a female advantage for quickly producing words from a particular semantic category has been reported (Gordon et al., 1986) but no sex difference for rapidly producing words beginning with a particular letter was found (Gordon et al., 1986). There are also some other studies which found no gender difference for either type of fluency measure (Hampson et al., 1992; Moffat et al., 1996) or a task of rapid articulation (Gouchie et al., 1991). It seems that language has evolved by a process of increasing hemisphere specialization. Therefore, studies on hemisphere specialization for language functions which reveal stronger lateralization in men than women and even gender related differences in interhemispheric transmission time in the human brain (Nowicka et al., 2001) may account for female superiority on verbal tasks.

Since handedness is related to cerebral language representation, it has often been associated with performance on native and foreign language verbal tasks. Left-handers differ from right-handers on cognitive task performance. One of the most striking differences between left- and right-handers' brains is the lateralization of language. It has been claimed that if a certain functional asymmetry (defined as the anatomical hemisphere of the brain in which a certain function, like language, is localized) is observed in right-handers, the corresponding function in left-handers will be less lateralized and possibly lateralized in the other direction (Springer et al., 1998). In other words, language localized to the left hemisphere (LH) for right-handers would be less localized to the LH, or even dominant in the right hemisphere (RH), for left-handers.

Although some studies found no relationship especially between verbal ability and relative hand skill in the two sexes (Bishop, 1990; Crow et al., 1998; Palmer et al., 1996; Resch et al., 1997), degrees of handedness may be important since it has been suggested (Bishop, 1990; Orton, 1937; Zangwill, 1960) that failure to develop unequivocal dominance in one hemisphere predisposes to pathology. Given the fact that left-handers are a more heterogenous population than right-handers in language function organization and patterns of interhemispheric communication, some studies showed inferior achievements of left-handers in foreign language achievement (Lamn *et al.,* 1999; Lamn, 1997). It seems that left-handers are less equipped for the developing of adequate phonological skills needed for reaching high levels of proficiency in L2. In addition, left-handedness seems to be a more affective factor than sex since studies have shown that left-handers of both sexes are overrepresented in the lowest level L2 classes and were underrepresented in the higher level L2 classes, compared with right-handers of both sexes (Lamn et al., 1999).

CAREER CHOICE AND LEARNING STYLES

Furthermore, success in L2 higher education learning is related to career choice. Discipline-based research (Willcoxson et al., 1996) has shown that specific learning style preferences are typically found in disciplines which belong to pure sciences such as Foreign Languages and Humanities and are different from those adopted by students in disciplines such as Civil Engineering and Computer Science or Mathematics, which belong to exact sciences. This finding indicates that common learning style preferences may act as a facilitating factor for students of Humanities who learn a foreign language.

Educational leaders nowadays recognize that the process of learning is critically important and the way individuals learn is the key for an educational improvement (Demirbas et al., 2003). An individual's preferred method for receiving information in any learning environment is the learning style of that individual. Learning can be defined as an internal process that is different for every individual and learning style can be described as the way individuals acquire new information. Each learner's preferred ways of perception, organization and retention of new information are distinctive and consistent. Learning styles have been extensively discussed in the educational psychology literature (Claxton et al., 1987; Schmeck, 1988) and specifically in the context of language learning by Oxford and her colleagues (Oxford, 1990; Oxford et al., 1991; Wallace et al., 1992; Oxford et al., 1993) and over 30 learning style assessment instruments have been developed in the past decades (Guild et al., 1985; Jensen, 1987).

Kolb (1984) suggested that an individual learner's style may be identified by assessing her/his position on each of the bipolar dimensions by using a test called Learning Styles Inventory (LSI). There are 12 open-ended questions that have four different alternative responses in LSI. Each question asks respondents to rank-order four sentence endings in a way that best describe their learning preference in any learning setting. After answering all 12 questions, four scores are calculated. These scores are clustered under four modes of the learning cycle which reflect the individual's tendency to learn through Concrete Experience (CE) or through the construction of theoretical frameworks (Abstract Conceptualization-AC) combined with the tendency to learn either through Active Experimentation (AE) or through reflection (Reflective Observation-RO). In the next stage, by subtracting CE from AC and RO from AE scores two combined scores are found out. These combined scores show the position of the individual learner in the two bipolar scales. More specifically, they refer to the major different ways by which students learn: the first (AC-CE) is "how a student perceives" new information or experience and the second (AE-RO) is "how a student processes what s/he perceives". In other words, these combined scores give the learning style preference of that individual. The learning style preferences resulting from the two bipolar scales were described by Kolb (1984) as accommodating (AE/CE), divergent (CE/RO), assimilating (RO/AC) and convergent (AC/AE). These four different learning styles, were labeled according to the individual's preferred information perceiving and processing modes. Each learning style has its own strengths and weaknesses but that does not mean that one is better than the other. More specifically: *Accommodating* learners are best at CE and AE, with their greatest interest lying in doing things (Kolb, 1984). They grasp their environments concretely through their feelings and utilize action to transform information obtained. They are risk-takers and enjoy seeking out new experiences. This kind of learners tends to solve problems in an intuitive, trial-and-error manner and instead of their own analytic ability, they rely on others for information. *Diverging* learners are best at CE and RO. This kind of learners are interested in people and tend to be imaginative and emotional. They have the ability to synthesize and/or assimilate a wide range of totally different observations into a comprehensive explanation that enables them to generate many ideas (Hsu, 1999). They are less concerned with theories and generalizations. Their approach to situations is in a less thoughtful, systematic or scientific way, therefore their abilities to make decisions are inhibited. *Assimilating* learners have the opposite learning strengths of accommodating learners. Their dominant learning abilities are AC and RO. They experience their world symbolically and transform it to information through thought. They are less interested in people and more concerned with abstract concepts, but are less concerned with the practical use of theories (Smith et al., 1996). It is more important for assimilating learners that the theory is logically sound and precise. *Converging* learners have opposite learning strengths of the diverging learners. Their dominant learning abilities are AC and AE. They bring a logical, pragmatic and unemotional perspective to any situation. They are more concerned with the relative truth than absolute truth. The knowledge of converging learners is organized, so that through hypothetical-deductive reasoning, they can focus their knowledge on specific problem. According to Smith and Kolb's description (1996), converging learners are unemotional and prefer to deal with things rather than people.

Results obtained using Kolb's Learning Style Inventory (1985) in discipline based research demonstrate some measure of agreement among researchers regarding the learning style preferences typically found in specified disciplines and more agreement if disciplines are subsumed under descriptions such as arts or sciences. It was found that arts students tend to favour divergent or assimilating learning styles (Kolb, 1985; Kruzich et al., 1986; Willcoxson et al., 1996), social science students tend to have accommodating (Kruzich et al., 1986; Wilson, 1986) and exact science students convergent learning style preferences (Katz, 1988; Reading-Brown et al., 1989; Willcoxson et al., 1996). Regarding L2 learning, there is a great deal of theoretical and empirical support (Jones, 1997; Reid, 1987; Rossi-Le, 1995) that students tend to favour kinesthetic and tactile styles (they prefer active participation/experiences and hands-on work). However, very few studies looked at the links between styles and discipline (e.g. science versus arts). Melton (1999) found that arts students favoured kinesthetic and individual styles, while science students did not. It was also found that science students have stronger preference for group styles, while arts students have a stronger preference for auditory and individual styles (Peacock, 2001).

A careful consideration should be given to learning styles since a mismatch between learning and teaching styles causes learning failure and frustration with implications for both learners and teachers (Drew et al., 2002; Felder et al., 1995). On the contrary, matching teaching styles to learning styles can significantly enhance academic achievement and student attitudes and specifically in foreign language instruction (Oxford et al., 1991; Wallace et al., 1992). Students learn best when they are actively involved in the learning process and when they are in learning situations that meet their learning style needs (Claxton et al., 1987; Earley, 1994; Felder et al., 1995; Hartman, 1995; Kramsch, 1993).

APPROACHES TO STUDYING

Learning styles are closely related to approaches to studying since students with undirected learning styles fail to adopt any consistent strategies when studying. Teachers who use teaching and learning strategies that correspond to their students' learning styles are more likely to reach a larger number of students. Research conducted by Malett et al., (1983) found that university students who became aware of their learning styles consciously adopted approaches to studying which corresponded to their preferred learning styles. This resulted in improvement of work habits, time on task and an increase in grade point averages. The choice of proper approaches to studying affects second language learning outcomes and it is among the most important variables influencing performance in second language. Choosing effective approaches to studying makes learning easier, faster, more enjoyable, more self-directed and more transferable to new situations and contributes to more independent, autonomous and lifelong learning (Allwright, 1990; Little, 1991; Oxford, 1990). Therefore, there is a need to identify and inculcate those approaches which are associated with success and ensure they are congruent with the academic values of higher education. Students' approaches to studying should be widely understood and accepted by teachers in higher education in order to improve the effectiveness of student learning.

Interviews with university students have shown that contrasting approaches to studying are adopted. Marton and Saljo (1976), in a study of how Scandinavian students tackled the task of reading academic articles and texts, identified two contrasting approaches, *deep* and *surface*. Students who adopted a deep approach started with the intention of understanding the meaning of the article, questioned the author's arguments and related them to both previous knowledge and personal experience. This approach contrasted with that of other students who started with the intention of memorizing the important facts and hence were described as adopting a surface approach. During the 1970s and 1980s, using a combination of large-scale surveys and in-depth interviews, Entwistle and his co-workers developed a series of inventories, each consisting of study orientations made up of a number of subscales. The Approaches to Studying Inventory (ASI) assessed, by means of a self-report type format, students' perceptions of their approaches to studying. There have been a number of versions of the ASI including a long form (64 items in 16 subscales), a short form (18 items in three scales) and a more recent version, the Revised Approaches to studying Inventory (RASI) (Entwistle et al., 1994). The RASI is one of the most widely used questionnaires consisting of 44 items and it has been designed to measure student approaches to studying in a higher education context. The items have been conceptualized and designed from six learning orientations, corresponding to six subscales of the subscales of the Inventory: *deep approach, surface approach, strategic approach, lack of direction, academic self-confidence and metacognitive awareness of studying.* However, only the concepts of deep, surface and strategic approaches are widely applied and understood by academics, while the others are not (Tait et al., 1996). For this reason, a shorter version of RASI, a 30-item version, is recommended (Duff, 1997) because it comprises items that relate only to these three approaches to studying.

Deep learning has been one of the most influential constructs to emerge in the literature on effective learning in higher education (Boyle et al., 2003). Students identified as having a *deep approach* report they try to work out the meaning of information for themselves, do not accept ideas without critical examination of them, relate ideas from their studies to a wider context and look for reasoning, justification and logic behind ideas. The deep approach refers to a deeper level of understanding whereby the learner understands the content, the argument and the meaning of the learning materials and is able to apply a critical point of view and can justify and interact with the learning materials. Deep processing involves processes of a high cognitive level, searching for analogies, relating to previous knowledge and theorizing about what is learned. Deep learners are intrinsically motivated by intrinsic interest (Boyle et al., 1003) and it was proved that high levels of intrinsic motivation are positively related to grades in higher education (Lin et al., 2003). In the deep approach, there is a personal commitment to learning, which means that the student relates the content to personally meaningful contexts or to existing prior knowledge. Ehrman (1996) describes deep processing as: an active process of making associations with material that is already familiar, examining interrelationships within the new material, elaborating the stimulus through associations with it and further development of it, connecting the new material with personal experience and considering alternative interpretations. The learner may use the new material to actively reconstruct his or her conceptual frameworks.

Students identified as having a *surface approach* see themselves as relying on rote learning of material, accepting ideas without necessarily understanding them, and emphasizing the acquisition of factual information in isolation to a wider picture and would express anxiety about their studies in terms of organization and volume of material. The surface approach involves a superficial mastery of the learning materials, which brings about a low level of conceptual understanding. Surface motivated students focus on what appears to be the most important items and memorizes them. Because of this focus, they do not see interconnections between the meanings and implications of what is learned. Surface learners in higher education are extrinsically motivated by the desire to obtain qualifications or a job (Boyle et al., 2003). Ehrman (1996) describes surface processing as: completion of the task with minimum conceptual effort, with the result that much less information will stay in memory, because it has been encountered much less and there is no emotional or cognitive investment in it.

Inventories developed to measure the above mentioned approaches have demonstrated a link between the intention to understand and learning processes which relate ideas and use evidence (Entwistle et al., 1983). Deep and surface approaches form almost unrelated factors in analyses of these inventories. In relation to everyday studying, a third dimension has been identified, a *strategic approach,* which describes an intention to achieve the highest possible grades through effort and well-organized studying. Students reporting a strategic approach perceive themselves as having clear goals related to their studies and being hard workers, ensuring that they have the appropriate resources and conditions for successful study, and feel that they are generally well organized (Sadler-Smith, 1996). Investigations using such inventories have indicated that a deep strategic approach to studying at university is likely to lead to high grades, while a surface approach combined with low scores on the strategic dimension is associated with poor academic performance (Au et al., 1999).

Research has shown that there is a clear relationship between a deep approach and a deep level of understanding an academic article (Marton et al., 1976). Another study (Svensson, 1977) has shown that only 23% of the students classified as surface learners passed all their semester examinations while 90% of the students classified as deep learners passed all their semester examinations. Ramsden and Entwistle (1981) examined the relationship between approaches to studying and self-reported ratings of of academic progress. Discriminant function analysis was conducted to discriminate between those who believed they were doing very well and those who believed they were doing badly. Organized study methods and a strategic approach were among the variables which characterized those students who believed they were doing very well. On the other hand, disorganized study methods and surface approach were found to be consistently related to low academic grades awarded (Watkins, 1982). On the whole, it was suggested (Drew et al., 1998; Murray-Harvey, 1993) that approaches to studying are important factors in determining academic performance with organized study methods and a strategic approach being the best predictors of high achievement (Harper et al., 1986). Appropriate approaches to studying make such a difference to learning success that many have attempted to design and execute training programmes on approaches to studying, especially for inexperienced learners (Ehrman et al., 2003). More specifically, in order to increase L2 proficiency some researchers and teachers have provided instruction that helped students learn how to use more relevant and more powerful approaches to studying. Positive effects of instruction emerged for proficiency in speaking (Dadour et al., 1996; O' Malley et al., 1985) and reading (Park-Oh, 1994) and led to increased L2 learning motivation (Nunan, 1997).

OUR RESEARCH FINDINGS

In view of the above findings, we undertook a three-fold research in a sample of 452 undergraduate students (146 males and 306 females) at the university of Thessaly, Greece. Two hundred and thirty-two of them were enrolled in the Faculty of Humanities and 220 in the Faculties of Civil Engineering and Computer Science.

In the first part of our research (Andreou, Vlachos, and Andreou, in press) we investigated the influence of level in L2, sex, handedness and Faculty choice on the performance of phonological, syntactical and semantic tasks in L2. A within-subjects mixed-design ANOVA (handedness X sex X faculty X L2 level) was performed on phonological, syntactical and semantic tasks. The main effect which was statistically significant (p< .05) for all three tasks was obtained for L2 level [phonology: $F(1) = 67.626$, p< .00; syntax: $F(1) = 4.128$, p< .04; semantics: $F(1) = 11.806$, p< .00], indicating that subjects with a professional degree performed generally better than those who did not have, in phonological tasks (13.88 vs 6.80 out of 20), in syntactical tasks (8.02 vs 6.11 out of 10) and semantic tasks (35.30 vs 25.67 out of 40). A statistically significant main effect for syntax and semantics was obtained for sex [syntax: $F(1) = 8.262$, p< .00; semantics: $F(1) = 5.093$, p< .02], indicating that females performed better than males in syntax (7.50 vs 6.57) and semantics (31.47 vs 30.80). No statistically significant main effects were found for faculty and handedness when taken alone but there were two-way statistically significant interactions of handedness X certificate for semantics [$F(2) = 3.992$, p< .01], of sex X faculty for syntax [$F(1) = 6.793$, p< .00] and semantics [$F(1) = 15.704$, p< .00] and of faculty X certificate for syntax [$F(1) = 6.123$, p< .01]. A three-way statistically significant interaction was also obtained for handedness X faculty X certificate for syntax only [$F(2) = 3.075$, p< .04].

In the second part of our research we investigated the relationship between Greek students' learning styles and performance in English phonological, syntactic and semantic tasks, in combination with their sex and discipline. Learning styles were assessed by Kolb's self-report Learning Style Inventory (LSI, 1985). In order to determine the relative contribution of each of the learning styles to performance on L2 verbal fluency tasks three multiple regressions were performed. When phonology served as the dependent variable, R was significantly different from zero [$R^2 = .23$, $F(4, 447) = 2.58$, p<.05]. Inspection of the predictor variables revealed that only divergent learning style (beta = .22, t = 1.96, p<. 05) significantly predicted scores on phonological tasks. For the regression on syntax and semantics R was also significantly different from zero [$R^2 = .39$, $F(4, 447) = 4.54$, p<.001 and $R^2 = .25$, $F(4, 447) = 8.04$, p<.001, respectively]. Scores on syntactical tasks were significantly predicted by accommodative learning style preference (beta = .19, t = 1.87, p<.05) and scores on semantics by divergent learning style preference (beta = .25, t = 2.31, p<.05).

In the third part (Andreou, Andreou, and Vlachos, 2004), we examined further how Greek students' approaches to studying in combination with sex, academic discipline and professional degree in English affect performance on verbal fluency tasks in English as a second language. Approaches to study were assessed by a 30-item version of Entwistle and Tait's RASI (Duff, 1997). The mixed design analysis of variance (MANOVA) (approaches to studying X sex X faculty X L2 certificate) which was computed for each verbal fluency task revealed statistically significant main effects for sex [$F(1) = 10.82$] and approaches to studying [F(1) = 3.26] on syntax, for faculty [F(1) = 10.86] on phonology and for certificate on phonology [F(1) = 250.16], syntax [F(1) = 25.71] and semantics [F(1) = 102.55]. Two-way statistically significant interaction effects were observed for sex X faculty on semantics [F(1) = 4.02] and for sex X certificate on phonology [F(1) = 8.93]. A three-way statistically significant effect was also obtained for sex X certificate X approaches to studying on syntax [F(1) = 2.46].

Table 1. summarizes in words the factors which contribute to high score achievement in university students' L2 tasks.

Table 1. Factors contributing to high score achievement in university students' L2 tasks

Variables	Verbal Phonology	Fluency Tasks Syntax	Semantics
Level (High/Low)	High*	High*	High*
Sex (Male/Female)	-	Female*	Female*
Learning Styles (Accomodative/Divergent/ Convergent, Assimilative)	Divergent*	Accomodative*	Divergent*
Approaches to studying (Deep/Surface /Strategic)	-	Deep*/Strategic*	-

*statistically significant (p< .05) differences

CONCLUSION

Our findings indicated that the students who reached a high level in L2 showed a superiority in all three linguistic codes, phonology, syntax and semantics. In other words, students who had obtained a professional degree in L2 performed better than those who had not, in all three tasks, phonological, syntactical and semantic. This finding confirms earlier findings, discussed in the context of the Linguistic Coding Deficiency Hypothesis (LCDH), which have shown that subjects who achieve high scores in L2 tasks have strong language aptitude skills (Ganschow et al., 1998; Ganschow et al., 1994; Karapetsas et al., 2001; Sparks et al., 1995).

Handedness alone did not influence our students' performance on L2 tasks, but only in combination with L2 level. This confirms earlier studies which found no relationship between language abilities and relative hand preference (Bishop, 1990; Crow et al., 1998; Palmer et al., 1996; Resch et al., 1997). However, some studies claim that degrees of handedness are important and that left handers are less equipped for the developing of adequate phonological skills needed for reaching high levels of proficiency in L2 (Lamn et al., 1999; Lamn, 1997) and probably that's why the combination of handedness and certificate played an important role in our results.

Gender was found to play an important role in our results, alone and in combination with faculty. Females performed better than males in both syntax and semantics confirming earlier studies which found a female advantage for verbal skills (Gordon et al., 1986; Stumpf, 1995). The fact that sex combined with faculty influenced our results could be explained by studies on hemispheric specialization for language functions which reveal stronger lateralization in men than women and a female superiority on verbal tasks. Stronger verbal skills on the part of females influences their career choice leading them to choose Faculties such as Humanities which belong to pure sciences rather than exact sciences.

The linguistic code which was mostly influenced by all factors was syntax. This is probably related to the native language spoken by the subjects tested in second language tasks. The native language of our sample was Greek which is a language with free word order while the second language tested was English, a language with strict word order (Goodluck, 1986). Therefore, all our factors had an impact on syntax probably because Greek syntax is completely different from English syntax. In Greek, the same sentence may be expressed in different word orders even with the subject missing while in English, words follow a strict word order in a sentence.

Concerning learning styles, our research findings suggest that university students prefer a divergent learning style while performing phonological and semantic tasks. It is concrete experience and reflective observation that these students apply on L2 phonology and semantics. They like to use their imagination, synthesize and generate ideas and they are less concerned with theories when they are to perform phonological and semantic tasks in L2. On the other hand, they prefer an accommodative learning style while performing syntactical tasks. They have a tendency to learn L2 syntax through a combination of concrete experience and active experimentation. They utilize action to transform information obtained and seek out new experiences when they are to perform syntactical tasks. Therefore, teachers should take into account that while teaching L2 phonology or semantics they should use pedagogic techniques that favour concrete experience and reflective observation such as handouts, videos, class or group discussions. They could also encourage note-taking and reading, write key information on the board, give oral explanations and instruction and generally encourage active participation. On the other hand, while teaching L2 syntax they should use techniques that favour concrete experience and active experimentation such as problem solving activities which involve practical experimentation. Where experimentation does occur, as in the learning of a foreign language, it consists of the oral or written testing of hypotheses. That is, reflection upon personal experience (upon responses to one's use of language) leads to concept development (the formation of new hypotheses about the construction of the language) and the testing of the concepts developed, again through personal experience.

Regarding approaches to studying, our findings are in line with previous research, which reveals that studying orientations are one of the important factors in determining academic performance (Drew et al., 1998; Murray-Harvey, 1993). However, our results suggest that approaches to studying alone or in combination with students' sex and professional degree in L2 seem to influence students' performance only on syntactical L2 tasks and not on phonological or semantic ones. This is probably related to the native language spoken by the subjects tested in L2 tasks. Their native language was Greek which, as it was mentioned above, is a language with strict word order as opposed to the subjects' L2 which was English, a language with strict word order. Therefore, a surface approach, which is based on rote learning and superficial mastery of the learning materials, seems to lead to lower performance on syntactical tasks in English as L2. On the other hand, a deep approach, which involves processes of a high cognitive level and intrinsic motivation, is positively related to higher performance on syntactical tasks in English as L2.

Based on our findings, two main aspects need to be addressed concerning approaches to studying. Firstly, there are students who habitually employ a surface approach to higher education studies in subjects which require a deep level approach. These students need study skills assistance to develop the capability of appropriately utilizing a deep approach. Secondly, there are students who would normally make appropriate use of the deep approach but because of factors such as surface assessment demands, high workloads, overprescriptive courses or an inhospitable learning environment, resort to a surface approach. This second problem can only be ameliorated if the factors influencing students towards a surface approach are addressed by curriculum design, instructional design or institutional policy. In general, research (Ramsden et al., 1981) indicates that the propensity of students who resort to a surface approach can be reduced by ensuring that questions and examinations demand a deep approach, workloads are reasonable and courses have sufficient flexibility to offer relevance and induce intrinsic interest. Any initiatives along these lines would be in keeping with the desire to produce graduates who are true independent learners as well as to reduce the use of a surface approach.

In conclusion, it is obvious both from previous studies and from our research findings that individual differences influence the way people learn and succeed in language study. Therefore, L2 level, sex, handedness, faculty choice, learning styles and approaches to studying may be important factors for teachers in higher education to take into account when designing and delivering their programmes and providing guidance for students. This is especially true in a higher education system where all students are being required to a) take the initiative in learning b) move away from an overreliance on lecturers c) accept that a student-centered approach to learning is active as opposed to passive and d) accept they should learn not just for the purposes of assessment but for their own intellectual growth, pleasure and fulfillment. This places demands on higher education teachers who need to design instruction that meets the needs of their students and enables the most learners possible to learn as much as they can and give them every advantage, including a program that enables them to start out in a relatively comfortable and stress-free way. This means giving them the opportunity to learn in their preferred way, which can happen in the interests of keeping classrooms paced to the majority or to a standard curriculum.

While this digest has focused on second language learning from the perspective of individual differences, it is important to point out that a wider, social and cultural, context of second language development has a tremendous impact on second language learning. Therefore, further research is needed to extend our knowledge on factors which may affect students' L2 learning. For example, further examination of gender differences in adult L2 learning styles will elucidate the influence of second language learners' cultural background and of the educational settings in which they learn the target language on the choice of their approaches to studying by gender. Although this study contributes useful information to the understanding of some of the individual differences among L2 adult learners, yet there is need for further research to cross-validate findings from the present study taking into account more/or different factors that may influence L2 learning.

REFERENCES

Allwright, D. (1990). *Autonomy in language pedagogy. CRILE working paper 6. Centre for Research in Education*. Lancaster: University of Lancaster.

Andreou, E., Andreou, G. and Vlachos F. (2004). Studying orientations and performance on verbal fluency tasks in a second language. *Learning and Individual Differences,* 15, 23-33.

Andreou, G., Vlachos, F. and Andreou, E. (in press). Affecting factors in second language acquisition. *Journal of Psycholinguistic Research,* 34 (4).

Au, C. and Entwistle, N. (1999). Memorizations with understanding in approaches to studying: cultural variant or response to assessment demands? *Paper presented at the European Association for Research on Learning and Instruction Conference.* Gothenburg.

Bishop, D. (1990). *Handedness and Developmental Disorders.* London: Mackeith.

Boyle, E., Duffy, T. and Dunleavy, K. (2003). Learning styles and academic outcome: The validity and utility of Vermunt's Inventory of Learning Styles in a British higher education setting. *British Journal of Educational Psychology,* 73, 267-290.

Carrol, J. (1973). Implications of aptitude test research and psycholinguistic theory for theory for foreign language teaching. *International Journal of Psycholinguistics,* 2, 5-14.

Chee, M., Tan, E. and Thiel, T. (1999.) Mandarin and English single word processing studied with functional magnetic resonance imaging. *Journal of Neuroscience,* 19, 3050–3056.

Claxton, C. and Murrell, P.(1987).*Learning Styles: Implications for Improving Educational Practice.* (ASHE-ERIC Higher Education Report No. 4). ASHE: College Station.

Cline, T. (2000). Multilingualism and dyslexia: challenges for research and practice. *Dyslexia,* 6 (1), 3-12.

Crow, J., Crow, R., Done, J. and Leask, S. (1998). Relative hand skills predicts academic ability: global deficits at the point of hemispheric indecision. *Neuropsychologia,* 36(12), 1275-1282.

Dadour, S., Robbins, J. (1996). University- level studies using strategy instruction to improve speaking ability in Egypt and Japan. In Oxford, R. (ed.) *Language Learning Strategies Around the World: Cross-cultural Perspectives* (pp. 1-25). Manoa: University of Hawaii Press.

Dehaene, S., Dupoux, E., Mehler, J., Cohen, L., Paulesu, E., Perani, D., Van de Moortele, P-F., Lehéricy, S. and Le Bihan, D. (1997). Anatomical variability in the cortical representation of first and second language. *Neuroreport,* 8, 3809–3815.

Demirbaş, O. and Dermikan, H.(2003). Focus on architectural design process through learning styles. *Design Studies,* 24, 437-456.

Dinklage, K. (1971). Inability to learn a foreign language. In Blaine G.B. and McArthur C. C. (eds.) *Emotional problems of the student* (pp. 185-206). New York: Regents.

Downey, D., Snyder, L. and Hill. B. (2000). College students with dyslexia: persistent linguistic deficits and foreign language learning. *Dyslexia,* 6 (2), 101-111.

Drew, P. and Watkins, D. (1998). Affective variables, learning approaches and academic achievement: A casual modelling investigation with Hong Kong tertiary students. *British Journal of Educational Psychology,* 68, 173-188.

Drew, F. and Ottewill, R. (2002). Learning styles and the potential for learning on institution-wide language programmes: an assessment of the results of the pilot study. *Language Learning Journal,* 26, 11-18.

Duff, A. (1997). A note on the reliability and validity of a 30- item version of Entwistle and Tait' s Revised Approaches to Studying Inventory. *British Journal of Educational Psychology,* 67, 529-539.

Earley, P.(1994).Self or group: cultural effects of training on self-efficacy and performance. *Administrative Science Quarterly,*39,89-117.

Ehrman, M. (1996). *Understanding second language learning difficulties.* Thousand Oaks, CA: Sage.

Ehrman, M. and Leaver, B. (2003). Cognitive styles in the service of language learning. *System,* 31(3), 393-415.

Entwistle, N. and Ramsden, P. (1983). *Understanding student learning.* London: Croom Helm.

Entwistle, N. and Tait, H. (1994). *The Revised Approaches to Studying Inventory.* Edinburgh: University of Edinburgh, Centre for Research into Learning and Instruction.

Felder, R. and Henriques, E. (1995). Learning and teaching styles in foreign and second language education. *Foreign Language Annals,* 28, 21-31.

Galloway, L. and Krashen, S. (1980). Cerebral organization in bilingualism and second language. In Scarcella, R. and Krashen, S. (eds.), *Research in Second Language Acquisition* (pp.74-80). Newbury House: Rowley, Mass.

Ganschow, L. and Sparks, R. (2000). Reflections on foreign language study for students with language learning problems: research, issues and challenges. *Dyslexia,* 6 (2), 87-100.

Ganschow, L., Sparks, R., Javorsky, J., Pohlman, J. and Bishop-Marbury, A. (1991). Identifying native language difficulties among foreign language learners in college: A foreign language learning disability?. *Journal of Learning Disabilities,* 24, 530-541.

Ganschow, L., Sparks, R., Anderson, R., Javorsky, J., Skinner, S. and Patton, J. (1994). Differences in anxiety and language performance among high- and low-anxious college foreign language learners. *Modern Language Journal,* 78, 41-55.

Ganschow, L., Sparks, L. and Javorsky, J. (1998). Foreign language learning difficulties: An historical perspective. *Journal of Learning Disabilities,* 31, 248-258.

Goodluck, H. (1986). Language acquisition and linguistic theory. In Fletcher, P. and Garman, M. (eds.), *Language acquisition* (2nd ed., pp. 49-68). New York: Cambridge University Press.

Gordon, H. and Lee, P. (1986). A relationship between gonadotropins and visuospatial function. *Neuropsychologia,* 24, 563-576.

Gouchie, C. and Kimura, D.(1991). The relationship between testosterone levels and cognitive ability patterns. *Psychoendocrinology,* 16, 323-334.

Guild, P.,and Garger, S.(1985*).Marching to Different Drummers.* Alexandria, VA: Association for Supervision and Curriculum Development.

Hampson, E. and Kimura, D.(1992). Sex differences and hormonal influences on cognitive function in humans. In Becker, J., Breedlove, S. and Crews, D. (eds.), *Behavioral Endocrinology* (pp. 357-398). Cambridge, MA: MIT Press.

Harper, G. and Kember, D.(1986). Approaches to studying of distance education students. *British Journal of Educational Technology,* 17, 212-222.

Hartman, V. (1995).Teaching and learning style preferences: transitions through technology. *VCCA Journal, 9,*18-20.

Hsu,C. (1999). Learning styles of hospitality students: Nature or nurture? *HospitalityManagement,* 18(1), 17-30.

Janowsky, S. , Chavez, B., Zamboli, D. and Orwoll, E.(1998). The cognitive Neuropsychology of sex hormones in men and women. *Developmental Neuropsychology,* 14(2/3), 421-440.

Jensen,G. (1987).Learning Styles. In Provost, J. and Anchors, A. (eds.).*Applications of the Myers-Briggs Type Indicator in Higher Education* (pp.181-206). Palo Alto: Consulting Psychologists Press.

Jones, N. (1997). Applying learning styles research to improve writing instruction. *Paper presented at RELC Seminar on Learners and Language Learning.*

Karapetsas, A. and Andreou, G. (2001). Visual field asymmetries for rhyme and semantic tasks in fluent and nonfluent bilinguals. *Brain and Language*, 78, 53-61.

Katz, N. (1988). Individual learning style: Israeli norms and cross- cultural equivalence of Kolb's Learning Style Inventory. *Journal of Cross- cultural Psychology*, 19, 361-379.

Kim, K., Relkin, N., Lee, K. and Hirsch, J. (1997). Distinct cortical areas associated with native and second languages. *Nature*, 388,171–174.

Klein, D., ·Milner, B., Zatorre, R., Meyer, E. and Evans, A. (1995). The neural substrates underlying word generation: a bilingual functional-imaging study. *Proceedings of the National Academy of Science USA*, 92, 2899–2903.

Kolb, D. (1984). *Experiential Learning: Experience as the Source of Learning and Development.* New York: Prentice- Hall.

Kolb, D. (1985). *Learning Style Inventory.* Boston: McBer and Co.

Kramsch, C. (1993).*Context and Culture in Language Teaching.* Oxford: Oxford University Press.

Kruzich, J., Friesen, B. and Van Soest, D.(1986). Assessment of Students and faculty learning styles: research and application. *Journal of Social Work Education*, 22, 22-30.

Lamn, O. (1997). Sinistrality and developmental reading difficulties. In Shirmon, J. (ed.), *Studies in the Psychology of Language* (pp. 228-247). Jerusalem: Magnes.

Lamn, O. and Epstein, R. (1999). Left handedness and achievements in foreign language studies. *Brain and Language*, 70, 504-517.

Lefebvre, R. (1984). A psychological consultation program for learning disabled students. *College Student Personnel*, 7, 361-362.

Lin, Y. G., McKeachie,W. and Kim,Y. (2003).College student intrinsic and/or extrinsic motivation and learning. *Learning and Individual Differences*, 13, 251-258.

Little, D.(1991). *Learner Autonomy 1: Definitions, Issues and Problems.* Dublin: Authentik.

Lujan-Ortega, V. and Clark-Carter, D. (2000). Individual differences, strategic performance and achievement in second language learners of Spanish. *Studia Linguistica*, 54, 280-287.

Malett, S., Kirschenbaum, D. and Humphrey, L. (1983).Description and subjective evaluation of an objective successful study improvement program. *Personnel and Guidance Journal*, 61, 341-345.

Marton, F. and Saljo, R.(1976). On qualitative differences in learning : I. Outcome and process. *British Journal of Educational Psychology*, 46, 4-11.

Melton, C. (1990). Bridging the cultural gap: a study of Chinese students' learning style preferences. *RELC Journal*, 21, 29-54.

Moffat, S. and Hampson, E.(1996). A curvilinear relationship between testosterone and spatial cognition in humans: Possible influence of hand preference. *Psychoendocrinology*, 21, 323-337.

Murray-Harvey, R.(1993). Identifying characterisitics of successful tertiary students using path analysis. *Australian Educational Researcher*, 20, 63-81.

Nowicka, A. and Fersten, E.(2001). Sex- related differences in interhemispheric transimission time in the human brain. *Neuroreport*, 12(18), 4171-4175.

Nunan, D.(1997). Does learner strategy training make a difference? *Lenguas Modernas,* 24, 123-142.

Obler, L. (1981). Right hemisphere participation in second language acquisition. In: Diller K. (ed.), *Individual Differences and Universals in Language Learning Aptitude* (pp. 53-64). Newbury House: Rowley MA.

O´ Malley, J., Russo, R., Chamot, A., Stewnen- Manzanares, G. and Kupper, L.(1985). Learning strategy applications with students of English as a second language. *TESOL Quarterly,* 19(3), 557-584.

Orton, S.T.(1937). *Reading, Writing and Speech problems in children.* New York: Norton.

Oxford, R.L.(1990*). Language Learning Strategies: What every Teacher Should Know.* Boston: Heinle and Heinle.

Oxford, R., Ehrman, M. and Lavine, R. (1991).Style Wars: Teacher-Student Style Conflicts in the Language Classroom. In Magnan, S. (ed.) *Challenges in the 1990's for College Foreign Language Programs* (pp. 1-25). Boston: Heinle and Heinle.

Oxford, R. and Ehrman, M. (1993). Second Language Research on Individual Differences. *Annual Review of Applied Linguistics,* 13, 188-205.

Palmer, R. and Corballis, M. (1996). Predicting reading ability from handedness measures. *British Journal of Psychology,* 87, 609-620.

Paradis, M. (1994). Neurolinguistic aspects of implicit and explicit memory: Implications for bilingualism and SLA. In Ellis, N.C. (ed.), *Implicit and explicit learning of languages* (pp. 393-419). Academic Press: San Diego.

Park- Oh, Y. (1994). Self- regulated strategy training in second language reading. *Unpublished doctoral thesis.* University of Alabama.

Peacock, M. (2001). Match or mismatch? Learning styles and teaching styles in EFL. *International Journal of Applied Linguistics,* 11(1), 1-20.

Pompian, N., and Thun, C. (1988). Dyslexic/ Learning Disabled Students at Dartmouth College. *Annals of Dyslexia,* 38, 278-284.

Ramsden, P. and Entwistle, N. (1981). Effects of academic departments on students' approaches to studying. *British Journal of Educational Psychology,* 18, 3-13.

Reading- Brown, M. and Hayden, R. (1989). Learning styles- liberal arts and technical training: what' s the difference? *Psychological Reports,* 64, 507-518.

Reid, J. (1987). The learning style preferences of EFL students. *TESOL Quarterly,* 21, 87-111.

Resch, F., Haffner, J., Pfueller, U., Strehlow, U. and Zerahn- Hartung, C.(1997). Testing the hypothesis of relationships between laterality and ability according to Annett's right- left theory: findings in an epidemiological sample of young adults. *British Journal of Psychology,* 88, 621-635.

Rossi- Le, L.(1995). Learning styles and strategies in adult immigrant ESL students. In J. M. Reid, *Learning styles in the ESL/ EFL classroom,* (pp. 87-111). Boston: Heinle- Heinle.

Sadler- Smith, E.(1996). Approaches to studying: Age, gender and academic performance. *Educational Studies,* 22, 367-379.

Schmeck, R. (1988). *Learning strategies and learning styles.* New York: Plenum.

Smith, D., and Kolb, D. (1996).*User's Guide for the Learning-Style Inventory: A Manual for Teachers and Trainers.*Boston: McBer and Company.

Sparks, R., Ganschow, L. and Pohlman, J. (1989). Linguistic coding deficits in foreign language learners. *Annals of Dyslexia,* 39, 179-195.

Sparks, R. and Ganschow, L. (1993). The impact of native language learning problems on foreign language courses: Connections between native and foreign language learning: Case study illustrations of the linguistic coding deficit hypothesis. *Modern Language Journal*, 77, 58-74.

Sparks, R., Ganschow, L. and Patton, J. (1995). Prediction of performance in first- year foreign language learning. *Journal of Educational Psychology*, 87, 638-655.

Sparks, R. and Javorsky, J. (1999). Students classified as LD and the college foreign language requirement: replication and comparison studies. *Journal of Learning Disabilities,* 32 (4), 329-349.

Springer, S. and Deutsch, G. (1998). *Left·brain right brain: Perspectives from cognitive neuroscience* (5th ed.). New York: W. H. Freeman and Company.

Stumpf, H. (1995). Gender differences in performance on tests of cognitive abilities: Experimental design issues and empirical results. Psychological and psychobiological perspectives on sex differences in cognition: I. Theory and research. *Learning and Individual Differences*, 7, 275-287.

Svensson, L. (1977). On qualitative differences in learning. III. Study skill and learning. *British Journal of Educational Psychology*, 47, 233-243.

Tait, H. and Entwistle, N. (1996). Identifying students at risk through ineffective study strategies. *Higher Education*, 31, 97-116.

Van Lancker, D. (1997). Rags to Riches: Our Increasing Appreciation of Cognitive and Communicative Abilities of the Human Right Cerebral Hemisphere. *Brain and Language*, 57, 1-11.

Wallace,B.and Oxford,R.L.(1992).Disparity in Learning Styles and Teaching Styles in the ESL Classroom :Does This Mean War? *AMTESOL Journal*, 1, 45-68.

Watkins, D.(1982). Identifying the study process dimensions of Australian university students. *The Australian Journal of Education*, 26(1), 76-85.

Willcoxson, L. and Prosser, M. (1996). Kolb's learning style inventory(1985): Review and further study of validity and reliability. *British Journal of Educational Psychology,* 66, 247-257.

Wilson, D. (1986). An investigation of the properties of Kolb's Learning Style Inventory. *Leadership and Organization Development Journal*, 7, 3-15.

Zangwill, O. (1960). *Cerebral dominance and its relation to psychological function.* Edinburgh: Oliver and Boyd.

In: Consciousness and Learning Research
Editor: Susan K. Turrini, pp. 137-164

ISBN 1-60021-333-2
© 2007 Nova Science Publishers, Inc.

Chapter 7

EVOLUTION AND THE PROBLEM OF MIND IN 19TH CENTURY ENGLAND

C. U. M. Smith

Vision Sciences, Aston University, Birmingham, B4 7ET, UK

ABSTRACT

Nineteenth century England was pervaded by a sense of progress engendered by the steam-powered industrial revolution. This sense of progress made itself felt in the worlds of science and philosophy. In particular, the worlds of biology and the other life sciences were pervaded by evolutionary ideas. In this contribution I discuss the consequences of these ideas for the problem of mind. Evolutionary thought took many forms in the nineteenth century but all of them saw man as part of the living world. This placed enormous stress on the mind-matter dualisms of earlier centuries which, in general, saw man not as part of Nature, but apart from Nature. The response to this stress took the form of various types of dual-aspect, parallelistic and epiphenomenalist theories. I examine these responses in the work of Richard Owen, Herbert Spencer, John Hughlings Jackson, and Thomas Henry Huxley. The evolutionary tradition, emerging from early nineteenth-century transcendental biology and associated with German Romantic thought and Samuel Taylor Coleridge, influenced the greatest of mid-century comparative anatomists, Richard Owen. Another early evolutionary tradition, stemming from the embryological thought of Karl von Baer, influenced the work of Herbert Spencer, the 'philosopher of evolution', and through him the neurology and neurophilosophy of John Hughlings Jackson, the 'father' of British neurology. Finally, a third tradition, originating in the work of natural historians during the European diaspora, culminated in the work of Charles Darwin and his champion Thomas Henry Huxley. The conflict between Huxley and Owen is well known and centred on differing understandings of the brain and mind. Huxley, by common consent, won the encounter. The Darwin-Huxley 'paradigm' consequently became the immensely successful orthodoxy of twentieth century life science. Yet the very success of this paradigm only increases the sharpness of the mind-body conundrum. This chapter discusses these nineteenth century controversies and interpretations with a view to gaining perspective on the problem of consciousness as we begin the twenty-first century.

1. INTRODUCTION

The problem of mind in the Western world has had a very lengthy gestation period. It only became well-defined during the scientific revolution of the sixteenth and seventeen centuries AD. The work of Kepler, Galileo, Descartes and others threw it into sharp relief. Descartes, in particular, is credited with formulating the problem for the modern world. By his technique of 'hyperbolic' doubt he finally arrived at the '*cogito*'. Although everything else, even the truths of mathematics, could be doubted, it was impossible to doubt, whilst doubting, that doubt was occurring. This seemed to Descartes bedrock on which his philosophy could be erected: *cogito ergo sum; je pense donc je suis.* Descartes published his 'discovery' in the 1637 *Discourse on Method.* Three years later, in 1640, Andreas Colvius, . minister in Dordrecht, wrote to Descartes to point out that the *cogito* was remarkably similar to passages in the writings of St Augustine some twelve hundred years before (Kenny, 1970, p.83). Descartes wrote back at once to say that he had been to the town library in Leiden to check the reference (Adam and Tannery, vol.3, p.247). It does not seem that Descartes plagiarised Augustine, although his education at the Lycée Henri IV at La Flèche would have included some of Augustine's works. Nevertheless, the relevant passages do seem very similar (see Smith, 1998a). If, for instance, we turn to Augustine's *De Civitate Dei* 10, 26 we find: 'I know without all fantastical imagination that I am myself..... I fear not academic arguments in these truths, that say, "what if you err?" *If I err, I am (si enim fallor, sum).* For he that has no being cannot err: therefore my error proves my being: which being so, how can I err in holding my being? For though I be one that may err, yet doubtless in that I know my being I err not....' (my italics). A similar argument may be found in *De Trinitate X*, 10, 4, the passage to which Descartes had been referred by Colvius. There has, of course, been much learned argument about the two *cogitos*. Indeed La Forge, who edited one of the first editions of Descartes' *L'Homme* in 1664, published two years later, in 1666, a treatise on physiological psychology based on *L'Homme,* in which he states quite bluntly that Descartes' 'sentiments concerning the nature of the soul' are fully in conformity with those of St Augustine (La Forge, 1666)

However , if we look back to St Augustine in the fourth century AD and examine the physiological part of his psychophysiology we find a fundamental difference. St Augustine was fully *au courant* with the medical thought of his time (see Bardy, 1953) and he makes use of the theories of the great Alexandrians of the third century BC: Herophilus and Erisastratus. His neurophysiology, accordingly, consists of pipe-like nerves and subtle fluids (see Smith, 1998a). Once again we can detect a strong similarity with the neurophysiology which Descartes published (posthumously) in *l'Homme* and elsewhere. The fundamental difference is this: there is as yet no well-defined concept of the inorganic. Augustine's hollow nerves are filled with 'a wind called the soul' *(Deus hunc flatum facerit, quae anima dicitur) (De Genesi ad Litteram, 7, 19, 25).* This 'wind' or *'pneuma psychikon'* is distilled from the *'pneuma zotikon'* in the ventricles of the brain. The *pneuma zotikon* is, in turn, derived from a vivifying *pneuma* in the surrounding cosmos via the lungs (for a fuller account, see Smith, 1976). There is at this time, as Adkins observes, no concept of the 'material' as opposed to the 'spiritual' (Adkins, 1979). It was not until the scientific revolution of the sixteenth and seventeenth centuries AD that this opposition became established. Coleridge was exaggerating when he wrote that 'Descartes was the first man who made Nature utterly lifeless ..... a subject for purely mechanical laws' (Coburn, 1949, pp.376-8), but not by much. This was the implication of the great transformation of thought occurring in the sixteenth and seventeenth centuries. The 'animal spirits' which filled the cerebral ventricles and hollow nerves of the Cartesian physiology were thus only spirits in the sense that brandy and whisky are spirits.

Just as Johannes Kepler reconceived astronomy in the pattern of a giant clockwork, so René Descartes reconceived neurophysiology in the pattern of the water-driven automata which he had seen in his youth in the grottoes of St Germaine en Laye. At the end of *L'Homme* (which he had the good sense to withhold from publication during his life time) he writes that all the behavioural movements of a human being 'follow from the mere arrangement of the machine's organs every bit as naturally as the movements of a clock or other automaton follow from the arrangement of its counterweights and wheels. In order to explain these functions, then, it is not necessary to conceive of this machine as having any vegetative or sensitive soul....' (Descartes, 1662/1972, p.202). This analogy is not, of course, available to St Augustine. The problem of mind is thus not so acute in the fourth/fifth century AD as it is in the seventeenth. Even so, Augustine is unable to answer the interaction problem. He is unable to say how the rational soul is able to move the body although he suspects a sort of tension (see Smith, 1998a). Human nature, he concludes, is unfathomable: *'humanae naturae occultata est'* (*De Quantitate Animae, XXXI*, 64). For Descartes the problem is still more difficult. As is well known he made a valiant attempt to marry his materialistic neurophysiology with his non-materialistic psychology in the pineal gland (see Smith, 1998b). But this never made any sense and he seems to admit this in a response to Princess Elizabeth of Bohemia who had pressed him on the topic: 'How can the human soul determine the movement of animal spirits' she writes '.... as it is merely a conscious substance?' (Adam and Tannery, vol.3, p.661). Descartes replies from Egmond a fortnight later 'It seems to me that the human mind is incapable of distinctly conceiving both the distinction between body and soul and their union, at one and the same time; for that requires our conceiving them as a single thing and simultaneously conceiving them as two things, which is self-contradictory' and he goes on, later in the same letter, to add somewhat despairingly, that too much pondering on these conundrums is a waste of life: 'it would be very harmful to occupy one's intellect often with meditating upon them, for it would be less able to find leisure for the functioning of the imagination and the senses.' (Adam and Tannery, vol.3, p.690)

2. EIGHTEENTH CENTURY REACTION

This then was the problem the seventeenth century bequeathed its successors. It was not long before the old idea that nerves were hollow conduits carrying 'spirits' to and from the brain was discredited. Leeuwenhoek had assured himself as early as 1674 that the optic nerve, at least, contained no cavity (Leeuwenhoek, 1674) and as the seventeenth century gave way to the eighteenth other microscopists agreed. The old neurophysiology had to go. It was, however, far from clear with what it could be replaced (see Smith, in press). Indeed in popular culture the old ideas lived on. Laurence Sterne happily assumes that the readers of *Tristam Shandy* are all familiar with animal spirits: 'You have all, I dare say, heard of the animal spirits, nine parts in ten of a man's sense and nonsense …. Depend on their motions and activity' (Sterne, 1760, p.1). As John Sutton remarks the language of the old physiology spills easily across the psychophysical divide 'from fibres and pores to passions and feelings and conscious and unconscious motivations' (Sutton, 1998).

In addition to the slow demise of the old time-worn neurophysiology, very significant developments were occurring in the biological sciences. The microscope was not only showing that nerves contained no cavity but that a drop of pond water teemed with miniscule life. Leibniz at the beginning of the new century drew the conclusion that there was continuity all the way from submicroscopic monad to man. In a letter to Charles Bonnet he predicted the existence of zoophytes, or plant animals, bridging the gap between plants and animals (Rieppel, 1988). He must have been delighted when Abraham Trembley later reported their discovery[1] in 1744 (Trembley, 1744). Trembley also showed that fresh water polyps could be divided indefinitely and from each small fragment a complete new polyp would regenerate. This seemed to imply that the 'soul', the 'principle of life', could not be confined to one small part, but must be 'smeared' out through the organism. This, taken together with Haller's concept of 'irritability' located, as he showed, in muscle fibres throughout the body, quite independent of the brain or the nerves (Haller, 1755), seemed to finally undercut the Cartesian iatromechanics. La Mettrie was not the only thinker, though perhaps the most audacious, to draw the conclusion that the old Cartesian distinction between *res extensa* and *res cogitans*, between an inert, passive, 'extended' matter and an 'unextended' consciousness had to go (see Smith, 2002). 'The power to acquire motive force and the faculty of thinking' he writes 'have in all ages been considered, like extension, to be essential properties of matter' (La Mettrie, 1745, p.127). For La Mettrie, Descartes was fundamentally mistaken: '…that genius made to open up new paths and lose his way' (La Mettrie, 1745, p.138). The body could not be a mere mechanism activated by impulses sent from the brain.

These developments in biology meshed well with the widening of horizons generated by eighteenth-century voyages of discovery. It became increasingly difficult to view humans as unique and different from the rest of the living world. The writings of Leibniz, Buffon and Bonnet popularised the ancient notion of a 'Great Chain of Beings'. Alexander Pope made the idea central to his widely-read *Essay on Man*[2]. Lord Monboddo in the mid-eighteenth century was acutely aware of the possibility that humans had evolved from the animal kingdom and, indeed, believed that the newly discovered organg-outans were actually examples of primitive humans and that voyagers had come across at least one human tribe with tails (Monboddo, 1774). La Mettrie, as usual, provided the most audacious formulation: 'The transition from animals to man is not abrupt. Man is distinguished from the ape only as the ape is distinguished from other animals' (La Mettrie, 1747, p.78). Then, at the end of the century first Erasmus Darwin (1803) and then Jean-Baptiste de Lamarck (1809) published extensive works supporting evolutionary theory.

---

[1] Zoophytes had been known to Aristotle (*de Anima, 413a21*) and, indeed, to Nemesius of Emesa (c 390AD) who points out that the 'sea nettle' though seemingly a plant should in fact be classified as an animal as it possesses an animal's sense of touch.

[2] 'Vast chain of being! Which from God began;/ Natures ethereal, human, angel, man,/ Beast, bird, fish, insect, who no eye can see,/ No glass can reach, from infinite to thee;/ From thee to nothing –…'*Essay on Man*, VIII.

3. NINETEENTH CENTURY

At the beginning of the nineteenth century the 'Great Chain of Being' was being given a new dynamism. The western world was alive with the hope of progress. The steam-based industrial revolution was breaking apart the old order of things. Evolutionists like Erasmus Darwin were deeply involved in these new developments (see Smith and Arnott (2005)) and believed with Thomas Wright that 'thanks to the sciences, the scene begins to open to us on all sides....' (Wright, 1750). Evolution theory was very much part of this new *zeitgeist*. But it was not, of course, the evolution theory with which we are familiar today. Although both Erasmus Darwin and Lamarck believed in 'survival of the fittest' their belief in the inheritance of acquired characteristics retained a crucial role for the 'will' of the individual. The Darwin/Weismann 'external'mechanism of 'random variation and selective retention' was still fifty years into the future. Other 'takes' on the evolutionary process were also prominent. In many cases it was conceived more as the etymology of the word suggests: the unrolling of a scroll. The end result was foreordained. Some looked back to Kant and Goethe in the latter part of the previous century and seemed to see the working out of indwelling 'archetypes'. In 1809-11 Lawrence Oken published the best known account of this idea in his *Lehrbuch der Naturphilosophie* (Oken, 1809-11). Others found a model in embryological development, especially that of Karl von Baer. Again the 'end', the adult form, was, in a sense, foreordained. Only in mid-century with Charles Darwin, and some would say not until the end of the century with August Weismann, did the totally non-teleological theory of random variation and natural selection of the results of that variation take hold. All these versions of evolutionary theory had their supporters as the nineteenth century wore on. In what follows we shall look at these three significant variants paying particular attention to their implications for the philosophy of mind. All three of them were faced, in one way or another, with the need to account for the existence of consciousness, subjectivity, in a world where there seemed no gap between humans and the infrahuman animals. 'How' as Darwin asked in one of his post-Beagle notebooks, 'does consciousness commence?' (Darwin, 1837, §35)

3.1. Richard Owen and Transcendental Anatomy

Even more than the earthquake and tsunami that killed nearly 100 000 and destroyed the great city of Lisbon in 1755, the revolution in France in 1789 and the subsequent breakdown of social order shook the confidence in 'reason' which characterised the earlier part of the eighteenth century. No longer was it quite so easy to agree with Pope's famous lines:

> 'All Nature is but Art unknown to thee,/ All chance, direction which thou canst not see;/ All discord, harmony not understood;/ All partial evil, universal good;/ And, spite of Pride, in erring Reason's spite,/ One truth is clear, *Whatever is, is right.*'
> *Essay on Man, X*

Voltaire was not the only thinker to ridicule Leibniz's idea that we live in the best of all possible worlds. The reaction from the optimism of the enlightenment took the form of a 'Romantic' turning inward to the world of the human individual, away from the mechanising spirit of the earlier eighteenth century. In his essay on Coleridge J.S.Mill writes that 'The Germano-Coleridgean doctrine… expresses the revolt of the human mind against the philosophy of the eighteenth century. It is ontological because that was experimental; conservative because that was innovative; religious because so much of that was infidel; concrete and historical because so much of that was abstract and metaphysical; poetical because that was matter-of-fact and prosaic' (Mill, 1859).

If Kant and Goethe, in their different ways, can be seen as the founding fathers of the Romantic response in Germany, Coleridge, in a less articulated way, can be seen as the root of the response in England[3]. He writes of 'the barren and worse than barren fig-tree of the mechanic philosophy' (Coleridge in White, 1972, p.33) and throughout his life strove to achieve a larger, synoptic, vision of the world, ridiculing scientific reductionism as 'psilosophy' rather than 'philosophy'(see Smith, 1999a). He would have had no difficulty in applauding William Blake's diatribe against the scientific specialisms of his day:

> 'The Atoms of Democritus
> And Newton's particles of Light
> Are sands upon the Red Sea shore
> Where Israel's tents do shine so bright'

> *Mock on, Mock on, Voltaire, Rousseau*, III

Throughout his life Coleridge was plagued by the dichotomy between the 'I am' and the 'it is'. 'If', he said, 'philosophy began with an "it is" rather than an "I am", Spinoza would be altogether true'. But Spinoza's pantheism, he believed, ended in atheism, and this he (Coleridge) could not accept. Crabb Robinson writes of Coleridge walking across the Somerset moors to collect a copy of Spinoza and of how 'in the course of a few minutes while standing in the room he kissed Spinoza's face in the title page, and said, "this book has been gospel to me." But in less than a minute he added "his philosophy is nevertheless false"' (Robinson, November 3, 1812).

Coleridge has been accused of having had the effrontery to die with just a few poems, and many of those unfinished, to mark his huge talent. But after his initial great poetic outpouring he spent the better part of the remainder of his life attempting to put together his philosophical ideas into a *magnum opus*. The tract which he variously called 'Theory of Life', 'Hints towards the formation of a more comprehensive theory of life', 'Physiology of Life', 'Nature of Life', 'The Idea of Life' etc,.would have formed a central part of this unfinished work (see Levere, 1981). He never managed to complete the *Theory of Life* during his lifetime but in 1848, fourteen years after his death, Watson published a manuscript left in the possession of his friend and protector, Dr Henry Gillman (see Smith, 1999a). Amongst the many who visited him at his last home with the Gillmans in Highgate and attended his lectures was J.H.Green, a young surgeon at St Thomas' Hospital in London. Green shared Coleridge's obsession with German Romantic philosophy and quickly became a devoted follower (see Jackson, 1982). Indeed, so fascinated was he with Coleridge's thought that he

---

[3] Critics would normally award the accolade of being first to react against the Newtonian eighteenth century to William Blake (1757-1827; *Poetical Sketches*, 1783). A little later William Wordsworth joined with Coleridge in the programmatic foreword to the *Lyrical Ballads* (1798). But it is (I think) fair to say that Coleridge (perhaps to the detriment of his poetic sensibility) had the greater impact in the world of the intellect.

spent many hours each week in his company and after Coleridge's death in 1834 spent the rest of his life attempting to systematise his disparate writings, eventually publishing them in 1865 as *Spiritual Philosophy* (Green, 1865)

In 1824 Green was appointed to the Chair of Anatomy at the Royal College of Surgeons and during the years 1824-27 gave a series of lectures on anatomy and comparative anatomy. It is interesting to note that he also held the chair of anatomy at the Royal Academy of Arts from 1825-52 where his lectures 'covered a wide philosophical range.... (and) were enriched with numberless references to the history of art and to the masterworks of ancient and modern sculpture and painting' (Simon, 1865, p.xvii). One of the surgeons attending Green's lectures on anatomy was a young man freshly arrived from Lancaster, via Edinburgh: Richard Owen. Owen, in fact did more than merely attend, he also acted as one of Green's demonstrators, making many dissections to illustrate the course (see Smith, 1997). Owen was strongly influenced by Green's approach. 'Here for the first time in England' he wrote later 'the comparative anatomy of the whole animal kingdom was described, and illustrated by such a series of enlarged and coloured diagrams as had never before been seen. The vast array of facts was linked by reference to the underlying unity, as had been evidenced by Oken and Carus' (Simon, 1865, xiv).

Richard Owen (1804-1892) went on to become one of the most significant figures in mid-Victorian society: Professor of Comparative Anatomy and Physiology at the Royal College of Surgeons and first Superintendent of the British Museum (Natural History)[4]. The influence of the Germano-Coleridgean philosophy strongly influenced his interpretations of what he saw in the dissecting room. He secretly encouraged Tulk in his self-imposed and thankless task of translating Oken's *Lehrbuch der Naturphilosophie* into English and was responsible for writing the laudatory article on Oken in the eighth edition of the *Encyclopaedia Britannica*. He believed that he could see in the living world a divinely inspired orthogenesis. In very evocative concluding passages to a discourse on limbs, delivered at the Royal Institution in 1849, he writes 'the Divine mind.....planned the Archetype and also foreknew all its modifications.... "Nature" has advanced with slow and stately steps, guided by the archetypal light, amidst the wreck of worlds, from the first embodiment of the Vertebrate idea under its old Ichthyic vestment, until it became arrayed in the glorious garb of the human form' (Owen 1849, p.86).

It is clear that for Owen the problem of consciousness was not so stark as it was for evolutionists such as Thomas Huxley. The Coleridgean tradition, as emphasised above, started from an 'I am', or, to use Cartesian terms, from the 'res cogitans' side of the divide. The problem of how 'subjectivity' could have emerged from inanimate matter did not arise. In the Coleridgean tradition Nature merely veils 'the Amighty Spirit'[5]. In the original version of the *Aeolian Harp* which Coleridge wrote in 1795 soon after he left Cambridge, he writes

---

[4] Owen's son published a biography in 1894, other biographical material is to be found in Rupke 1994, Sloan, 1992.
[5] Coleridge, *This Lime Tree Bower my Prison:*
'.......So my friend
Struck with deep joy may stand as I have stood
Silent with swimming sense; yea gazing round
On the wide landscape, gaze till all doth seem
Less gross than bodily; and of such hues
As veil the Almighty Spirit, when yet he makes
Spirits perceive his presence'
To distinguish it from Spinoza's pantheism this position is conventionally known as panentheism

that '….God would be the universal soul/Mechanised matter th'organic harps/And each one's tunes be that which each calls I' (Coleridge, 1912, vol.2, p.1022-23). This is not to say, of course, that Owen would have subscribed to all the detail of Coleridge's metaphysics, still less to the cloudy panpsychism of Schelling, but the major thrust of his philosophical anatomy blunts the sharp problem which 'mind' presents to Huxley and others in the Cartesian tradition. Thus Owen, summing up his review of the plant and animal kingdoms in the sixth of the inaugural lectures he gave at the Royal College of Surgeons in 1837, says '….we cannot fail to perceive how many important characters they possess in common: and how grand a series of Instruments they form, by which the great end is at last obtained, of making Matter subservient to the manifestation of Mind' (quoted in Sloan, 1992, p.261). Thus it is not surprising that in the great debate at Oxford in 1860 when the Darwin-Huxley interpretation of the brain's evolution challenged the Owenite interpretation, it was the Bishop of Oxford, a theologian coached by Owen, who entered the lists on Owen's side (see Smith, 1992, 1997).

3.2. Spencer's Evolutionary Psychobiology

Although now largely forgotten, Herbert Spencer (1820-1903) was, at the end of the nineteenth century, one of its foremost philosophers[6]. His influence was far-reaching and, according to his biographer, his work 'was the best synthesis of the knowledge of his time' (Elliot, 1975). His thought was saturated with evolutionary ideas: indeed he was known as the philosopher of evolution and the idea holds together the whole of his system, from cosmology through biology and anthropology to sociology and psychology.

However, although he is credited with inventing the term 'survival of the fittest', his evolution is not the evolution which his fellow Midlander, Charles Darwin, promoted in 1859. Indeed, towards the end of his life, he published four essays in the *Contemporary Review* on the 'inadequacy of natural selection' arguing throughout and with great fervour against natural selection and for the inheritance of acquired characters (Spencer, 1893)[7]. Spencer is, instead, quite clear where the leading idea of his evolutionary philosophy originated. It originated in the embryological researches of Christian Pander and Karl Ernst von Baer in the early years of the century. Looking back in mid-career Spencer writes that 'that which really *has* exercised a profound influence over my thought is the truth which Harvey's embryological enquiries first dimly indicated, which was afterwards more clearly perceived by Wolff and which was put into definite form by von Baer – the truth that all organic development is a change from a state of homogeneity to a state of heterogeneity … the formula of von Baer has acted as an organising principle' (Spencer, 1864; 1891 vol.3). Spencer's model for evolutionary change is thus embryological development. It is consequently no surprise to find that his first publication on the subject, which appeared

---

[6] Spencer's fame and influence may be judged by the fact that although he was known to be uninterested in academic distinctions and made a habit of turning them down, he was nevertheless offered more than twenty two such distinctions ranging from doctorates to fellowships and presidencies of learned societies all over the world.

[7] It must, however, be said that the theory that Spencer found so objectionable was Weismann's not Darwin's. Darwin , with his theory of pangenesis, was far from averse to the inheritance of acquired characteristics (see Darwin, 1868, vol.2 chapter 27).

(anonymously) in the *Leader* of March 20 1852, was simply entitled 'The Development Hypothesis' (in Spencer 1891).

Spencer's formulation of von Baer's embryological 'law' runs as follows: 'Evolution is an integration of matter and a concomitant dissipation of motion; during which matter passes from a relatively indefinite, incoherent homogeneity to a relatively definite, coherent heterogeneity; and during which the contained motion undergoes a parallel transformation' (Spencer, 1870, p.396). This somewhat convoluted definition occasioned more than a little derision amongst some of his early readers[8]. However, we can see what he means. His idea looks back not only to von Baer but also to the *Naturphilosophen* of the turn of the century. It did seem to many that the lines of descent being traced out by these philosophical biologists could be interpreted in these Baerian-Spencerian terms. Spencer was quite explicit: he believed that this 'advance from homogeneity of structure to heterogeneity of structure .....is the law of all progress' (Spencer, 1857). He applied his model not only to the phylogenies which he had met in Carpenter's comparative physiology (Carpenter, 1839) but also to the development of human societies, from tribal groupings to industrial democracies, to the growth of languages, the arts, astronomy, geology and, last but far from least, to psychology (see Smith, 1982a)

The Principles of Psychology was the first major work which Spencer attempted and, as he wrote to his father, it broke his health (Spencer, 1904, pp. 463-4). It was published in 1855, three years after 'The Development Hypothesis'. It is pervaded with evolutionary ideas. But, like Descartes before him, to make a start he had to find bedrock, he had to find of what, if anything, we have the right to be sure. This he discovered in what he called his 'Universal Postulate'. In place of Descartes' ontological argument Spencer put a more epistemological proposition. That of which we have the right to be sure is that of which the negation is inconceivable. What does Spencer mean? He gives an explanatory example: 'It is unbelievable that a cannon ball fired from England should reach America; but it is not inconceivable. Conversely, it is inconceivable that one side of a triangle is equal to the sum of the other two sides – not simply unbelievable. The two sides cannot be represented in consciousness as becoming equal in their joint length to a third side, without the representation of a triangle being destroyed; the concept of a triangle cannot be framed without a simultaneous destruction of a concept in which these magnitudes are represented as equal. That is to say, the subject and predicate cannot be united in the same intuition – the proposition is unthinkable. It is in this sense only that I have used the word inconceivable' (Spencer, 1865). But this equation of 'knowledge of the highest validity' with analytical truth is, in fact, not the only definition Spencer gives. At the beginning of the *Psychology* he provides other instances: 'Whilst looking at the sun a man can no more conceive that he is looking into darkness, than he can conceive that the whole is greater than its parts..... we cannot while cold conceive that we are warm.....etc ' (Spencer, 1855, pp. 27-8). These propositions remind us, of course, of the *cogito*. It is impossible to believe when warm that we are anything but warm. Sensory experience, Hebert Feigl's 'raw feels', are irrefutable (Feigl, 1967). The only difference between these two instances of 'knowledge of the highest validity' is, says Spencer, that 'in the one instance the antecedents of the conviction are

---

[8] The mathematician Kirkman thought that Spencer's definition of evolution should be translated into a plainer English, and offered the following gloss.: 'Evolution is a change from a no-howish untalkaboutable allalikeness, to a somehowish and in general talkaboutable not alikeness, by a continuous somethingeleseification and sticktogetheration' quoted in Flugel and West, 1964, p.96.

present only on special occasions, whilst on the other they are present on all occasions' (Spencer, 1855, p.28).

It is important to recognise that Spencer did not regard these instances of 'knowledge of the highest validity' as *a priori* truths in the scholastic sense. Indeed, the very phrase 'knowledge of the highest validity' implies that while some things are unquestionably more certain than others, nothing is ultimately indubitable. He fully agreed with Mill that all knowledge enters through the doors of the senses, a position he dubbed 'the Experience Hypothesis'. When he came to write *The Principles of Psychology* he believed that he'd hit upon an important way of reconciling this hypothesis with 'its antagonist hypothesis of forms of thought' (Spencer, 1855, p.23n). This reconciliation, he believed, could be effected by an application of evolutionary theory to mind. Such an application, he wrote, 'furnishes a solution to the controversy between the disciples of Locke and those of Kant (Spencer, 1855, p.578; also 1868, vol.2, p.409).

In other words, Spencer, in the middle of the nineteenth century, was proposing the evolutionary explanation of the Kantian categories popularised in the twentieth century by Popper (1972), Campbell (1974a, 1974b) and Lorenz (1977). It is not, says Spencer, the experience of the individual which provides the peculiar certainty of the Kantian categories, or of the axioms of geometry, but the cumulative and inherited experience of countless lives which have gone before[9]. In the second edition of the *Psychology* he expresses this insight with great force: 'Space–relations have been the same not only for all ancestral man, all ancestral primates, all ancestral orders of mammalian but for all the simpler orders of creatures. These constant space-relations are expressed by definite nervous structures, congenitally framed to act in definite ways and incapable of acting in different ways. Hence the inconceivableness of the negation of a mathematical axiom, resulting as it does from the impossibility of inverting the actions of correlative nervous structures, really only stands for the infinity of experiences that have developed these structures (Spencer, 1872, p.419).

Ultimately, then, the analytic truths of the 'universal postulate' are, for Spencer, derived from the ages of evolutionary experience. But these truths, along with 'raw feels', play crucial roles in Spencer's *Psychology*. They not only form the bedrock on which he builds his philosophical system but they also act as a quasi-Darwinian selective force in cognition. For Spencer, as for John Stuart Mill, logic was the 'analysis of the mental process which takes place whenever we reason' (Mill, 1843, p.2) not, as for us (to take a modern definition), the study of 'pure form' (see Stebbing, 1950, p.489). Spencer argued that reasoning consisted in the attainment (evolution) of increasingly coherent states of consciousness. 'A discussion in consciousness' he writes 'proves to be a trial of strength between different connections in consciousness – a systematised struggle serving to determine which are the least coherent states of consciousness' (Spencer, 1865). In this struggle the least coherent states fall apart and the more coherent survive. The most firmly interconnected states, those that cannot in any circumstances be 'torn asunder', form the ultimate test against which the other states measure themselves. And these ultimately unbreakable states are, of course, the states of

---

[9] Michael Bradie has distinguished theories which attempt to use evolutionary models to account for the growth of ideas, theories etc as the *Evolutionary Epistemology of Theories (EET)* to contrast them with the *Evolution of Epistemology of Mechanisms (EEM)* (Bradie, 1986). Spencer's division is not quite the same. He is using evolutionary models to account for the origins of the Kantian categories over phylogenetic time on the one hand, and on the other to account for the emergence of conclusions from thought processes within individual minds.

consciousness described by the Universal Postulate. It is not difficult to see how thoroughly Spencer's *Psychology* is steeped in evolutionary ideas.

This absorption in evolutionary thought is evident throughout the *Psychology*. 'If the doctrine of evolution is true', he writes, 'the inevitable implication is that Mind can be understood only by observing how mind is evolved' (Spencer, 1870, p.291). In both the first and second editions of the *Psychology* Spencer shows how the objective indices of mentality grade insensibly from philosopher to protozoan. How do we know this? Spencer is clear that we know this with as little and as much certainty that we know that other human minds exist. If we once grant this we cannot deny that animal minds also exist. Paralleling the evolution of nervous systems there is, he asserts, an evolution of consciousness. But here, from our twenty-first century, post-Darwinian perspective, we might enter a caution. Spencer's mind-set had been formed by early nineteenth century beliefs in progress and Baerian embryology. It was natural for him, as it is not natural for us, to assume that consciousness reached a pinnacle in *Homo sapiens*[10]. In this sense he is at one with Richard Owen who, as we noted above, saw the evolutionary process culminating in human mentality. One hundred and fifty years later we are still groping to find the neural correlatives of consciousness. We still have no answer to the 'hard problem', of how 'qualia' or 'raw feels' are related to, or arise from, the goings on in the matter of the brain. The notion of an 'evolution of consciousness' remains deeply obscure: we do not know how, if at all, to tie it into the evolution of nervous systems.

Spencer, however, had, if not a theory, then at least a suggestion. A suggestion, moreover, consistent with his general evolutionary law: a movement from an indefinite, incoherent, homogeneity towards a definite, coherent, heterogeneity. Nerve centres, in his view, are at first poorly organised masses where 'information processing' is inefficient and sluggish. Later, with repetitive use, the centres become better organised, more intricate, more differentiated. The elements of these differentiated centres become, moreover, more tightly interconnected and thus more 'coherent'. This speculation has received support in more recent times, though only in embryogenesis. There is nowadays good evidence that the adult differentiated cortex arises from a pre-existing more homogeneous and labile 'pro-cortex' (O'Leary, 1989). Re-routing experiments in the foetal brain have shown that what would normally develop into auditory or somatosensory cortex is fully capable of dealing with input from, for instance, the optic nerve (Sur, Garraghty and Roe, 1988; Roe, Pallas, Kwon, Sur, 1992)). Vice versa it is possible to show that the destination of output fibres from a patch of cortex depends on the position of that patch in the whole of the cortex. If, for instance, patches of visual cortex are transplanted in the late foetal rodent to the sensorimotor region it develops output axons to the spinal cord; vice versa, a patch of presumptive sensorimotor cortex transplanted to the visual area sends its output axons to the superior colliculus (O'Leary and Stanfield, 1989). It seems that Spencer was quite right in believing that the nervous system, at least as represented by the mammalian cerebral cortex, develops from a pluripotent homogeneity towards a dedicated, comparatively hard-wired, heterogeneity.

Spencer gives a number of examples to illustrate this 'evolution' from an undifferentiated to a differentiated condition. Most of them, perforce, are instances drawn from ontogenesis.

[10] I am not, of course, intending to say that there has not been an evolution of 'intelligence' - there can be little doubt that there has - but that we have, as yet, no way of telling whether there has been an evolution of 'raw feel', of 'qualia'. To take just a Primate example, why should we suppose that 'pain' or 'redness' is any less intense, or different, in the Prosimii than in the Hominidae?

Speech, for instance, is learned slowly and with difficulty by the infant. This implies, says Spencer, that the nerve centres underlying articulatory behaviour are poorly differentiated. But 'the concomitant states are vivid and for the moment all-embracing' (Spencer, 1870, p.560). Later, however, speech becomes easy, well-formed, automatic. The underlying centres have, by this token, become highly differentiated and tightly organised. 'Nerve energy' now encounters little resistance as it flows through these centres. Correspondingly 'consciousness', the other side of the coin, loses its early intensity and lapses to the low levels we associate with automatic behaviour[11]. Similar interpretations can be made of other behaviours we acquire in childhood: walking, the upright stance etc.

Spencer does not necessarily believe that the 'seat of consciousness' lies in the nerve centres which govern behaviour such as articulacy and locomotion. Rather, he believes that consciousness is the 'internal aspect' of activity in 'higher centres'. He argues that a nerve centre, early on, while only poorly organised, is unable to cope with the rush of nerve currents flooding into it. It does not, at this stage, possess the smooth channels necessary to allow the escape of energy easily and automatically to the effector organs at the periphery[12]. Instead some of the brimming 'nervous energy' escapes 'centripetally' to 'higher centres' and there 'awakens a feeling' (Spencer, 1870, pp.107-8). Connected with this interpretation is the observation that feelings always have a temporal dimension, however short. A flash of lightning, says Spencer (quoting Huxley), is instantaneous, yet the sensation lingers on. This, according to Spencer, is due to the massive sensory inflow saturating the 'lower centre', so that an overflow surges up a centripetal pathway to a 'higher centre' and, reverberating there, provides the physical aspect of the sensation (Spencer, 1870, p.556).

What did Spencer have in mind when he used the term 'higher centre'? His concept remains quite acceptable today. Higher centres, according to Spencer, are those parts of the brain to which information from several or all sense modalities is brought, correlated and co-ordinated. At first glance Spencer seems to be in some difficulty here. On the one hand he wishes to assert (with Carpenter) that these centres represent the climax of the evolutionary process (Carpenter, 1839, p.453). But on the other they do not seem to fit his definition of an evolutionary climax.. It does not seem that these 'higher centres' show the 'definite, coherent, heterogeneity' which, as we have seen, is for Spencer definitive of an evolutionary climax. Quite the contrary: by his own account they are characterised by relatively homogeneous, poorly differentiated, tissue. In this relatively homogeneous matrix Spencer imagines that waves of neuronal activity ripple to and fro in a poorly co-ordinated, time-consuming fashion until they find an escape to the periphery. It is this reverberation in the centre before the nerve energy finds a way out to the periphery that Spencer believes constitutes the objective correlative of consciousness.

Yet this seeming contradiction in Spencer's evolutionary psychology is far more apparent than real. We need only remember Spencer's grounding in von Baer's embryology and Carpenter's zoology. In *The Principles of General and Comparative Physiology* Carpenter

---

[11] Spencer is, of course, writing long before microscopists had revealed the synaptic interconnections between neurons or the concepts of synaptic facilitation had been invented.

[12] The notion of a flow of nerve energy through pathways between cerebral centres seems to lie half way between the time-honoured ideas of animal spirit flowing through tube-like nerves and twentieth-century ideas of synaptic facilitation. It would be interesting to attempt a translation of Spencer's mid nineteenth-century psychophysiology into modern terms where synaptic resistances (nowadays understood at the molecular level) would take the place of Spencer's nineteenth-century 'channels' and action potentials the place of his 'nerve currents'.

writes (p.458): 'In tracing the progressive complication of the psychical manifestations during early life of the human being, a remarkable correspondence may be observed with the gradual increase in endowments which is to remarked in the ascending animal scale'. In short, here as elsewhere, 'ontogeny recapitulates phylogeny'. Hence Spencer sees the 'higher centres' of the lower vertebrates as homologues of the 'lower centres' of the higher vertebrates. (Spencer, 1870, p.105). It follows that, in the phylogenetic series, evolutionary advance progressively transfers nerve centres from 'incoherent homogeneity' to 'coherent heterogeneity', from random to 'hard-wired', as Spencer's general theory requires. 'The seat of consciousness' Spencer writes 'is that nervous centre to which mediately or immediately, the most heterogeneous impressions are brought (Spencer, 1870, p.105). Hence the 'seats of consciousness' in lower forms may be transformed into reflex centres in higher forms. In this way Spencer begins to provide an answer to Darwin's early perplexity (quoted above) as to how far through the animal kingdom consciousness stretches (see also Smith, 1978). Spencer would say, quite simply, that consciousness extends right through the animal kingdom (or at least the vertebrates), but, due to progressive encephalisation, the centres in which reverberatory activity provides its physical correlative in lower forms are left behind and only support reflex automatisms in higher forms.

The whole of Spencer's theory is, of course, open to a very obvious objection. Why should the mere difficulty of 'nervous discharge' and the consequent 'neuronal reverberation' form the physical correlative of consciousness? Romanes was quick to see this. Why, he asked, should 'reverberatory activity' be the neural correlative of consciousness? It is not obvious, he wrote, that 'complexity in itself … (has) anything to do with the rise of consciousness, except insofar as it may be conducive to what we may call ganglionic friction which may be expressed by delay in response' (Romanes, 1883, p.74n). A century and a half into the future we have developed a multitude of techniques for examining the neural correlatives of consciousness ranging from multiple microelectrode implants to various forms of neuroimaging. We are well on the way to determining what in the nervous system correlates with the rich world of subjectivity we all live through. Spencer's evolutionary theory may yet prove surprisingly fruitful.

3.3. John Hughlings Jackson's Philosophical Neurology

Some of the fruits of Spencer's thought were plucked by one of the most significant neurologists of the English nineteenth century: John Hughlings Jackson (1835-1911) (Smith, 1982b). Jackson's writings abound with the names of philosophers but one stands out: that of Herbert Spencer. 'I need scarcely mention the name of Herbert Spencer' he writes 'except to express my vast indebtedness to him' (Taylor, 1958, vol.2, p.395). It is clear from even the most cursory reading of Jackson's voluminous writings that he found the key to making sense of the bewildering phenomena of the neurological ward in Spencer's *Principles of Psychology*[13]. 'In the doctrine of evolution' he writes in his 1889 address to the Leeds

---

[13] It is noteworthy that in 1861, before any references to Spencer occur in Jackson's writings, he published a small treatise for private circulation amongst his friends entitled 'Suggestions for studying diseases of the nervous system on Professor Owen's vertebral theory' (Jackson, 1863). This is another instance of the pervasive nature of evolutionary thought in the nineteenth century. Jackson does not get very far with his classification of diseases on Owenite principles but it is interesting to note that the segmental view of the skull which he takes

meeting of the British Medical Association, 'we have principles which no doubt apply to the whole organism and to every one of its diseases' (Taylor, 1958, vol.2, p.395). That it is Spencer's concept of evolution (not Darwin's) that he has in mind is made clear later on in the same address when he writes: 'the evolutionary ascent is from the least to the most modifiable'.

Jackson's principal interest in Spencer's evolutionary theory is, however, not so much 'ascent' as 'descent'. Towards the end of his life Spencer recalled discussing his evolution theory with Tyndall and the physicist asking, 'But how will it all end?' to which Spencer replied, 'Equilibration'. 'But what happens next', asked Tyndall. 'Dissolution' said Spencer (Duncan, 1908, vol.1, p.555). It was this inverse to evolution, dissolution, which seemed to Jackson to hold the key to neurological disease. Dissolution, for Jackson, was 'the reverse of the process of evolution ... a process of 'undevelopment'....a 'taking to pieces' in order from the least organised, from the most complex and the most voluntary, toward the most organised, most simple and most organised' (Taylor, vol.2, p.46). Spencer's thought shines through this passage.

Jackson also makes use of another of Spencer's *aperçus*: 'survival of the fittest'. He maintains that during neurological disease the surviving behaviour represents the patient's 'fittest state'. 'The assertion is', he writes, 'that each person's normal thought and conduct are, or signify, survivals of the fittest states of what we might call the topmost 'layer' of his highest centres. Now suppose that from disease the normal highest level of evolution (the topmost level) is rendered functionless ... I contend that his positive symptoms are still survivals of his fittest states, are survivals on the lower, but *then* the highest level of evolution. The most absurd mentation, and the most extravagant activities in insane people are the survivals of their fittest states....(their) illusions, etc., are (their) mind' (Taylor, vol.2, pp.46-7). At the back of Jackson's mind as he wrote these passages is his analogy of the brain to the governing bureaucracy of a large organisation., either that of the nation itself, or of the Navy (Taylor, vol.2, pp.22, 55, 58). When one member of the Admiralty board is indisposed, he writes, the rest compensate by working a little harder and all goes on much as before. But if and when the entire upper echelon is removed, the consequences are likely to be serious. The State or Navy is now controlled by the less well-informed second level and is likely to perform half blind. The best the lower stratum can achieve is less well adapted to the circumstances. These poorly adapted responses are, for Jackson, the 'fittest' that the reduced organisation (brain) can achieve[14].

The crucial element of Jackson's neurophilosophy, brought out in the preceding quotation, is that the subjectivity of the patient is, quite simply, the subjectivity of what remains of his brain. It is not the balked, hindered, subjectivity of the normal, healthy, brain: it is the fittest state of which the brain's reduced organisation is capable. 'If a man takes a felt hat lying on the floor to be a black cat' he writes 'it is as certain that, negatively, he does not see the felt hat as that, postively, he does see a black cat....To say that the patient cannot

---

from Owen helped him make sense of the type of localised epilepsies which he had observed on his rounds during the early 1860s and to which he was later to give his name.

[14] Contemporary views of the functional architecture of the brain are not, of course, as simple as Jackson's metaphor suggests. Nevertheless most neuroscientists would still largely agree with William James' view that the neural correlatives of consciousness are widespread throughout the brain and that elimination, by disease or injury, of one or more elements leads to a re-organisation leading to a 'lower level' or 'less adapted structure'.

really *see* a black cat "because there is not one", is of no avail. His nervous system is not ours... He sees a black cat; we see a felt hat. The thing outside rouses in him the image of a black cat; it *rouses in us.....* the image of felt hat' (Taylor, 1958, vol.2, p.24). The patient is not mistaken when he disagrees with our interpretation. 'His illusions are not caused by the disease, but are the outcome of what is left of him (of what his disease has spared him).... His illusions etc. are his mind' (Taylor, 1958, vol.2, p.47). It is tempting to see here a neurological version of Spencer's psychophysiology outlined in the previous section.

How, then, did Jackson see the relation of mind to brain? His views are closely tied to his practice in the neurological wards at Queen Square. He was always concerned to distance himself from those who slipped into the habit of regarding the brain as a 'solid mind'. To advance from the neurophysiology of sensory nerve fibres, to sensations in sensory centres that are then compounded into ideas in higher centres and finally into elaborate mental states in the highest centres is, he says, common practice, but deeply incoherent. 'The real crudity' of this form of argument is veiled, he writes, by technicalities, the common sense is blinded by scientific verbiage; what meaning can be attached to 'unconscious sensation' that becomes by compounding 'conscious sensation'? The first, he says, is contradictory, the second tautological (Taylor, 1958, vol.2, p.28). These 'psychologico-materialistic theories' are, he concludes, 'not really clear: they hinder progress in neurology'. We still need Jackson's clarity. A century and half of further progress in neurology and the neurosciences has led to huge advances in understanding the brain and in treating neurological patients, but the obscurantist language remains. We still too easily pass from brain to mind and back again. This is a theme which has surfaced several times already in this chapter. Coleridge, it will be remembered, had only derision for those who believed that a sensible body could be achieved by combining a myriad insensible elements.

Jackson, however, is no two-substance dualist. Some have accused him of being a Leibnizian parallelist, others note that he quotes with approbation Lewes' dual aspect identity theory, whilst yet others note his liking for the idea of psychoneural concomitance. Jackson is himself not too bothered about how his views might be classified[15]. Indeed they probably varied from time to time and in different publications and we have to remember that Jackson had not had the advantage (disadvantage?) of a formal philosophical training. His approach is to apply his high intelligence and speculative intellect to his life-long observations of patients in the National Hospital. Like Spencer, he takes subjectivity to be primary[16]. He agrees with Spencer in arguing that the division between the objective and the subjective world is derived developmentally from an originally undifferentiated awareness (see Smith 1982a). . 'Object consciousness' and 'subject consciousness' are, says Jackson, merely divisions of convenience. They are subdivisions which allow us to make sense of the world. 'Each is by itself nothing; each is "only half of itself"... ideas come out of subject consciousness and then constitute "object consciousness"'.

What does he mean by this? Jackson has often been accused of being an awkward and inelegant stylist. Indeed, according to his early friend and mentor, Jonathan Hutchinson, he acknowledged this deficiency himself: 'I am only a Bedlamite theorist' (Hutchinson, 1911,

---

[15] When a critic suggested that Jacksons's position resembled Leibniz' 'two-clocks' theory he responded: 'It may be: it matters nothing for medical purposes whether it is or not' (Taylor, 1958, vol.2, p.84).

[16] The persistence of the Augustinian-Cartesian analysis is clear. A malign spirit, as Descartes imagines, might be responsible for systematically misleading us about the 'external' world; but we cannot doubt when we have a 'raw feel' that we are indeed having that 'feel'.

vol.2, p.950) and in another place he remarks that writing was for him like driving a team of eight horses. Others said of his writings that they resembled the peace of God, they passed all understanding. But part of the problem is the extreme difficulty of the ideas he is trying to express. He is having to go against the grain of Western language. He recognises that in many cases he has to resort to 'Irishisms'. 'What is called introspection of consciousness', he writes, 'is of states of consciousness already "come out of" subject consciousness. Subject consciousness, that which has these states (popularly "contemplates", "reflects on", "arranges", "attends to" etc.) is not known in any such way. To put the matter Hibernically; we only know, in the ordinary sense of the word know, subject consciousness - on its becoming object consciousness.... Subject consciousness is something deeper than knowledge..... it *is* us in an emphatic sense... It is thus a constant to object consciousness which is continually changing' (Taylor, 1958, vol.2, p.113)

We can see (just) what he means. Subject consciousness is by its very nature ungraspable. Interestingly, Jackson is saying the same things which existentialist and other philosophers were saying in the middle of the twentieth century. Jean Paul Sartre writes, 'The consciousness which says "I am thinking" is precisely not the consciousness which thinks'; Edelman writes of 'the remembered present'; Ned Block distinguishes between 'phenomenal' and 'access' consciousness. Heidegger's student Eugen Fink has an interesting metaphor: 'Man's mind', he writes, 'is like Midas of the legend: everything he touched turned to gold; even food and drink turned into hard metal for him. Likewise, everything we think turns into the hard solid form of "being", of something that "is"' (Demske, p.198). It is this uncatchable 'spontaneity' (to use Sartre's phrase) which, for Jackson, forms the 'bottom' of the mind. It 'solidifies' into 'object consciousness'. Initially, there is the 'raw feel', a state of 'being', our 'ownmost self' (to quote Heidegger's neologism) an instant later it has been 'objectified', we look back on it, we know what we feel.

The 'bottom of the mind', this ongoing Sartrean spontaneity, is, according to Jackson, fabricated of 'constants'. He believes, with Spencer, that these constants - space, time, mass etc. - have an evolutionary origin. They are consequently the deepest structures of our mentality. As an example he devotes a long discussion to one of these constants - the time constant. The sense of time must have puzzled us all. St Augustine famously remarked of time that when no one asked he knew, but that when someone asked he knew not.

What gives us our sense of the flow of time? Isaac Newton, it will be remembered, considered it to be a smooth, continuous, steady flow from the past towards the future. But how do we know this? If time is like a river how can we detect its flow if we are immersed in it, if we cannot see a stationary object. It seems that there must be some fixed point against which we can measure it. What can this fixed point be? Jackson points out that our conventional measures are quite arbitrary. They are keyed into astronomical phenomena such as the rotation of the earth, or, in more recent times, the vibration period of atoms such as Caesium in specified conditions. But we have no need of such external standards, says Jackson, to sense the passage of time. We must, he thinks, have an internal standard against which to measure it.

This internal standard, says Jackson, derives from the cerebral re-re-representation of the cardiac systole. He points out that the heart is 'the most autonomous of all organs'. An excised frog's heart can be kept beating for several days, as can that of a dog. Systolic contraction is complete, not graded as with other types of muscle. He argues that the cardiac rhythm is one of the Kantian-like 'forms' which has become incorporated into the brain during evolution.

He works the representation of the heart rhythm into his theory of the evolved stratigraphy of the brain. It is represented in the medulla, re-represented in (he says) 'the region of the corpus callosum', and finally re-re-represented quite generally throughout the cerebral cortex. This tripartite layering is derived from Herbert Spencer where it may be traced to sociological roots. It is interesting to note that triune theories of the brain crop up time and again from Plato in classical antiquity (again with a sociological origin) to Paul MacLean in our own times (MacLean, 1990) But that is another story!

According to Jackson it is this rhythmicity originating in the heart rhythm which forms the physiological substratum of the time sense. It is from this that the time-constant has been evolved. It is, moreover, (he says) 'the most simple and the most strongly organised' of all the nervous arrangements of the highest centres. It is indissolubly part of our self-image; our self-understanding is rooted in temporality.

The time sense, Jackson goes on, is a 'generalisation' of the 'machinery' which, in lower animals, ensures the rhythmical beat of the heart. During phylogenesis the third-order representation of this rhythm becomes 'entirely detached' from the lower cardiac centres. These merely retain the menial work of ensuring that the body's plumbing is kept going efficiently. The third-order representation loses all contact with this low level activity. Its origin has, as he writes, 'been forgotten' (Taylor, 1958, vol.2, p.113). The higher order representation is, in a sense, 'smeared' throughout the most recently evolved layer of the brain. A modern analogy is with a hologram. Each small pixel of a hologram contains a fuzzy image of the whole. This extended, detached, figuration of the cardiac rhythm forms part of the 'physiological bottom of the mind' (Taylor, 1958, vol.2, p.114). 'It is that' he writes 'by which time, in the sense of succession of our objective states, is known'.

Jackson acknowledges he has been writing only of the *physical bases* of the time constant. The subjective correlative is something else again. 'Suppose', he writes (perhaps referring to Leibniz's famous image in the *Monadology*), 'that I could see into a man's brain and could give a correct and thorough account of what went on in it whilst he was having the colour red (thinking of a red object), that would be no sort of explanation of the (his) colour itself, but only of its physical concomitant' (Taylor, 1958, vol.2, p.116). Similarly with the physiological basis of the time constant.

Our subjective sense of the passage of time, he argues, is not itself in time. 'There could be no objective sequences for us....unless we ourselves were going on at some rate independently of, and so to say, "out of" these objective sequences' (Taylor, vol.2, p.119). If, to repeat myself, time is like a river in which we are immersed, how can we detect its flow unless we can see a stationary object, perhaps the river bank? Jackson is back to the central puzzle of his neurophilosophy: the relation of mind to brain. Accordingly he ends this section by quoting the idealist philosopher T.H.Green: 'The relation of events to each other as in time implies their equal presence to the subject which is not in time. There would be no such thing as time if there were not a self-consciousness which was not in time' (Green, 1882, p.55).

Is this 'Bedlamite' philosophising.? I don't think so. I think it shows, as Hutchinson observed, the mark of a powerful philosophical mind. The anonymous writer of the obituary notice in the *British Medical Journal* likened Jackson's mind to that of another great Londoner: Samuel Johnson. He had, he says, a Johnsonian ability to cut through superficialities to the essentials. In his rounds at the National Hospital, and at medical conferences, he was not one to waste words. His students and colleagues learnt to wait, but were seldom disappointed. Jackson was struggling in the turgid prose just quoted to tell us something. He was struggling against the tide that seemed to be leading inexorably to the conflation of mind and brain. He was struggling against the intellectual slackness of taking the brain, as he says, to be a 'solid mind'. In many passages he points out the intellectual confusion and the neurological dangers lurking in this assessment. The danger of this confusion has not diminished in the years since Jackson walked the wards at Queen Square.

Sir Gordon Holmes writes, in 1954, of how Jackson's work 'remains a live and vitalising force in the thought of all who seek depth as well as width of knowledge in the field of neurophysiology and clinical neurology, and who wish to understand more than the reading of instruments of precision can tell them' (Holmes, 1954) and Charles Mercier, in his recollections of Jackson in the 1913 *British Medical Journal*, writes that '..his speculations on the ultimate nature of mental processes and their connection with brain processes are the most profound and, over a wide field, the most consistent and explanatory that have ever been attained; and they will undoubtedly form the foundation of a future system of psychology that is yet to be elaborated'.

Although Jackson's neuroscience nowadays seems that of another age, his questions, like those of Samuel Johnson, still strike to the heart of the matter. There is, of course, much interest, nowadays, in biological clocks (see Dunlap, 1999; Schantz and Archer, 2003). It does turn out that autonomous oscillators (though not related, of course, to the cardiac rhythm) are found in many (if not most) tissues. But the relation of this biochemistry and molecular biology to our sense of the passage of time? Few today touch this issue. Hughlings Jackson remains one of the few, the very few, to have understood the issue and to have attempted a philosophically-informed neurological response. His early twenty-first century epigoni in what has become known as 'consciousness studies' seldom penetrate so far or see so much. The encomiums of Jonathan Hutchinson, Arnold Pick, Gordon Holmes and the others were fully justified.

3.4. Thomas Henry Huxley and 'Epiphenomenalism'

With Thomas Henry Huxley (1825-95) we enter a very different 'thought world'. It is not for nothing that he is known as 'Darwin's bulldog'. At the height of his powers in 1860 he contrived a very public confrontation with Richard Owen, the greatest anatomist of his time. The Oxford meeting of the British Association for the Advancement of Science where Owen's anti-Darwinist views were represented by the Bishop of Oxford, 'Soapy Sam' Wilberforce, has been described and analysed in many places and it would be otiose to do so again here. Suffice it to say that Huxley, by this time a convinced Darwinian, by common consent won the encounter and the Darwin-Huxley paradigm dominated the rest of the nineteenth century.

Huxley was born at Ealing in 1825, the son of a struggling schoolmaster. In an autobiographical fragment he says that his greatest wish as a boy was to be a mechanical engineer and he goes on to ruminate that although the Institute of Mechanical Engineers would certainly not own him, he had been all along a sort of mechanical engineer *in partibus infidelium*. It is interesting to note that Herbert Spencer, another of Huxley's sparring partners, though in this case on friendly terms, started his career as a railway engineer in the

English Midlands (1837-41). The mechanistic paradigm, initiated by Descartes and reinforced powerfully by the steam-driven industrial revolution, is never far from the Victorian mind[17].

Huxley, however, did not become an engineer but was apprenticed to medicine and during his initial training at Sydenham College in London came under the influence of Marshall Hall who was at that time working tirelessly to establish the concept of the reflex arc (see Smith, 1999b). Hall's work on reflexes eliminated any need for an immaterial 'soul' or 'vis nervosa' in the spinal cord and showed that its responses could be explained on a purely mechanistic basis. This interpretation was taken up by a number of other figures prominent in the non-conformist medical schools of mid-century London. Huxley was exposed to this radical thinking at a young and impressionable age. As a medical student in inner London he was also exposed to the atrocious conditions under which the poor lived. Huxley came from a different generation and was exposed to different experiences, both intellectually and socially, from his more 'establishment' later antagonist, Richard Owen. This may well have contributed a large part to the animosity between the two (see Smith, 1997).

But Huxley's radicalism long antedates his experiences as a medical student. Even as a boy his notebook records arguments with his parents against the 'establishment'. He was particularly incensed that Dissenters should have to pay rates to support an established Church with whose opinions they sharply disagreed:. 'However small the contribution the demand was wrong in principle' (Huxley, 1903, vol.1, p.14). We can also read in this notebook of his early metaphysical convictions: 'Had a long argument with Mr May' he writes 'on the nature of the soul and the difference between it and matter. I maintained that it could not be proved that matter was essentially – as to its base –different from soul. Mr May wittily said, soul was the perspiration of matter' (Huxley, 1903, vol.1: November 22, 1840). How little the fifteen-year-old Huxley's views changed over the course of a long and controversial life!

Huxley's philosophical interests continued throughout his life. His notebooks and manuscript papers held at Imperial College London are filled with jottings and transcriptions on metaphysics and philosophy. He was sufficiently interested in philosophical matters to write essays on Descartes and George Berkeley and a full-scale account of David Hume in the *English Men of Letters* series (1879). The position which he elaborates in these manuscript jottings and published works is fully in line with the reflexology he learnt from Marshall Hall, Laycock and Carpenter in his student years. This is not to say that these pioneers would have necessarily drawn Huxley's large conclusions. Carpenter, for one, in two long articles he published in the *Contemporary Review*, in a paper to the *Metaphysical Society*, and elsewhere, strongly disagreed and sought to preserve a role for 'free will' outside the cerebral machine (Carpenter, 1872, 1875).

Unlike Owen who, as we saw, looked back to the 'Germano-Coleridgean' tradition, Huxley was quite clear that it was René Descartes who had the true vision of a modern physiology. In particular, he sought to develop the physiological stance which Descartes had initiated in the book which he had suppressed in his own lifetime (due to ecclesiastical pressure) – *L'Homme* or *Treatise of Man*. Descartes was Huxley's hero. He entitles the fourth volume of his collected essays 'Method and Results' in conscious homage to his great

---

[17] Yet another significant mid-Victorian biologist, W.B.Carpenter, had wished in his boyhood to become an engineer but was forced by lack of parental resources to take up an apprenticeship in medicine. His mother ever-after felt that it had been a mistake not to let her eldest son have his way (Carpenter, 1888).

predecessor. At the beginning of his 1874 essay on 'Animal Automatism' he praises him as a 'great and original physiologist', having done for 'the physiology of motion and sensation that which Harvey had done for the circulation of the blood and opened up that road to the mechanical theory of these processes, which has been followed by all his successors' (Huxley, 1874) and in his essay on Descartes he says that 'the spirit' of the central passages in *L'Homme* is 'exactly that of the most advanced physiology of the present day' (Huxley, 1870, p.184).

Huxley devotes many pages to a discussion of the consequence of Descartes' neurophysiology: the 'beast-machine'. In *Animal Automatism* he quotes Malebranche: '...cats, dogs and the other animals....eat without pleasure, cry without grief; believe without knowing; desire nothing; know nothing... ' (Malebranche, 1841, in Huxley, 1874, p.218n). He goes on to describe Goltz' experiments on frogs (Goltz, 1869) which he says he has repeated and that he has confirmed Goltz' observations[18]. Descartes, he writes, would have taken them to amply confirm his own assessment. He brings into discussion a French army sergeant, F---, with a bullet wound in the left parietal lobe, studied by Dr Mesmet who '...drinks, smokes, walks about, dresses and undresses himself, rises and goes to bed at the accustomed hours' and even sings as if he were, as Huxley says, one of Vaucauson's automata, (Huxley, 1874, pp.226-35) and finally cases of mesmerism, somnabulism and split personality. These provide acute tests for the Cartesian. Are they conscious or not? How should we treat them? As mere mechanisms or as sentient, though damaged, human beings?

Huxley's position as a Cartesian was of course made doubly difficult by his being at this time a convinced Darwinian. 'The doctrine of continuity', he writes, 'is too well established for it to be permissible for me to suppose that any complex natural phenomenon comes into existence suddenly without being preceded by simpler modifications; and very strong arguments would be needed to prove that such complex phenomena as those of consciousness, first make their appearance in man' (Huxley, 1874, p.236). The Darwinian world does not allow, to quote one of Darwin's early notebook entries, a 'soul' to be 'superadded' (Darwin, 1837, §37). If animals were automata, then why not humans also? The logic seemed unbreakable.

Huxley, although a good German scholar, was not attracted to the solution proposed by Kant and the followers of his critical philosophy (Kant, 1781). Instead, he opted for epiphenomenalism memorably summed-up in his phrase 'Mind is to brain as whistle is to steam engine' (Huxley, 1874, p.240). This mature position cannot but remind us of the phrase used by Mr May to the fifteen year old Huxley a quarter of a century before: soul is but the perspiration of matter. In this sense Huxley is thoroughly materialistic. Indeed, in his essay on Descartes he asserts that 'sooner or later (we shall) arrive at a mechanical equivalent of consciousness, just as we have arrived at a mechanical equivalent of heat' (Huxley, 1870, p.191). In his second contribution to the *Metaphysical Society*, of which he was one of the founding members, he mocked the more conventionally minded with a paper entitled 'Has the frog a soul and of what nature is that soul, supposing it to exist'.

Epiphenomenalists see mind as a mere lazy looker-on at the world's affairs. Mind seems just an effervescence created by deeper goings on within the brain, having no leverage on its

---

[18] In the 1850s and 1860s Goltz showed by a long series of experiments that decerebrate frogs were fully capable of numerous complex co-ordinated behavioural movements. He went on to show similar results in decorticate dogs. These latter results were, however, successfully challenged by localisationists such as David Ferrier.

output. This view has received support in more recent times from the work of Libet and co-workers, whose neurochronology has been interpreted as showing that consciousness comes late on the scene of willed-action (Libet, 1983; 1993). Huxley was ever a controversialist. He was well aware of the hornet's nest he was stirring up. If free-will is an illusion, it must be our deepest illusion (see Smith, 1991). It is very much definitive of who we are. Moreover, without the notion of freely acting agents it would be impossible to apply the core concepts of praise and blame. Without these concepts how can society exist? How can legal systems be set up or operate? Huxley was aware of these consequences. But, he says, as a scientist I have more important things to do than spend time finding answers. The world, he says, 'is full of misery and ignorance, and it is the plain duty of each and all of us…to attempt to make it a little less so' (Huxley, 1868).

Nonetheless, Huxley wants to dispel one illusion: that he is a 'crass' materialist. He argues, as he'd argued as a fifteen year-old, that 'we cannot find the absolute basis of matter, we know only its properties; neither know we the soul in any other way' (Huxley, 1903, vol.1). All knowledge, he agrees with Locke and Hume, enters through the doors of the senses. We form our ideas of primary, just as much as our ideas of secondary, qualities by long-continued (and unconscious) analysis of our sensations. 'Suppose' he says, 'I prick my finger with a pin. I immediately become aware of a condition of my consciousness – a feeling which I term pain etc. This feeling is in myself alone,' he goes on 'it is not something which inheres in the needle …. it is a state of consciousness' (Huxley, 1871, pp.251-2). Similarly with touch, colour, smells, tastes etc. their *esse* is *percipi*. 'But that which perceives or knows is termed mind or spirit, and therefore the knowledge which the senses give is, after all, a knowledge of spiritual phenomena'. But not only secondary qualities are known in this way, but also the so-called primary qualities. Pain is localised, two pinpricks a distance apart give rise to new ideas - co-existence, number, distance, relative place or direction and so on. Primary qualities such as number, extension etc. are as much dependent on mind as are colour, pain etc. Similarly the sense of touch defines self and non-self, ego and non-ego; finally the proprioceptive senses, the senses of effort and fatigue, the correlation between muscular movement and effort, provides us with our primitive concepts of solidity, power, work, energy. 'If' he concludes (and in more than one place) 'I were obliged to choose between absolute materialism and absolute idealism, I should feel compelled to accept the latter alternative' (Huxley, 1871, p.279).

This analysis is very similar to that which we can find in Herbert Spencer's *Psychology*. This is not surprising as Spencer and Huxley were firm friends. Both were members of the highly exclusive X-club (founded in 1864 , some 240 meetings over thirty years) and Huxley not only read the proofs of *First Principles,* the first volume of Spencer's vast *Synthetic Philosophy,* but his papers at Imperial College London contain over eighty letters written to Spencer. As late as 1880 Huxley was jotting down analyses of Spencer's 'Universal Postulate' and trying out possible conclusions that might be drawn from it (Huxley, 1880). Spencer concludes his *Psychology* with the doctrine of so-called 'transfigured realism': both mind and matter are ultimately unknowable (see Smith, 1983). And Huxley, in a letter to Charles Kingsley, says much the same: he writes of the 'absurdity of imagining we know anything about either spirit or matter' (Huxley, 1863, 346-52).

Has Huxley made out his case? We can see that his thought flows smoothly from that of his great forerunner, René Descartes. If we go back to some of his earliest jottings as a boy at Coventry in 1840, we find him writing '….*cogito ergo sum* is the only thing we certainly know' (1903, vol.1, p.15). This, as we have seen, led Huxley to a species of absolute idealism, or solipsism. Descartes, of course, had an escape route from this dead end: a version of the ontological proof for a good and benevolent Deity. This allowed him to establish the veracity of the external world: such a Being (by definition) would and could not deceive. But St Anselm's proof is not, of course, available to Huxley the agnostic. He would have regarded it as a mere playing with words, worthy only of the flames. It is, perhaps, possible to argue, as David Deutsch and others have argued, that extremes meet: absolute idealism is ultimately indistinguishable from absolute materialism (Deutsch, 1997, pp.85-6). But neither monism answers to experience. The world appears to us under two aspects: the 'mental' and the 'physical'. Neither Huxley nor his philosopher friend Spencer were able to solve the conundrum which Descartes left the modern world. A conundrum made more acute by the acceptance·of an evolutionary theory which leaves no doubt that humans as well as all the other members of the living world are connected, without interruption, to the inorganic world of macromolecules, molecules, atoms and fundamental particles. It may be that the problem of consciousness in a material world is insoluble by us as McGinn and the so-called 'New Mysterians' believe (McGinn, 1990), or it may be that researches into the fundamental nature of matter will show us the way to an answer (see Schwarz, Stapp and Beauregard, 2004; Smith, 2006; Stapp 2005).

4. CONCLUSION

In her well-known book, *A Distant Mirror*, Barbara Tuchman described how the calamitous 14th century provides some useful lessons for our own (slightly) less calamitous times. In looking in some depth at the work of four 19th century evolutionists interested in the mind-brain problem I have hoped to hold a mirror up to the work of consciousness researchers in our own times and to show what is new and what is not. There were, of course, many other biologists, psychologists and philosophers interested in the 'hard problem' of the relation of mind to brain in the nineteenth century, too many in fact to list here, but the four reviewed above provide examples of those who took an evolutionary approach.[19]

Of the four, Richard Owen was the least troubled by the problem.. This was because, as we saw, his view of the world stemmed unambiguously from the so-called 'Germano-Coleridgean' tradition where the mind-body problem hardly arose. This tradition originates in a panentheistic metaphysics. The material world, as Coleridge put it, 'veils the Almighty Spirit'[20]. Owen is thus not troubled by the traditional mind-brain 'hard problem': how consciousness, subjectivity, qualia, call it what you will, can be accommodated in a world of things. He concludes, as we noted, by arguing that Nature strove 'through the wreck of worlds' to achieve at last 'the great end... of making Matter subservient to the manifestation of Mind'. This clearly echoes Coleridge's mature position and harks back to the Romantic biology of previous century.

---

[19] For an exhaustive account which discusses most of the significant figures in the nineteenth century evolutionary biology of mind, see R.J Richards, 1987. Richards does not, however, devote much space to the philosophical issue of the 'hard problem'.

[20] Coleridge: *This Lime tree Bower my Prison*: see footnote 5.

With Herbert Spencer we enter a different world. The sources of Spencer's evolution theory were, as we noted, embryological, especially the embryology of Ernst von Baer. The ideas which, as a young man, he absorbed from von Baer, pervade his neuropsychology. Using these ideas he was able to construct a pioneering evolutionary psychology, both from the 'interior', *res cogitans*, side of Descartes' divide, and from the external, *res extensa,* side. Yet, when pressed, he retreats to a position hardly different from Berkeleyan idealism. He claims that our familiar categorisation of experience into objective and subjective evolved during infancy from an originally undifferentiated consciousness.. He would argue that when a modern neurophysiologist observes an oscilloscope trace, or examines a Golgi-stained cortex, that is as much a subjective experience as when he or she feels the heat of a Bunsen flame. This is what he means by his doctrine of 'transfigured realism'. 'Our only course' he concludes 'is to recognise our symbols as symbols only; and to rest content with that duality in them which our constitution necessitates' (Spencer, 1870, p.162).

John Hughlings Jackson's experience was very different from that of either Owen or Spencer. He was daily confronted with the often cruel experiments which disease processes conduct on the brain. He found the best way of making sense of the distressing results of these 'experiments' was Herbert Spencer's evolutionary psychology. He, too, recognised the magnitude of the 'hard problem' and never ceased to warn his colleagues not to glibly overlook it. But in the end he felt that, as a practicing neurologist, his efforts were best directed to treating his patients. How best to maintain consistency when speaking and writing about the mind-brain interface was secondary.

Finally we come to Thomas Henry Huxley. Like Hughlings Jackson, he felt that the world was too full of practical problems form him to squander over-much of his time on the philosophy of mind. He is best known for his espousal of animal (and by implication, human) automatism and for the linked doctrine of epiphenomenalism. We saw that this assessment of how brain and mind were related had appealed to him from his boyhood. Huxley was by conviction a materialist but not, as he insists, a 'crass materialist'. Like Spencer, when pressed, he retreated, like his great predecessor René Descartes, into a species of absolute idealism. Of nothing but our own subjectivity ('there is pain now') have we the right to be sure. And, like Spencer, though without the philosophical analysis, he had perforce to rest content with the duality in our experience. 'Matter' and 'mind' are ultimates which we cannot reach beyond.

Thus, in conclusion, we can see that through the millennial growth of neuroscience and psychology, from the time of St Augustine to the present, there glimmers the same ultimate assessment. At bottom, all we know for certain is that we, as individual consciousnesses, exist. Yet, as Schopenhauer said, to deny that an external world also exists does not so much require philosophical rebuttal as psychiatric treatment. Nevertheless, how it is that our world consists of both mind (qualia, raw feels, subjectivity) and matter (which, according to the Cartesian settlement, has none of these things), and how the two are related, remains a mystery. Evolution theory, in showing that there is no break in the chain from elementary particle to man, sharpens that mystery. Does all Nature have this dual aspect? Was Spinoza, in spite of Coleridge's strictures, perhaps right after all? Is there some way in which sense can be made of the resulting panpsychism? (see Smith, 2000). Can the break with seventeenth century concepts of matter made by the great physicists of the early twentieth century point the way to an answer? These are the questions with which, it seems to me, the twenty-first century opens.

REFERENCES

Adam, C. and Tannery, P (1974-1986): *Oeuvres de Descartes*, 2nd edition, 11 vols., Paris.

Adkins, AWH (1979): *From the Many to the One*. London: Constable.

Bardy, G (1953): St Augustin et les medicines. *L'Année Théologique Augustinienne, 13*, 327-346.

Bradie, M (1986): Assessing Evolutionary Epistemology. *Biology and Philosophy, 1*, 401-59.

Campbell, DT (1960): Blind Variation and Selective Retention in Creative thought as in Other Knowledge Process. *Psychol. Rev. 67*: 380-400.

Campbell, DT (1974a): Evolutionary epistemology. *In Philosophy of Karl Popper*, ed. P.A.Schilp. La Salle: Open Court.

Campbell, DT (1974b): Downward Causation in Hierarchically Organised Systems. In Ayala, FJ and Dobzhansky, T., eds. *Studies in the Philosophy of Biology*. London: Macmillan

Carpenter, JE (1888), ed.: *Nature and Man, Essays Scientific and Philosophical*. London: Kegan, Paul, Trench and Co.

Carpenter, WB (1839): *Principles of General and Comparative Physiology*. London: Churchill.

Carpenter, WB (1872): What is common sense? *Metaphysical Society*. London.

Carpenter, WB (1875): On the doctrine of human automatism. *Contemporary Review, 25*, 397-416; 940-62

Coburn, K (1949): *Philosophical Lectures of Samuel Taylor Coleridge*. London: Pilot Press.

Coleridge, EH ed. (1912): *The Complete Poetical Works of Samuel Taylor Coleridge*. Oxford: Oxford University Press.

Darwin, CR (1837): Old and Useless Notes. In Barrett PH (1980): *Metaphysics, Materialism and the Evolution of Mind: Early Writings of Charles Darwin*. Chicago: Chicago University Press.

Darwin, CR (1868): The Variation of Animals and Plants under Domestication, 2 vols., London: Murray; facsimile edition (1998): Johns Hopkins University Press.

Darwin, E (1803): *The Temple of Nature*. London: J.Johnson.

Demske, JM (1970): *Being, Man and Death*. Lexington: University Press of Kentucky

Descartes, R (1662): *De Homine*. Leiden; trs. And ed. T.S.Hall, 1972, *Treatise of Man*, Cambridge, MA: Harvard University Press.

Deutsch, D (1997): *The Fabric of Reality*. London:Allen Lane, The Penguin Press.

Duncan, D (1908): *Life and Letters of Herbert Spencer* (2 vols.). New York: Appleton.

Dunlap, JC (1999): Molecular bases of circadian rhythms. *Cell, 96*: 271-90.

Elliot, HSR (1975): Herbert Spencer. *Dictionary of National Biography*. London: Oxford University Press

Fiegl, H (1967): *The 'Mental' and the 'Physical'*. Minneapolis: University of Minnesota Press.

Flugel, JC and West DJ (1964): *One Hundred years of Psychology*. London: Duckworth.

Goltz, FL (1869): *Beitrage zur Lehre von den Functionen der Nervencentren des Frosches*. Berlin.

Green, JH. (1865): *Spiritual Philosophy: founded on the teaching of the late Samuel Taylor Coleridge*, ed. Simon, J. London: Macmillan.

Green, TH (1883): *Prolegomena to Ethics*, ed. Bradley, AC. Oxford: Clarendon Press.

Haller, A von (1755): *A Dissertation on the Sensible and Irritable Parts of Animals*. London: Nourse.

Hutchinson, J (1911): *British Medical Journal*, vol.2.

Huxley, L (1903): *Life and Letters of Thomas Henry Huxley*, 2 vols. London: Macmillan.

Huxley, TH (1845): *Notebook 3*. Imperial College London.

Huxley, TH (1868): On the Physical Basis of Life. In Huxley, 1893.

Huxley, TH (1870): On Descartes 'Discourse touching the Method of Using One's Reason Rightly and of Seeking Scientific Truth. In Huxley, TH (1893).

Huxley, TH (1871): Bishop Berkeley on the Metaphysics of Sensation. In Huxley, TH, 1897, *Hume with helps to the study of Berkeley*, London: Macmillan.

Huxley, TH (1874): 'On the Hypothesis that Animals are Automata and its History'. *Fortnightly Review, XVI*, 714-36.

Huxley, TH (1880): Idealism on Spencerian Principles. Paper at Imperial College, London.

Huxley, TH (1893): *Method and Results*. London: Macmillan.

Jackson, H (1982): Coleridge's collaborator, Joseph Henry Green. *Studies in Romanticism 21*: 161-79.

Jackson, JH (1863): *Suggestions for studying diseases of the nervous system on Professor Owen's vertebral theory*. Printed for private circulation, in library of Royal Society of Medicine, London.

Kant, I (1781): *Critique of Pure Reason* trs.Kemp Smith, N., 2003. Basingstoke: Palgrave Macmillan.

Kenny, A (1970): *Descartes: Philosophical Letters*. Oxford: Clarendon Press.

La Forge, L (1666): *Traité de l'Esprit de l'Homme, de Facultés et Fonctions, et de son union avec le corps, suivant les Principes de René Descartes*. Paris.

La Mettrie, JO de (1745): *Histoire Naturelle de l'Ame*. La Haye: Jean Neaulme.

La Mettrie, J.O de (1747): *L'Homme Machine*. Leiden: Elie Luzac Fils.

Lamarck, J-B de (1809): *Philosophie Zoologique*, Paris; trs. H.Elliot (1984), *Zoological Philosophy*. Chicago: Chicago University Press.

Leeuwenhoek, A.van (1674): More observations from Mr Leeuwenhoek. *Phil.Trans.Roy.Soc 9*: 178-82.

Levere, TH (1981): *Poetry Realised in Nature*. Cambridge: Cambridge University Press.

Libet, B et al. (1983): Time of conscious intention to act in relation to onset of cerebral activity (readiness potential): the unconscious initiation of a freely voluntary act. *Brain, 106*: 623-42.

Libet, B (1993): The neural time factor in conscious and unconscious mental events. In *Experimental and Theoretical Studies of Consciousness (Ciba Symposium, 174)*, pp.123-137. Chichester: John Wiley and Sons.

Lorenz, K.(1977): *Behind the Mirror: A Search for the Natural History of Human Knowledge*. New York: Harcourt Brace Jovanovich.

MacLean PD (1990): *The Triune Brain*. New York: Plenum Press.

Malebranche, N (1841): *Feuillit de Conches. Meditations Metaphysiques et Correspondance de N.Malebranche: 9th Meditation*. Paris

McGinn, C (1990): *Problem of Consciousness: Essays towards a Resolution*. Oxford: Blackwell.

Mill, JS (1843): *A System of Logic*. London: Longmans.

Mill, JS (1859): *Dissertations and Discussions*, London: Longmans, Green, Reader and Dyer.

Mondboddo, Lord (1774): *The Origin and Progress of Language* (vol.1.). Edinburgh: J.Balfour and T.Cadell, pp.281-6.

Oken, L (1809-11): *Lehrbuch der Naturphilosophie.* trs. Tulk, A. (1847) *Elements of Physiophilosophy*. London: Ray Society.

O'Leary, DDM (1989): Do cortical areas emerge from a protocortex? *Trends in Neuroscience, 12*: 400-406.

O'Leary, DDM and Stanfield, BB (1989): Selective elimination of axons extended by developing cortical neurons is dependent on regional locale. Experiments using fetal cortical transplants. *Journal of Neuroscience 9*: 2230-46.

Owen, R (1849): *On the Nature of Limbs*. London: John van Voorst.

Owen, RS (1894): *Life of Richard Owen*, 2 vols. London: Murray.

Popper, KR (1972): *Objective Knowledge: An Evolutionary Approach*. Oxford: Clarendon Press.

Richards, RJ (1987): *Darwin and the Emergence of Evolutionary Theories of Mind and Behaviou*r. Chicago: University of Chicago Press.

Rieppel, O (1988): The reception of Leibniz's philosophy in the writings of Charles Bonnet (1720-1793). *J.Hist.Biol., 21*, 119-45.

Robinson, H.Crabb (1932) *Diary, selections*, ed. Morley, E.J.. Manchester: Manchester University Press.

Roe, AW, Pallas, SL, Kwon, YH and Sur, M (1992): Visual projections routed to the auditory pathway in ferrets: receptive fields of visual neurons in primary auditory cortex. *Science, 250*: 818-20.

Romanes, GJ (1883): *Mental Evolution in Animals*. London: Kegan Paul, Trench

Rupke, NA (1994): *Richard Owen: Victorian Naturalist*. New Haven, Ct.: Yale University Press

Schantz, M.von and Archer, SN (2003): Clocks, genes and sleep. *Journal of the Royal Society of Medicine, 96*: 486-9.

Schwarz, JM, Stapp, HP and Beauregard, M. (2004): Quantum physics in neuroscience and psychology: a neurophysical model of mind-brain interaction. *Phil.Trans.Roy.Soc.B., 360*: 1309-27.

Simon, J (1865): Memoir of the author's life. In Green, 1865.

Sloan, PR (1992): *The Hunterian Lectures in Comparative Anatomy*, May-June 1837. Chicago: Chicago University Press.

Smith, CUM. (1976): *The Problem of Life: An essay in the origins of biological thought*. London: Macmillan.

Smith, CUM (1978): Charles Darwin, the Origin of Consciousness and Panpsychism. *J.Hist.Biol., 11*, 245-67.

Smith, CUM. (1982a): Evolution and the Problem of Mind: Part 1, Herbert Spencer. *J.Hist.Biol., 15*, 55-88.

Smith, CUM (1982b): Evolution and the Problem of Mind: Part II, John Hughlings Jackson. *J.Hist.Biol., 15*, 241-262.

Smith, CUM (1983): Herbert Spencer's Epigenetic Epistemology. *Stud.Hist.Phil.Sci., 14*, 1-22.

Smith, CUM (1991): Kant and Darwin. *J.Social.Biol.Struct., 14*: 35-50.

Smith, CUM (1992): 'The Hippopotamus Test: A controversy in nineteenth century brain science'. *Cogito 1: Supplement to the Italian Journal of Neurological Sciences 1*: 69-74.

Smith, CUM. (1997): Worlds in Collision: Owen and Huxley on the Brain. *Science in Context, 10*, 343-65.

Smith, CUM. (1998a): Descartes' Visit to the Town Library, or how Augustinian is Descartes' Neurophysiology? *J.Hist.Neurosci., 7*, 93-100.

Smith, CUM. (1998b): Descartes' pineal neuropsychology. *Brain and Cognition, 36*: 57-72.

Smith, CUM. (1999a): Coleridge's 'Theory of Life. *J.Hist.Biol., 32*, 31-50.

Smith, CUM (1999b): T.H.Huxley and Neuroscience. *Physis: Rivista Internzionale de Storia della Scienza, XXXVI*: 355-65.

Smith, CUM (2000): 'Evolutionary biology and the 'hard problem'. *Evolution and Cognition, 6*, 162-75.

Smith, CUM. (2002): Julien Offray de la Mettrie (1709-1751). *J.Hist. Neurosci., 11*,110-124.

Smith, CUM. and Arnott, R. (2005): *The Genius of Erasmus Darwin*. Aldershot: Ashgate.

Smith, CUM. (2006): The'hard problem' and the quantum physicists: Part 1, the first generation. *Brain and Cognition, 61*: 181-8

Smith, CUM. (in press): Brain and Mind in the 'long' Eighteenth Century. In Whitaker, H, Smith, C.U.M., Finger, S., eds., *Mind, Brain and Medicine: Essays in Eighteenth Century Neuroscience*. New York: Springer

Spencer, H (1855): *The Principles of Psychology*. London: Longmans, Brown, Green and Longmans.

Spencer, H (1864): Reasons for Dissenting from the Philosophy of M.Comte, in *Essays: Scientific, Political and Speculative*, 3rd edition, 1891. London: Williams and Norgate.

Spencer, H (1865): Mill versus Hamilton: the test of truth. *Fortnightly Review*. In *Essays II*, pp. 383-413.

Spencer, H (1870; 1872): *The Principles of Psychology* (2nd edition), 2 vols. London: Williams and Norgate.

Spencer, H (1870): *First Principles*. London: Williams and Norgate.

Spencer, H (1893): The inadequacy of 'natural selection'. *Contemporary Review 63*: 153-66; 439-456.

Spencer, H (1904): *An Autobiography*. London: Williams and Norgate.

St Augustine: *Civitate Dei*, trs. J.Healey (1931), *The City of God*. London: Dent.

St Augustine: *De Genesi ad Litteram*. In *Oeuvres de St Augustine*, vols 48 and 49; ed and trs P.Agäesse and A.Soignac, 1972, *Études Augustiniennes*. Desclée de Brouwer: Paris.

St Augustine: *De Quantitate Animae*. In *Oeuvres de St Augustine*, vol.5; ed and trs. P.de Labriolle, 1948. *Études Augustiniennes*. Desclée de Brouwer: Paris.

Stapp, HP (2005): Quantum interactive dualism. *J.Consc.Stud., 12*, 43-58.

Stebbing, LS (1950): *A Modern Introduction to Logic*. London: Methuen.

Sterne, L (1760): *Tristram Shandy*. London.

Sur, M, Garraghty, PE and Roe, A (1988): Experimentally induced visual projections into auditory thalamus and cortex. *Science 242*: 1437-41.

Sutton, J. (1998): *Philosophy and Memory traces: Descartes to Connectionism*. Cambridge: Cambridge University Press.

Taylor, J. (1958): *Selected Writings of John Hughlings Jackson* (2 vols.). New York: Basic Books.

Tuchman, BW (1978): *A Distant Mirror: The Calamitous 14th Century*. .New York: Random House.

Trembley, A (1744): *Memoires pour servir a l'histoire d'un genre de polypes d'eau douce, a bras en formes de cornes.* Leiden and Paris.

White, RJ (1972): *The Collected works of Samuel Taylor Coleridge: Lay Sermons.* London: Routledge and Kegan Paul.

Wright, T. (1750): *An Original Theory or New Hypothesis of the Universe.* Facsimile reprint with introduction by Hoskin MA (1971). London: MacDonald.

In: Consciousness and Learning Research
Editor: Susan K. Turrini, pp. 165-199

ISBN 1-60021-333-2
© 2007 Nova Science Publishers, Inc.

Chapter 8

CONSCIOUSNESS AND VOLUNTARY ACTION

Richard A. Sieb
Edmonton, Alberta, Canada

ABSTRACT

Human beings are enormously successful in interacting with their environment. The two most important developments allowing us to do this are consciousness and the ability to create a variety of voluntary new or novel intentional actions. The two are intimately connected, as one does not occur without the other. Consciousness is subjective; subjective may be defined as the having of or the adopting of a particular point of view or perspective. Voluntary new or novel intentional actions are actions which are newly created at the time through the choice or free will (voluntary) of the person for some specific purpose (intentional). A detailed description of various different types of voluntary new or novel intentional actions and where and how they are generated in the brain is given. These actions are always created with respect to the point of view or perspective of the person and this point of view or perspective is shown to be equivalent to consciousness. Hence consciousness is a point of view or perspective created in the brain from perception which is utilized to create and generate specific voluntary new or novel intentional actions. A basic nonlinear emergent mechanism, responsible for a large number of natural phenomena, is described and utilized to explain the generation of consciousness and the creation and generation of voluntary new or novel intentional action. This mechanism results in the formation of new or novel explicit stable states which are shown to be equivalent to consciousness and are able to generate voluntary new or novel intentional actions. A detailed comparison of the properties of these nonlinear explicit stable states and the properties of consciousness results in the conclusion that the two are identical. Since these states are physical, consciousness is given a physical basis and can have physical effects. The link between consciousness and voluntary new or novel intentional action is also established. Consciousness is shown to be natural, material, and functional. It is a physical development which has evolved for a special purpose: the creation of voluntary new or novel intentional actions. These actions allow the person to respond in a rapid, versatile, and purposeful manner to changes in the environment. This is extremely important for the survival and success of the individual in a rapidly changing and complex environment. Supporting empirical evidence and ideas for future research are also given.

INTRODUCTION

Human beings are enormously successful in interacting with (and hence adapting to) their environment. We can make changes in our environment at will, and any changes that may occur in our environment are rapidly perceived and appropriately responded to. We interact with our environment through our sensory and motor capabilities. Our motor capabilities or movement may be of two types: automatic or conscious (voluntary). Automatic movement is movement that has been programmed into our nervous system in some way. It may be hardwired (prewired) into our nervous system through genetically controlled development or acquired through learning processes (our nervous system has a certain plasticity in that its structure is modifiable so as to incorporate new experience) and includes various reflexes, learned skilled movements and movement sequences, and other programmed movements. Automatic movements are generally stimulus specific (that is, they are set-off by a specific stimulus or specific type of stimulus), rapidly initiated without deliberation in a mechanistic like fashion, not made by choice or free will (not voluntary), unconscious, rapidly performed, stereotyped (always the same), reliable, accurate within a specific context (if performed in the wrong context, they may be extremely inappropriate; they are not adaptable to change), and not goal specific. We may learn complex automatic motor skill sequences consisting of long complex sequences of movements; where the performance of one movement in the sequence serves as the stimulus for the next movement in the sequence, which serves as the stimulus for the next movement, and so on. Consciousness is not involved in the performance of automatic movements, except in the initial creation and performance of such movements before they are learned. Conscious or voluntary movement is always newly created at the time for some specific purpose (to attain some goal). Conscious movement is usually rather loosely tied to sensory stimulation (that is, it often does not occur immediately after sensory stimulation), requires consciousness, evolves more slowly than automatic movements because a delay occurs between the initiating stimulation and the actual movement (it is deliberated) during which the specific movement is composed, is usually more controlled and less rapidly performed, is variable and flexible, and is context and goal specific (is always created and performed with regards to a specific situation). Consciousness may actually interfere with and impede the performance of automatic movements. If you consciously consider making a certain reflex action (such as the rapid removal of your hand from a hot stove), this consciousness probably will interfere with the automatic performance of the reflex action in that situation. If you are playing a game (tennis, billiards, any other game or sport) against an opponent who has a lot of automatic motor skill in that game or sport, you can interfere with your opponent's performance by complementing them on their skill. This complement tends to focus their attention and consciousness on their own individual skilled movements (which were mostly performed automatically and unconsciously), interfering with the skilled automatic performance of these movements. Consciousness seems to engage a creation or modification mechanism for movement (the creation of new movement), which interferes with the automatic performance of movements. This tactic has often been used to gain advantage over an opponent. Conscious or voluntary movements may be of a ballistic type, where the velocity of the movement is the prime consideration (a certain velocity is chosen with which to move a part of the body). Throwing a ball to a certain target location or using a hockey stick to impart force to a puck to drive it to a certain location are some examples. In other conscious movements, the achievement of a certain location or position may be the most important consideration. Such movements might include reaching for or putting down an object in a certain location or assuming specific postures or positions for parts of the body. In other conscious movements, the nature of the trajectory of the movement might be an important consideration. For example, when dancing, movements must be smooth and graceful; if carrying an explosive or delicate object, it would be advantageous to use slow, smooth, and extremely controlled movements; if carrying a heavy object, it is easier on the back to use slow and steady motions. Conscious movements may also be of the pursuit type, where a part of the body is directed to follow or pursue a moving object. In consciously-directed or voluntary movement sequences, each different movement in the sequence is separately composed consciously or voluntarily; one movement does not mechanistically set-off the next, as in automatic skilled movement sequences. At any rate, in conscious-type movements, consciousness seems to arise from sensory perception and to direct the motor system to compose a new specific movement for a specific purpose, as specified by sensory perception. In other words, the individual chooses to generate a new specific movement for a specific purpose; he or she demonstrates free will or choice. Movements made by choice or free will are known as voluntary movements. The directedness or urge to make a movement is known as movement intention. An intentional movement is of or about something. Conscious movements are always voluntary and intentional. Automatic movements are not made by choice or free will and are therefore involuntary. There is also no urge or directedness to make them and they are not of or about something, so automatic movements are not intentional. Conscious movements, but not automatic movements, are also always new or novel. They are always newly created (according to the current circumstances) to fulfil some purpose or to attain some goal. Conscious movement is but one type of conscious action. Other types of conscious action might include conscious generation of saccadic eye movements, speech, writing, thought, and emotion. All these actions may be consciously generated when an individual chooses to do so for some purpose or goal. They may be collectively referred to as voluntary new or novel intentional actions.

Consciousness and the ability to produce voluntary new or novel intentional actions are probably the two most important human developments responsible for the success of the human species in interacting with its environment. These two developments are intimately related, as one does not occur without the other. The ability to consciously generate ever more increasingly complex new or novel behaviours and sequences of behaviour (voluntary new or novel intentional actions) has allowed humans to master their constantly changing environment and to triumph over their own and other species. These developments also allow individual human beings to succeed and thrive (compete) among the many inhabitants of the complex societies they live in. The ability to respond in a quick, versatile, and purposeful manner to the many different and constantly changing situations that occur in our daily lives is of paramount importance for success and survival in our society. If our consciousness or ability to create voluntary new or novel intentional actions is lost; then we are lost, as we lose our ability to function and survive in our society and the world.

For centuries people have been trying to explain consciousness. This is abundantly illustrated by the large number of papers that have been written on the subject and collected on the website of David Chalmers [2006]. Philosophers such as Socrates, Plato, and Descartes had their own explanations for consciousness. There have been many different kinds of theories that have arisen since to try and explain consciousness and it seems sometimes that just about everyone has their own special theory of what consciousness is. There have been monist (consciousness and the physical world are of one and the same material) and dualist (consciousness and the physical world are each of different material) theories and physical (consciousness is of physical substance and can be explained by physical or scientific principles) and non-physical (consciousness is not physical and cannot be explained by physical or scientific principles) theories invoked to explain consciousness. Some theorists have concluded that consciousness is unexplainable (consciousness is not explainable because it is too hard to explain, it does not exist, because the necessary scientific principles have not yet been discovered, or because the human brain cannot grasp what consciousness is at the current state of the brain's evolution) or that it is epiphenomenal (consciousness is a by-product of or a non-functional attachment to brain function) and has no function. Some say that consciousness is universally present in all things (panpsychism). Among the theories that say that consciousness is physical are those that utilize quantum mechanics to explain consciousness and those that portray consciousness as some fundamental entity (something that cannot be broken down into smaller units and still maintain its properties and identity). Other theories (to which I subscibe) portray consciousness as a natural physical state that can be explained using current scientific principles. However, no theory to date has successfully explained the true essence of consciousness and consciousness has escaped true scientific explanation. In this composition, I attempt to explain the true essence of consciousness in materialistic (physical) terms using current scientific knowledge and principles.

The main problem in explaining consciousness is accounting for its subjectivity (What is this subjectivity? How and why does it arise? How can it be accounted for physically? What is it for? How can it have physical effects? How and why did it evolve?). I try to answer these questions in the following pages. Consciousness is defined by its subjectivity, ie. that is what consciousness is. To say that something is subjective is to say that it is an internally-generated perspective or point of view. Hence consciousness is an internal perspective or point of view built from external (sensory) input and previous experience [McCrone,2001]. In other words, consciousness is an internal context built from perception (external sensory input interpreted in terms of previous experience). This subjectivity (perspective or point of view, consciousness) is created, stabilized, and maintained for a short period of time, during which it is available (over this short period of time) for producing effects in other systems, including those involved in the generation of action. These aspects of consciousness are evident from our everyday knowledge of our own consciousness. In order to be stabilized, to be maintained for a short period of time, and to have effects on other systems; this subjectivity (point of view, perspective, consciousness) must be a physical state of some kind (hence the subjectivity is said to be explicit, which means that it is a definite realized physical state that can produce effects in other systems). If this subjectivity was not a physical state of some kind, then such subjectivity would be non-physical (and not describable by scientific principles) and this would raise all sorts of problems in trying to explain how a non-physical state can have physical properties and effects. Consciousness therefore must consist of explicit stable states of some kind that are created and maintained over short periods of time and are available during this time for the activation of other systems. These explicit stable states might be considered as "episodes" of consciousness. These states of consciousness might be differentiated by their content. The content of consciousness consists of various conscious experiences or qualia. In this sense, consciousness might be considered a personal point of view or perspective whose content consists of various qualia (conscious experiences).

Qualia apparently arise from the neural processing of perception and consist of various colours, tastes, smells, textures, sounds, shapes, pains, motion, experiences of self (I, me), experience as an agent (I am doing this), and other experiences (of meaning, of knowing, on the tip-of-the-tongue, of familiarity, of being somewhere before, of an emotion-love, hate, pain, fear, sadness, anger), depression, etc. It is the qualia that fill and differentiate our consciousness, give it meaning, and that may differentiate its effects.

How and why might such subjectivity evolve in the first place? One answer might be: for the production of specific voluntary new or novel intentional actions. As mentioned above, consciousness and voluntary new or novel intentional action always occur together. Voluntary new or novel intentional action does not occur (is not created) without consciousness. Whenever you wish to create a new or novel action for some reason, this is a conscious event and consciousness must be present. One cannot create a voluntary new or novel intentional action without consciousness (unconsciously). Consciousness may also not occur without there being some creation of voluntary new or novel intentional action. That is, consciousness itself is generated only when one chooses to generate some new or novel action for some reason. The idea that consciousness can occur without content (that is, without qualia) is not supported by this theory; as this would mean that there would be nothing to give consciousness any composition or substance. There would be nothing to differentiate consciousness and give it meaning. There would be no way for consciousness to specify specific new voluntary new or novel intentional actions or have any function. There would be no reason for consciousness to be generated. I hope to provide support for the preceding points during the course of this writing.

Subjective systems may also be adaptive; that is, able to respond to change [McCrone,2001]. Such systems might be expected to self-organize to control their own behaviour. The ability to form new or novel explicit stable states could be one way that a subjective system could do this (that is, self-organize to control its own behaviour, be adaptive, respond to change). The subjectivity (point of view, perspective aspect) of consciousness may be thought of as being the creation of something new or novel and personal in response to some environmental change, which is then utilized in the composition of some new or novel personal action in response to that change. Voluntary new or novel intentional action is always composed according to the subject's own particular point of view or perspective (their consciousness). Hence the subjectivity of consciousness is created anew at each moment of time from perception and utilized. This subjective system of consciousness is consequently always continuously adapting (responding to change) and self-organizing to control its own behaviour. Since consciousness and the ability to create voluntary new or novel intentional action always occur together, then the function of consciousness might be for the creation of specific voluntary new or novel intentional actions, and consciousness might have evolved to do so. Consciousness, therefore, probably exists to some degree in lower animals, especially mammals. The qualia (which make up the content of consciousness and are derived from perception) might determine the specifics (modality, action domain, parameters) of the action. If some ability has evolved (like to be conscious), then it must have evolved for some purpose. It seems ludicrous to think that something has evolved for no purpose at all or by accident. Also, for something to persist (like consciousness), it must be of some use. If some development was of no use, it would be lost, in accordance with the old adages of biology-use it or lose it and if something is of no use, it will be selected out.

In this composition, I try to show how such subjectivity (as found in consciousness) might arise in the brain and be utilized (in the production of voluntary new or novel intentional actions and action sequences). Since a nonlinear emergent mechanism for the production of the explicit stable states ("episodes") of consciousness is advanced in this writing, it might be beneficial to begin with a description of a basic mechanism of nonlinear emergence, which is responsible for an enormous number of physical and biological phenomena. Such a mechanism probably operates in the brain and the role of such a mechanism in the generation of consciousness and voluntary new or novel intentional action is supported by much empirical data. After this, I describe where and how various types of voluntary new or novel intentional actions are produced in the brain. Then I describe where and how a point of view or perspective (consciousness) might arise in the brain. I next describe the relationship between consciousness and the generation of voluntary new or novel intentional action. Following this, I discuss how consciousness might be generated in the human brain.

NONLINEAR EMERGENCE

Events may be produced by other events linearly or nonlinearly. Linearly produced events are determined and defined by their precipitating determinant causal events [Newman,1997]. Sunburn, a rainbow, a car crash, etc. may be caused by sunshine. Sunburn, a rainbow, or a car crash can be traced back to and directly related to the properties of sunshine (ultraviolet waves, a mixture of all the spectral colours or wavelengths, bright and blinding when viewed directly). They are directly caused by and are defined by the properties of sunshine. A dog attack, tripping over a rock, a headache, etc. may result from jogging. A dog attack, tripping over a rock, or a headache can be directly traced back to and directly related to (and caused by) the properties of jogging (rapid bouncing motion, unexpected obstacles to be avoided, vibratory shock to the head). They are directly caused by and defined by the properties of jogging. Evacuations, atrocities, internment, starvation, death, etc. may be directly related to and caused by the properties of war (danger, hate, no food, fighting, etc.). Again, these events are directly caused by and defined by the properties of war. A car stops, a child stops, a car hits the child, etc. may be caused by a speeding car and a child running. The car stops, a child stops, or the car unhappily hits the child are directly caused by and defined by the properties of a speeding car and a child running (uncontrolled speed on the part of the car and child, inadequate observation of danger or obstacles on the part of the driver and child, inadequate reflex avoidance response on the part of the driver and child, careless or negligent driver or child). A ticket, a warning, a chase, etc. may result from a car running a stop sign in the presence of police. The giving of a ticket, a warning, or the occurrence of a car chase are directly caused by and defined by the properties of running a stop sign in the presence of police (a symbol requiring vehicles to stop, a law requiring cars to stop, enforcers of the law). No events or properties are created or emerge which cannot be traced back to and defined by the properties of the causal events during the linear production of events. The causal lineage of events is determined and set. Thus the production of events can be predicted with great accuracy. A large number of natural events occur in this manner, as can be seen from the given examples. The complete behaviour repertoire of machines and many animals is probably of this linear nature. Nonlinear events are determined, but not defined (nonlinear emergence), by their precipitating determinant causal events [Newman,1997]. The resulting events are entirely different from (have new properties) their initiating events. The initiating events cannot be determined or defined from the resulting events, since the resulting events are entirely new or novel. Thus in nonlinear emergence, there is the production of something new, with entirely new properties, which cannot be determined from the initiating events. Nonlinear emergence commonly occurs when two or more events interact in some way and something new emerges from this interaction. A common type of such nonlinear emergence arises when positive feedback (excitatory interaction) between release and dissipation events leads to exponential growth of these events and the activation of inhibition; the latter limiting the growth, producing a new balanced (stable) state [Scott,1996;1999;2000]. The main crux of this mechanism is that energy or some other quantity is dissipated and feeds back to cause the release of more of this energy or other quantity, which causes more dissipation of the energy or other quantity, which causes more release, and so on. This positive feedback interaction causes an exponential growth in the turnover (release and dissipation) of the energy or other quantity. Positive feedback might be a way of amplifying activity. However, the release and dissipation events also lead to the activation of inhibitory influences (factors which inhibit release, factors which inhibit dissipation) which inhibit the growth, producing a balanced stable state. This stable state is a new or novel state arising in a nonlinear fashion and which can then participate in the production of new or novel events by acting on other systems. The stable state may directly produce a new or novel event and may even be part of the new or novel event.

A large number of natural phenomena may be established in the above manner as new or novel nonlinear emergent events [Scott,1996;1999;2000]. When a candle is lit, wax vapour burns and energy is dissipated as heat and light. This dissipated heat melts more candle wax, producing more wax vapour, which burns, producing more heat, and so on. The positive feedback interaction between energy dissipation (heat) and energy release (stored chemical energy of the candle wax is released when dissipated heat melts more wax) results in exponential growth of these events (dissipation and release). However, inhibition also occurs from these dissipation and release events (heat diffusion away, cooling effect of surrounding air, cross-sectional area of candle-determines rate of energy release, density and composition of candle, etc.), which limits the growth. A new balanced (stable) state emerges and propagates down the candle (nonlinear diffusion)[Scott,1996;1999;2000]. Via production of this stable state, the interacting events condition a flame, a nonlinear emergent (a balanced disposition of heat and light). A nerve impulse may be initiated (emerge) and transmitted by this nonlinear mechanism. Nerve axon membrane has a resting potential with the inside negative with respect to the outside because $Na+$ ions are pumped out against concentration and electrostatic gradients. Thus electric energy is stored in the membrane capacitance. Depolarization (reduction in resting potential) discharges this capacitance by causing membrane $Na+$ channels to open (energy release) and $Na+$ ions to enter the axon (energy dissipation), causing further depolarization (and $Na+$ channel opening), causing further $Na+$ entry, causing further depolarization, etc. The resultant positive feedback interaction leads to exponential growth (runaway increase in $Na+$ permeability). This interaction also produces inhibition (increased positive charge inside the axon acts to prevent $Na+$ ions from entering, re-polarizing influences, changes in conformation of sodium channels, outside $Na+$ depletion, etc.), that limits the growth, producing a stable state. This stable state is a nonlinear relation that propagates (local circuit action) at a constant speed and amplitude along the axon (nonlinear diffusion), conditioning the nerve impulse phenomenon. Aquatic, optical, and lattice solitons (waves); the folding of proteins; and cell membranes may also be examples of nonlinear emergence via this mechanism [Scott,1996;1999;2000]. For example, in aquatic waves, when some object enters water, it pushes water molecules outwards (dissipation). Other surrounding water molecules then move in behind to take the place of the displaced water molecules (release), pushing more water molecules outwards (more dissipation), causing more release, and so on. This positive feedback interaction would result in an exponential growth of these dissipation and release events. However, inhibitory influences are also activated (weight and density of water, interference from other waves and disturbances in the water, electrostatic attraction or repulsion of water molecules, etc.) which act to inhibit this growth and result in a balanced stable state. Thus a wave of a certain amplitude and velocity (the balanced stable state) travels across the water. The wave is a nonlinear emergent produced by this nonlinear mechanism. Any business may be thought of as a nonlinear emergent produced by the above mechanism. The release and dissipation of the resources of a business may be analogous to the release and dissipation of energy of a biological or physical system. This release and dissipation of resources could enter a positive feedback cycle and exponential growth until it activates, and is limited by, inhibition (amount of resources, ability and speed of restoring resources, the working speed of workers, work interruptions, number of workers, hours of work, etc.). A stable state is established and the functioning company is the nonlinear emergent, conditioned by this nonlinear relation. Many social (family, organization, nation, etc.) and nonsocial (body, cell, etc.) groupings may be regarded as nonlinear emergents. Any one of these groupings emerges in a nonlinear fashion from the positive feedback interaction of its component parts. In each case, something with new properties and capacities emerges from the positive feedback interaction of component units, which cannot be directly related back to and defined by the component units.

Nonlinear emergence appears to arise from a particular dynamics in this case (this is not to preclude that there are other mechanisms of nonlinear emergence). There must be established a positive feedback interaction between release and dissipation events, leading to exponential growth and the activation of inhibition, which limits (balances) the growth, producing a new stable state. The formation of a stable state (which is lacking in the linear production of events) is important. This state is fixed for a period of time, ie. it is made explicit (that is, it is fully realized physically, it is a discreet physical object which can be directly utilized in the production of other explicit states)[O'Brien and Opie,1999]. Because this explicit state persists for a short period of time and can produce explicit states in other systems (it is integrated)[O'Brien and Opie, 1999], it resembles a type of working memory or active short-term memory. It is a relation through which interacting events produce particular nonlinear emergents. Because they serve as standpoints for the determination of effects on other systems, these nonlinear emerging stable states may also be considered system perspectives or "points-of-view" [Mandik,2001;McClamrock,1994], which are in effect projected outwards. They therefore are a type of subjectivity (they are a point of view or perspective, they may also be called phenomenal) and are intentional (they are of or about something, they have a directedness, they are representational). Both the intentional and subjective properties of these states are natural (scientifically explainable) properties of these explicit states [O'Brien and Opie,1999] and either (the intentional aspect or the subjective aspect; a representation or a point of view) may be thought of as the cause of further events.

This gives the impression that the system's subjectivity (as a point of view, perspective) causes further physical events. This is one way that subjectivity can be thought of as causing physical changes or events. These nonlinear explicit stable states are physical in that they arise from physical events, occupy space-time, can be described scientifically, and can cause physical effects. Since they are composed anew each time, they are always new or novel and hence always produce new or novel effects or events. A similar mechanism may be involved in the production of voluntary new or novel intentional actions (to be described later).

It might be noticed in the preceding that many of the nonlinear emergent states produced by the described mechanism occur in nonliving physical systems and are described as system points of view or perspectives. It might seem strange to describe a nonliving system as having a point of view or perspective. However, I think it is acceptable, because the new or novel effects produced by a nonliving physical system operating in the described manner might be thought of as arising from a certain standpoint (point of view or perspective) of that system. This may be a virtual attribution, as one is projecting living qualities to a nonliving system. However, the nonlinear states produced arise from the same type of dynamics in living and nonliving systems and I think they are therefore analogous. This is important for scientific study, as the study of the generation, dynamics, and manipulation of such states might be easier in nonliving systems than in living systems.

The importance of positive feedback in brain function might be shown by its further development, refinement, and utilization in the basal ganglia for the control of movement [Sieb,1987]. The basal ganglia are a collection of large nuclear masses underlying the cortical mantle. They consist on each side of the caudate nucleus, the putamen, the globus pallidus, the substantia nigra, and the subthalamic nucleus. The main receiving areas of the basal ganglia are the caudate nucleus and the putamen (collectively known as the striatum). These areas receive excitatory input from all parts of the cerebral cortex (the caudate-from association areas, the putamen-from sensorimotor areas). The caudate and putamen project an inhibitory output to other parts of the basal ganglia: the globus pallidus, substantia nigra, and subthalamic nucleus. The interconnections of the basal ganglia are very complex, but the two main output areas of the basal ganglia are the globus pallidus medial segment and the pars reticulata of the substantia nigra. The core pathway of the basal ganglia is thought to be this striato-pallido-nigro pathway. The projection of the association cortex (including the prefrontal cortex) to the caudate is excitatory, from the caudate to the globus pallidus medial and lateral segments and the pars reticulata of the substantia nigra is inhibitory, from the globus pallidus medial segment and substantia nigra to the ventral anterior thalamic nucleus (the pallido and nigro projections go to different parts of the nucleus) is inhibitory, and there is an excitatory projection from the ventral anterior thalamic nucleus back to the parts of the association cortex from whence the pathway was originally activated from. Inhibition (of the globus pallidus and the substantia nigra by the caudate) of inhibition (of the ventral anterior thalamic nucleus by the globus pallidus and substantia nigra) produces excitation (of the ventral anterior thalamic nucleus); so in effect, activation of this loop by cortical association areas produces a positive feedback activation of the cortical association areas. This positive feedback activation could be tempered by inhibitory influences, resulting in the emergence of new explicit stable states of activation in these cortical association areas. The inclusion of the inhibitory links in the circuit may provide more of a precise control of this association cortical activation. This loop could have some importance in the fine control of cognitive function, perhaps even in the generation of consciousness. It might play a role in the generation and maintenance of qualia. The sensorimotor cortex (involved in the production of movement) has an excitatory projection to the putamen, which in turn has inhibitory projections to the globus pallidus medial (to a different area than from the caudate) and lateral segments and the pars reticulata of the substantia nigra (to a different area than from the caudate), and the subthalamic nucleus. The medial segment of the globus pallidus and the substantia nigra then have inhibitory projections to different areas of the ventral lateral thalamic nucleus. The ventral lateral thalamic nucleus then has an excitatory projection back to the supplementary motor cortex (part of the sensorimotor cortex involved in the production of voluntary new or novel intentional action-described later). Thus there is another intricate positive feedback loop through the basal ganglia involving the sensorimotor cortex, perhaps for the fine development and control of sensorimotor cortical activation and movement. To further complicate matters, the caudate and putamen both have an inhibitory projection to the globus pallidus lateral segment, which has an inhibitory projection to the subthalamic nucleus. The subthalamic nucleus also receives an inhibitory input from sensorimotor cortex. The subthalamic nucleus then has an inhibitory projection to the globus pallidus medial segment and an excitatory projection to the substantia nigra pars reticulata. This extremely complex positive feedback circuitry involving the sensorimotor cortex, especially the supplementary motor cortex, is known as the motor loop. It probably has some complex function in the generation and fine control of movement; an involvement in the generation of new or novel movement patterns (like in voluntary new or novel intentional movements) or in the incorporation of such things as target acquisition phases into the latter stages of a movement. These phases occur in the latter stages of a movement and make sure the movement reaches its correct target position [Sieb,1987]. This circuit might also be involved in sequencing movements and other control mechanisms. Whatever the purpose of these complex positive feedback loops; the importance of positive feedback to brain function, especially motor function (including the generation of voluntary new or novel intentional actions), should not be underestimated. This is illustrated by the dramatic conditions that result from pathology in the basal ganglia. These conditions include Parkinson's Disease, Huntington's Chorea, athetosis, ballismus, and dystonia. These are all characterized (depending upon where in the basal ganglia circuitry damage or pathology occurs) by uncontrolled involuntary motor activity and postures. The generation of voluntary new or novel intentional movements is also seriously impaired.

VOLUNTARY NEW OR NOVEL INTENTIONAL (ADAPTIVE) ACTION

Our production of voluntary new or novel intentional (adaptive) action is essential for our survival. We voluntarily (by choice, free will) produce such action and it is always directed towards some goal (intentional). We have the ability to create this action continuously moment by moment. It is not predetermined by any existing internal determinant conditions (we fully create and determine it at the time; hence we demonstrate free will, choice), so it is always new or novel and it always has a purpose (to reach or satisfy some goal). This action is usually preceded to some degree by the effortful cognitive processes of planning and deliberation, and the outcome is monitored for success and future learning. Focussed attention is usually involved in the preparation and execution of this action. These actions are usually only loosely bound to immediate stimulation (unlike reflex and other programmed actions), but are heavily dependent on task context and memory of previous learned associations. Because these actions are intentional, they are always represented in some manner in the nervous system (brain); that is, they are representational. This representation probably consists of some pattern of neural activation, which is created from perception. This pattern of neural activation activates a specific action-producing system, in a specific manner, to produce a specific action. The creation of this action allows us to respond to our continuously changing environment in a rapid, versatile, and purposeful manner. We are not bound by stereotyped inflexible reflexive or programmed-type responses (including learned responses) typical of lower animals and machines (predetermined action); but have a high capacity to create new or different responses as the situation demands. Reflex and programmed-type responses are direct responses to immediate sensory stimulation. They are fast, stereotyped, and inflexible because they must be rapid, accurate, and reliable. They do not necessarily fit changing circumstances (context). Voluntary new or novel intentional actions, on the other hand, must be controlled, variable, flexible, and purposeful. They normally are created to fit changing circumstances (context). Hence no machine at present can be said to be capable of producing voluntary action, as every machine was built and programmed by a human being and so some external (human) source has predetermined all its responses (and hence they are not created by the subject machine's choice or free will, as voluntary responses would be). Most animal behaviour appears to be genetically prewired (hardwired) or learned in some way (such as conditioning) and hence is of the programmed or predetermined variety. It cannot therefore be said to be voluntary. However, some animals (especially mammals) appear to be capable of creating some voluntary new or novel intentional actions.

Our production of voluntary new or novel intentional actions or action sequences has reached its highest development in language (speech, writing) and reasoning (thinking). In communicating with others, we are continually composing voluntary new or novel intentional word sequences. For example, in writing this composition, I choose to put words together in new or novel sequences, so as to convey various ideas to the reader. This is thus voluntary new or novel intentional action. Whenever you have a conversation with someone else, both individuals involved choose to convey their ideas to each other by continuously ordering words in newly created sequences. The same applies for the writing and passage of email messages among people. Broca's Area in the left lateral frontal cerebral cortex seems to be involved in the motoric production of speech through its connections with the sensorimotor cortex [Joseph,1990]. Broca's Area may be directed by Wernicke's Area in the left superior temporal cortex and the supramarginal and angular gyri of the inferior parietal cortex. Damage to Broca's Area may produce expressive aphasia [Joseph,1990]. Wernicke's Area in the left temporal cortex seems to be involved in the comprehension of speech [Joseph,1990]; while the supramarginal and angular gyri of the inferior parietal cortex may be involved in perception and the storage of the motor programs of speech and of patterns of perception. Corresponding areas in the right hemisphere may be involved in integration of the emotional aspects of speech [Joseph, 1990]. Damage to Wernicke's Area may produce receptive aphasia [Joseph,1990]. Damage to the supramarginal and angular gyri may produce deficits in the selection and activation of learned motor patterns, including those involved in speech [Joseph,1990]. Similarly, Exner's Area, which is adjacent to Broca's Area in the left lateral frontal cerebral cortex, appears to be involved in the production of the motoric aspects of writing, through its connections with the sensorimotor cortex [Joseph,1990]. Exner's Area also might be driven by Wernicke's Area and the supramarginal and angular gyri cortex. In thinking, we are continually modifying thoughts and arranging and rearranging thoughts (these may be considered as reactivated memories of perception) in voluntary new or novel intentional sequences. Since the supramarginal and angular gyri of the inferior parietal cortex are involved in perception and the storage of patterns of perception, perhaps this cortex plays a large role in our voluntary new or novel intentional generation of thought. Whenever we have a thought about a past event, a present event, or a future event; the thought consists of the reactivation of a memory of that event (reactivation of a pattern of perception). This memory consists of a reactivation of a perception of the event. Satisfactory thought processing, therefore, must require satisfactory operation of learning and memory mechanisms in the brain. These in turn probably depend on proper functioning of the entorhinal cortex-hippocampal-subicular circuit of the medial temporal area of the brain. This circuit has been found to be necessary for the formation and consolidation of new memories (and hence new learning). Damage to this circuit has been found to cause a remarkable pathology in which the affected individual is unable to form and consolidate new memories (such as in Korsakoffs Syndrome, caused by a deficiency of vitamin B1). These individuals have impaired recent memory and cannot remember things just seen or events that have just occurred. Some thought might depend on the proper functioning of this circuit. However, since long term memory is intact in such pathological conditions of this circuit, any thought utilizing long term memory might still be possible. Whether to solve a problem or to plan a course of action (such as the writing of this composition), we are continuously choosing to create new or novel sequences of thoughts. Hence such creation may be considered production of a type of voluntary new or novel intentional action. The creation of voluntary new or novel intentional actions and action sequences may be seen abundantly in our muscular motor action (skeletal and ocular):going to a store, reaching for a certain cup, playing a game, fixing something, scanning a crime scene, etc. In going to a store, we create a voluntary new or novel intentional sequence of actions (we create voluntary new or novel intentional individual actions as well within the sequence) to proceed from our present location to the store. We may get dressed (picking out clothing of a certain look and colour), check our finances (thinking about what we wish to purchase), close and lock the door of our house, proceed out the yard, walk through the streets (creating voluntary new or novel intentional action in response to events or sights encountered or any obstacles to be avoided), enter the store, collect desired items in the store, pay for them, and return home. Each time we go to a store or proceed to various other locations, we create a voluntary new or novel intentional sequence of actions to satisfy our goal of going to these various locations. Throughout our waking moments, we are also continuously composing individual voluntary new or novel intentional skeletomotor actions as the situations demand. We may reach for a certain cup, we may shake hands with someone, we may open a book to a certain page, we may kick the dog, etc. In fact, our entire day's activity may be looked upon as a long complex sequence of voluntary new or novel intentional activity. In playing games or fixing things, we again compose voluntary new or novel intentional individual skeletomotor actions and sequences of actions, as the situations demand, to accomplish our goal of winning the game or fixing something. The production of such voluntary new or novel intentional skeletomotor (muscular) actions probably depends on the supplementary motor cortex and its connections to the sensorimotor cortex. Fried and coworkers [2004] found that low levels of electrical stimulation of the supplementary motor cortex sometimes produced an urge (this might be looked on as an expression of the free will or choice to make a movement, an expression of the voluntary nature of making the movement) to move a certain body part; while higher stimulation levels at the same site produced actual muscle contraction in the same body part. This might indicate that the choice or free will to make a movement is a direct product of neural processes operating in the supplementary motor cortex that generate movement and suggests that the supplementary motor cortex may be involved in the generation of voluntary new or novel intentional movement. The ability to compose voluntary new or novel intentional skeletomotor action may be lost, with damage to the supplementary motor cortex [Joseph,1990]. When scanning a crime scene, we compose voluntary new or novel intentional saccadic eye movements or sequences of such movements, so that our eyes move appropriately over the crime scene to glean relevant information to solve the crime. When entering a room, we may scan the faces of the people in the room (by making voluntary new or novel intentional saccadic eye movements) to see if any are familiar. The creation of voluntary new or novel intentional individual saccadic eye movements or sequences of saccadic eye movements probably depends on the frontal eye fields and its connections to the supplementary eye region (part of the supplementary motor cortex) and sensorimotor cortex and/or the superior colliculi. The ability to make sequential conjugate saccadic scanning (exploratory) eye movements may be lost with damage to the frontal eye fields [Joseph,1990]. Such damage may make it difficult to explore the surrounding environment. The ability to make individual saccadic eye movements to certain locations in the orbit is controlled by the superior colliculus. The superior colliculi may be driven by the frontal eye fields to produce voluntary new or novel intentional sequences of conjugate saccadic scanning eye movements. Voluntary new or novel intentional action may also include emotional reactions. Emotional responses are produced by what is often referred to as the third motor system [Holstege et al,1996]. The first motor system (the pyramidal system) begins in the sensorimotor cortex and is involved in the production of skilled movements of the extremities (as well as some gross movements of other body parts), such as those of the hands, fingers, thumbs, lips, and tongue; through direct connections with the motor neurons and interneurons of the spinal cord [Afifi and Bergman,1986]. The second motor system (extrapyramidal system) also begins in the sensorimotor cortex, but passes to other structures (the basal ganglia, the cerebellum, the reticular formation nuclei, the red nuclei, the vestibular nuclei, the superior colliculi, the inferior olives) before passing to other areas or the spinal cord [Afifi and Bergman, 1986]. The extrapyramidal pathways appear to be involved mostly in the control and regulation of skeletomotor movements. The system that composes emotional responses may be considered a motor system because various degrees and composition of emotional reaction are composed, depending on the situation, by a definite response system. This composition of emotional reactions appears to depend on the transfer of incoming sensory and cognitive information to the amygdaloid nuclei of the brain from the sensory pathways, the reticular formation, the specific and nonspecific nuclei of the thalamus, the olfactory pathways, the cingulate cortex, the hypothalamus, and the frontal cortex [Afifi and Bergman,1986;Perryman et al,1987;Turner et al,1980;Van Hoesen,1981]. The amygdaloid nuclei project to a large number of target areas in the brain, noticeably the brainstem (these areas include the central grey-is involved in the arrest of ongoing behaviour, freezing, or the production of fight/flight behaviours; the dorsal motor nuclei of the vagus nerves-produces changes in heart rate; the hypothalamus-produces changes in blood pressure and other autonomic changes; the parabrachial nuclei-produces changes in respiration such as panting and respiratory distress during panic; the nuclei reticularis pontis caudalis-produces startle, orientation, maintenance of attention; the trigeminal motor nuclei-produces jaw movements; the facial motor nuclei-produces facial expressions; the ventral tegmental area-increases dopaminergic, noradrenergic, and cholinergic actions in the cerebral cortex via activation of the dopaminergic nuclei, loci coeruleus, and nuclei basalis of Meynert respectively leading to increased vigilance, cortical processing, and learning), which are involved in the behavioural, humoral, and autonomic signs of emotional reactions [Davis et al, 1991;Holstege et al,1996;Kapp et al,1990;LeDoux,1990; Weinberger et al,1990]. Much of this wiring system appears to be innate, but subject to plastic change (learning) in the amygdaloid nuclei or their afferent projections [Davis et al,1991]. We may be very angry in one situation (shouting, red face, violent gestures, aggressive facial features, increased respiration, increased heart rate and blood pressure, etc.), but not so angry in another (firm speech, no red face or gestures, fixed facial features, little increased heart rate or blood pressure). We may be petrified and cringing with fear in one situation, able to flee in another. We may show love to one person, anger to another. One can see that new emotional reactions are continuously being created to fit any circumstances that might arise. Hence they may be considered as voluntary new or novel intentional actions. All the different kinds (domains) of actions discussed above are similar in that they are voluntary new or novel intentional responses. They are created in response to new specific situations and contexts. This ability to produce voluntary new or novel intentional actions in different action domains may also be seen to a much more limited extent in certain lower animals (especially mammals). The production of such responses is very important for survival and may have evolved for such a purpose.

Our ability to produce voluntary new or novel intentional actions and action sequences may have evolved first in the skeletal motor system. The development of this system may have led to the success of early man and the emergence of Homo sapiens as the dominant species [McCrone,1999]. Consider for example, the discovery and use of tools and weapons by early man and how they must have helped him gain mastery over other animals, humans, and the environment. The skeletal motor system is intimately related to perception, as elements of perception are closely tied to specific skeletal motor responses [Allott,1994]. Much of this relationship may be prewired-genetic [Allott,1994]. The reason for this close relationship can be seen when one observes how the skeletomotor system is structured. The sensorimotor cortex involved in the production of most skeletomotor movements involves a number of adjacent cerebral cortical areas with sensory and motor functions. They are Brodmann's Areas 1,2,3 (primary sensory cortex), 4 (primary motor cortex), 5 (association sensory cortex), and 6 (lateral-premotor cortex, medial- supplementary motor cortex)[Brodal,1981]. These areas are all complexly interconnected with one another and function together as a unit in the execution, control, and guidance (regulation) of skeletomotor movements [Jones et al,1978;Kuypers and Catsman-Berrevoets,1984]. These areas all contribute to the corticospinal (pyramidal) tracts (primary motor cortex-40%, sensory cortex-30%, premotor cortex-30%) which directly activate the spinal motor neurons and interneurons involved in the production of skeletomotor movements [Afifi and Bergman,1986;Joseph,1990]. Sensory information from the peripheral sensory receptors passes to the primary and association sensory cortex via the dorsal collumn-medial lemniscal system (discriminative touch-pressure, vibration, position-kinesthetic sensation), spinothalamic tracts (crude touch, temperature, pain), and vestibular (balance, position, motion) pathways. Input from muscle (muscle spindles), tendon (golgi tendon organs), joint, and cutaneous receptors can directly activate the sensorimotor cortex and corticospinal tracts producing muscle action necessary to maintain limb position, stability, and posture. These latter circuits are known as transcortical reflexes or loops. Thus sensory input can directly access the skeletomotor movement-generating (corticospinal) pathways to generate skeletomotor movement [Ganong,1996;Joseph,1990]. Since the preceding sensorimotor structure is genetically determined, this means that our central nervous system may be prewired or genetically programmed so that sensory input and basic skeletomotor response are intimately related. Since perception is also sensory determined (perception is external sensory stimulation interpreted in terms of previous experience), this means that perception and basic skeletomotor response may also appear to be intimately related and occur together. The neural structure involved in the production of saccadic eye movements, speech, writing, thought, and emotion might have evolved from this basic structure of the skeletomotor system [Allott,1994; McCrone,1999], as these different action systems each have a comparable basic organization for the generation of its particular type of action. These different action domains each appear to have a genetically-determined (prewired) brain structure and basic response in all these systems might also be intimately related to perception, just as skeletomotor action is. Such action could be said to be elicited unconsciously (without consciousness) by a prewired (programmed) structure and is of an automatic nature. Voluntary new or novel intentional action is produced when perception is reorganized and re-represented in some way, so that it becomes a new or novel representation capable of activating the voluntary new or novel intentional action-producing domains and producing a specific new or novel action. These voluntary new or novel intentional action producing areas are not involved in producing the basic sensory (perceptual) motor responses. There appear to be different specific frontal cortical areas for the activation of each of the voluntary new or novel intentional action domains. These are the supplementary motor cortex (skeletomotor movements), the frontal eye fields (saccadic eye movements), Broca's Area (speech), Exner's Area (writing), and the orbitofrontal cortex (emotion)[Joseph, 1990;Pandya and Yeterian,1990;Sieb,1995]. Each of these areas in turn may be activated by a different specific dorsolateral prefrontal cortical region (this cortex extends over the dorsolateral convexity of the cerebral cortex, in front of the frontal regions just mentioned), each of which has different specific inputs and projects to different specific target areas [Pandya and Yeterian,1990;Sieb,1995]. Thus each of the voluntary new or novel intentional action-producing domains may be engaged differentially via a different specific dorsolateral prefrontal region and frontal region. This structure provides a location and organization whereby the domain of voluntary new or novel intentional action can be differentially selected and engaged. This differential selection and engagement may be driven by input from the inferior parietal and inferior temporal cortex [Haggard,2005]. The inferior parietal cortex may be where perception occurs [Mattingley,1999]. It may be here that perception may be reorganized into a new or novel representation (this may give rise to conscious awareness, as described next) which is then utilized in the generation of voluntary actions. Sirigu and coworkers [2004] found an altered time of perceived conscious awareness of making a voluntary movement in patients with damage to the parietal cortex, while Lau and coworkers [2004] found greater activation in the supplementary motor cortex and intra-parietal sulcus during the generation of voluntary movements rather than during the involuntary generation of such movements. The evolution of this ability to produce a variety of voluntary new or novel intentional actions would give increased reproductive and survival success.

POINT OF VIEW OR PERSPECTIVE

Voluntary new or novel intentional action is always produced from the subject's own particular point of view or perspective. This point of view or perspective arises from perception. It is unique to that individual at that time. It cannot be known (experienced) by another. It is what is known as subjectivity-the having of or the adopting of a particular perspective or point of view [Alter,2001; McClamrock,1994;McCrone,2001]. This point of view or perspective is "what it is like" or "how it feels" to be that particular person at that particular time. It is the essential basis of consciousness.

The formation of a particular point of view or perspective is essential for the production of voluntary new or novel intentional (adaptive) action. A point of view or perspective is a particular way of looking at particular information. As mentioned above, perception is directly associated with production of a basic type of action, since our nervous system is genetically structured (programmed) to do so. Perception is thought to occur in the inferior temporal and inferior parietal cortex [Mattingley,1999]. The inferior parietal cortex is found at the junction of the parietal, temporal, and occipital lobes of the cerebral cortex of the brain. It is the area where pathology results in the production of most cases of hemilateral neglect (contralateral neglect)[Mattingley,1999]. In hemilateral neglect, perception and consciousness of sensory input (the sensory field) is lost on the contralateral side to where the pathology is found. Such individuals may be unaware of or not conscious of the sensory space on their affected side. They may shave or wash only one side of their faces; they may be completely unaware of and ignore the affected side of their body. When drawing a scene or various objects from view, they may draw only one side of the scene or one side of the object; they may draw only the portions of the scene or object perceived consciously on the unaffected side. The inferior parietal cortex consists of the supramarginal and angular gyri, part of area 7, and cortex partly coextensive with the posterior superior temporal gyrus. The inferior parietal cortex has some neurons which are multimodally responsive, receiving highly processed input from somesthetic, visual, and auditory association areas of the cortex; the frontal lobe (including movement-related areas); and other higher order assimilation areas throughout the neocortex [Joseph,1990]. The inferior parietal cortex is consequently involved in the creation and assimilation of cross-modal associations (auditory, somesthetic, and visual equivalents of events, actions, feelings, and ideas)[Joseph,1990]. In other words, the inferior parietal cortex is involved in perception. In order to produce voluntary new or novel intentional action, perception (which remember is directly associated with production of a basic type of action) must somehow be reorganized and re-represented in a new or novel manner [Gershenson and Heyligher,2004]. Such a reorganization and re-representation of perception could occur in the inferior parietal cortex through the formation there of new or novel stable states from perception via the nonlinear emergent mechanism described previously. These new or novel stable states are not entirely predictable and probably do emerge in a nonlinear fashion, which is typical of complex systems (consisting of interacting elements) like the brain [Gershenson and Heyligher,2004]. These new stable states (built from positive feedback and inhibition) also appear to be maintained over a short period of time (a type of active short term memory, working memory), making them available for a short period of time for the production of specific behaviors or actions. Since these stable states are newly created each time, they may always result in the production of new or novel behaviours or actions. Since these new stable states arise from perception and are involved in the production of new or novel intentional actions (they serve as standpoints for the production of such actions), they may be thought of as newly created points of view or perspectives of the subject. Thus a newly-created point of view or perspective is available for the production of new or novel action. Since by definition, consciousness is a point of view or perspective (since it is subjective), perhaps these newly created nonlinear stable states are therefore equivalent to consciousness. If this is so, then consciousness would have a physical basis; it is nonlinearly-produced stable states arising from perception. The action produced via these stable states can consequently be thought of as being made by the choice or free will of the subject and as having a specific purpose or direction; hence these actions may be thought of as voluntary new or novel intentional actions. The nonlinearly-produced explicit new stable states (points of view, perspectives) produced in the inferior parietal cortex may access the voluntary new or novel intentional action-producing systems by being routed from the inferior parietal cortex to the cortex responsible for selecting, planning, and executing voluntary new or novel intentional action. Research indicates that this would probably be the dorsolateral prefrontal cortex (see below). Through this cortex, the appropriate voluntary new or novel intentional action-producing system is selected and activated. Research indicates that the frontal and parietal lobes together form a circuit that creates and monitors new motor plans in advance of their execution and from the activation involved creates a conscious intention to make the movement [Haggard, 2005]. The same might be true for the other voluntary new or novel intentional action domains (eye movements, speech, writing, emotion, thought); the frontal and parietal lobes together might form a circuit for the creation and monitoring of new motor plans in each of these domains also, with the conscious intention to make the action arising from the activation involved. Hence the dorsolateral prefrontal cortex might be the place where the appropriate domain of voluntary new or novel intentional action is selected and engaged. Perhaps attention is involved here. Attention could lower the threshold of activation to input from the inferior parietal cortex of a specific region of the dorsolateral prefrontal cortex which is involved in the production of a specific domain of voluntary new or novel intentional action.

The nonlinear emergent mechanism outlined previously possesses the characteristics and properties necessary for the production of such points of view or perspectives (consciousness) necessary for the production of voluntary new or novel intentional actions: it may occur in the cerebral cortex, it may occur in the appropriate area (the inferior parietal cortex) which appears to be involved in perception and consciousness, it may arise from perception, it may result in the reorganization and re-representation of perception, it may result in the production of new or novel explicit perceptual stable states, it is not entirely predictable, its explicit stable states are maintained over a short period of time (active short term memory), and it produces new or novel explicit stable states which are readily available for the production of voluntary new or novel intentional action.

The nonlinear production of new or novel explicit stable states supports the view that consciousness is produced over short temporal integration periods or epochs ("episodes") from sensory perception of the external world. This enables explanation of many of the properties of consciousness and explanation of many conscious-related phenomena. The view that consciousness is produced over short temporal integration periods is supported by the fact that it takes time for a specific conscious experience to be produced. This might be the time required for the integration of a specific type of state, like the nonlinear stable states described above. Thus specific sensory stimulation applied to the sensory pathways or sensory cortex must be maintained for a short period of time (several hundred milliseconds) before the sensory input is experienced consciously; that is, before the subject becomes consciously aware of it [Libet,1985]. Libet called this time, the time to achieve neural adequacy. This may be the time required for the positive feedback of perceptual processing to build up and form an explicit new stable state. The temporal evolution of the preparatory activation occurring in the premotor areas of the brain during the generation of a voluntary skeletomotor movement also indicates that it must take a short period of time for consciousness to be produced. The temporal order of occurrence of consciousness and premotor preparatory activation also has important implications for any role consciousness might have in the generation of the movement. If consciousness were to arise before the preparatory cortical activation, then consciousness could be the cause of the preparatory cortical activation and the movement. If consciousness were to arise after the preparatory cortical activation had already began; then consciousness could not have caused the movement, but is a consequence of the preparatory activation. Studies by Libet and coworkers [1983] found that the preparatory activation (readiness potential) of premotor cortical areas may begin more than 1 sec before a voluntary movement (of the right hand) actually begins, but the conscious intention to make the voluntary movement (of the right hand) does not occur until about 206 ms before the movement actually begins [Haggard,2005]. Conscious intention to make the movement occurred more than 500 ms after the preparatory activity (readiness potential) began. Since an effect cannot precede it's cause, it therefore cannot be said that consciousness caused the movement, because the preparatory activity required for making the movement occurred well in advance of the conscious intention to make the movement. Hence the preparatory activity involved in causing the movement most likely led to the production of the conscious intention; conscious intention is a consequence of the preparatory activity. This again might suggest that it takes a short period of integration time to form and stabilize a state of activation necessary to produce conscious experience (like the new stable states produced by the nonlinear mechanism previously described).

The experiments of Libet have been successfully replicated [Haggard and Eimer,1999;Sirigu et al,2004], but are still controversial. Haggard and Eimer [1999] used a modification of Libet's experiments to study the relation of selection to conscious intention. They allowed their subjects to freely choose either the right or left hand when they performed a voluntary movement. This time it was found that the generalized readiness potential in premotor cortical areas did not correlate with the time of judgement of the appearance of conscious intention. This supports the time difference between the appearance of the generalized readiness potential and appearance of conscious intention, but contradicts Libet's assumption that this readiness potential caused the conscious experience. Haggard and Eimer further studied the situation by looking at the lateralized readiness potential that occurred during the performance of the voluntary movement. The lateralized readiness potential is an internal marker of selection. It is the point where the activity in the hemisphere contralateral to the selected hand exceeded the activity in the hemisphere ipsilateral to the selected hand. Importantly, they concluded that the process of selection must be over just before the lateralized readiness potential begins. Haggard and Eimer [1999] found that conscious intention was linked to the lateralized preparatory activity to perform a specific movement (as evidenced by the lateralized readiness potential). Conscious intention thus arises after the selection process (that is, after the choice is made to make a specific movement) as a consequence of the lateralized cortical activity generating a specific voluntary movement. Hence the free choice to make a voluntary movement appears to involve unconscious processes; that is, processes operating automatically and unconsciously. This unconscious selection process then generates a specific voluntary movement, as well as consciousness. Free choice is probably a perceptual process. Perception occurs automatically and unconsciously (as evidenced by the generalized readiness potential). If perception occurs in the inferior parietal cortex, then the choice to make a specific voluntary movement could be made here. The making of such a choice here could entail the formation of a new or novel nonlinear explicit stable state from perception via the described nonlinear mechanism. This state could take many different forms, but assumes a single form (stabilizes to a certain form) that would result in the production of a specific voluntary movement. This is tantamount to making a choice to produce a specific movement. As discussed previously, this state also represents consciousness. Thus conscious intention arises just after the choice is made to make a specific movement (through perception) and hence is correlated with the lateralized activation that produces the specific movement. This selection process might be expressed in the passage of activity from the inferior parietal cortex to the dorsolateral prefrontal cortex in a lateralized fashion. Consequently, the activity producing a specific voluntary new or novel intentional skeletomotor movement is lateralized from the inferior parietal cortex on through the motor system. The production of conscious intention after the choice is made to make a specific voluntary movement makes the advent of consciousness more efficient and precise. Consciousness would consequently not be wasted in representing alternative actions which are not selected and which would undoubtedly cause much interference and confusion.

The production of each new explicit stable state (point of view, perspective) via the described nonlinear mechanism might represent the production of a new episode of consciousness. Any part or element of perception that is active during an integration period for a new perceptual stable state (episode of conscious perception) might become part of a single conscious perception. This might explain the observation that our consciousness at any one time consists of many perceptual elements consciously experienced at the same time. Thus any perceptual element that is active during a conscious perceptual integration period might become part of the same conscious perception, even though they might become active at slightly different times during that integration period. Within a certain temporal interval of activation (the conscious perceptual integration period), various perceptual elements will be part of the same conscious perception (that is they will be consciously perceived as occurring simultaneously). If elements of perceptual activation are active outside a single conscious perceptual integration period, then they might be incorporated into a different conscious perceptual integration period and consciously perceived as occurring at a different time (consciously perceived serially or sequentially). This suggests that consciousness might be played out in episodes, much like the scenes (frames) of a film running through a movie camera. This results in the serial production of episodes of conscious perception. Each episode of consciousness that is so formed might represent a particular point of view or perspective for the subject that is maintained for a short period of time. Each point of view or perspective (episode) is thus available for a short period of time for the creation of action. Voluntary new or novel intentional action is thus continuously created. The integration periods might slightly overlap each other during production and thus would appear to succeed one another seamlessly. This idea that it takes a short period of time (an integration period) for conscious perception to arise supports the notion that consciousness is produced by the continuous sequential building of new nonlinearly-produced explicit stable states. The time it takes to build one of these nonlinear explicit stable states would be the time it takes to integrate a single conscious episode. If consciousness is formed over short integration periods or episodes, then it is not produced continuously (that is, without perceptual integration periods or episodes). If consciousness was formed continuously, it would be difficult to see how consciousness could be associated with the production of something new or novel (such as voluntary new or novel intentional action). There would be no reorganization or re-representation of perception which is necessary for such production. As mentioned a number of times, continuous and direct perception is directly associated with a basic programmed-type of action.

The idea that consciousness is produced in short integration periods or episodes (as nonlinearly-produced explicit stable states), rather than being produced continuously, may be supported by some consciousness-related phenomena. For example, some complex figures are bistable when perceived consciously; that is, they may be consciously perceived, with equal probability, in more than one way (this means they have different conscious representations that have an equal probability of being perceived). The Necker Cube or the Rabbit-Vase (the head of a rabbit or a vase may be consciously perceived when the figure is viewed directly) figures are examples of figures which have two different equally-probable conscious perceptions, which may alternate with one another, when the figure is viewed directly. The fact that these different conscious perceptions of the same figure occur alternately, suggests that they are different representations being produced serially or sequentially. Just such a situation might occur if a conscious perception arose from the integration of information over a short integration period (as from the integration of a nonlinearly-produced stable state). Each different conscious perception of the figure would result from integration over a separate (different) integration period (the creation of separate nonlinear explicit new stable states). If conscious perception were to occur without integration over short periods of time (as without the formation of nonlinearly-produced explicit stable states-such as continuously), then it is hard to see how the different conscious perceptions of a bistable figure would alternate sequentially with one another. In change blindness, an individual is often unaware of or not conscious of (blind to) small changes that might occur in a scene or event. For example, if a complex picture is shown to a subject, then removed, and then shown again with small changes made in its content; the subject often does not consciously notice (is not aware of) the changes. Consciousness seems to depend on focussed attention. Focussed attention might be necessary to produce and maintain an intensity of activation of perceptual elements needed for the production of nonlinear explicit stable states. If the small changes made in the content of a viewed scene do not attract the attention of the subject, then they may not be included as part of the activation integrated into a new nonlinear explicit stable state and so are not perceived consciously. However, even if consciousness was produced continuously, such changes might still not be expected to be consciously perceived, if attention is not focussed on them. However, if the changes were made while the subject was viewing the scene or picture, they may attract the attention of the subject and consequently be perceived consciously. Similarly, in inattentional blindness, an individual is often not conscious of or is unaware of things in a scene or event that do not catch his or her attention. This further suggests that attention seems to be necessary for the formation of consciousness. Thus during the viewing of a complex picture or live action of some sort there may be various items that do not catch the subject's attention and therefore remain out of the subject's consciousness. In a familiar example I have seen on film, subjects were told to count the number of times a basketball was passed, during a game. During the game, an individual dressed in a gorilla suit ran through the court. Most of the subjects when questioned afterwards were unaware of the presence of the individual in the gorilla suit, since their attention was devoted to the task of counting passes and was not attracted by the individual in the gorilla suit. This shows that in order for the gorilla suit to be processed consciously, it must attract the attention of the subjects in some way. Only then could the intensity of activation be high enough and/or the threshold of activation be lowered enough to produce conscious perception of the gorilla suit. Again this could be accomplished if consciousness was produced over short intervals of time (as in the formation of nonlinear explicit stable states). Various illusions also support the idea that consciousness is produced in episodes. One such illusion occurs when a red light and a yellow light are set next to one another (maybe about 6 inches apart) and flashed alternately repeatedly, the red light first and then the yellow light. At long intervals between the two flashes, both the red light and the yellow light are separately perceived consciously as flashing, with the yellow light as flashing just after the red light. Hence the conscious integration periods (nonlinear explicit stable states) for each light flash do not overlap and each light is consciously perceived as flashing separately. If the interval between the two light flashes is gradually shortened, an interval size is reached where the red light appears to move from its position to the yellow light position and to change colour from red to yellow midway. This may occur because at this short interval of separation of the light flashes, the conscious integration period for the red light flash is not completed before the conscious integration period for the yellow light flash begins, and so the two conscious integration periods (respective nonlinear explicit stable states) overlap. This might give the appearance of the red light moving towards and changing into the yellow light. This illusion is even harder to explain if consciousness was produced continuously. In the wagon wheel illusion, when a wagon wheel moves below a certain speed, each part of the wheel rim can have attention fixed on it and can be consciously perceived. Thus each part of the wheel is represented by its own separate integration period (nonlinear explicit stable state). Each part of the wheel is therefore separately consciously perceived and the whole wheel is consequently consciously perceived as moving in the direction of travel. However, if the wheel travels at a rate of speed that is faster than the time required for integration of a conscious integration period (or nonlinear explicit stable state) of a single part of the wheel, then conscious integration periods (and nonlinear explicit stable states) might partially overlap and the conscious perception of the direction of rotation of the wheel might be in the opposite direction (a reversal) to its actual direction of travel. Hence the illusion might arise where the whole wheel might be perceived as turning in the opposite direction to travel. This illusion seems to occur in moving films and in continuous light (natural observation). Such reversal might not occur if consciousness was produced continuously, as there would be no conscious integration periods (nonlinear explicit stable states) to overlap. If a disk has the colors red, yellow, and blue painted on it in alternate stripes and then is spun; at a low speed, one may be consciously aware of the disc turning in the direction of travel. Above a certain speed, however, the disc might seem to travel in the opposite direction (a reversal) to which it is actually travelling. This again may indicate that consciousness is produced in episodes for the same reason as in the previous example. If a light is repetitively turned on and off, on and off, at a slow rate, each on-off cycle can be separately consciously perceived. However, if the rate at which the light is turned on and off is gradually increased, a rate is reached in which the individual on-off cycles cannot be separately perceived consciously and the light appears consciously to be on continuously. This again might suggest that consciousness is formed in episodes, rather than being generated continuously. At a low repetitive rate, each on-off cycle is processed separately as a single conscious episode (nonlinear explicit stable state). At a high cycle rate, cycle rate is so fast that the sequentially-produced conscious integration periods (nonlinear explicit stable states) for individual on-off events may overlap in their construction and the light appears consciously to be on continuously. This may be what happens with our common home lighting systems using alternating current. The lights are actually flashing on and off at such a high rate, that they consciously appear to be on continuously. It is certainly hard to explain this phenomenon if consciousness was produced continuously. A movie camera may operate similarly. The frames (scenes) of a film are fed fast enough through the camera so that the individual frames are not consciously perceived as separate (conscious episodes or nonlinear explicit stable states for each frame are formed so rapidly, that they overlap), but are consciously perceived as one continuous changing scene. The same effect can be obtained with a child's cartoon book. If a cartoon character is drawn on successive pages with his limbs in a slightly different position on successive pages, when the pages are flipped at a high enough speed, the character appears to move his limbs. When each page is examined individually, the cartoon character is consciously perceived as stationary (in' one position), because a separate conscious integration period (nonlinear explicit stable state) is composed for each page. However, when the pages are flipped at high speed, conscious integration periods (nonlinear explicit stable states) overlap and the character appears to move. In binocular rivalry (a type of perceptual rivalry), each eye simultaneously views a different stimulus (object, picture). This results in a rivalry between the two stimuli for conscious perception and the two stimuli may alternate with one another in conscious perception; first one is consciously perceived, then the other, then the first again, then the other, and so on. Such rivalry might also be explained if consciousness is produced in episodes, rather than continuously. If consciousness was produced continuously, then such rivalry might not be expected to occur; conscious perception in this case might be a combination of the two stimuli. If consciousness is formed in episodes, however, each stimulus may form its own conscious episode (nonlinear explicit stable state), so that each episode appears alternately in conscious perception (the rivalry condition).

The consciousness-generating mechanism outlined above might also explain some other consciousness related phenomena. In certain people, conscious experience in one sensory modality is linked to conscious experience in another sensory modality. This is called synesthesia. For example, colored words. Here conscious perception of a certain spoken word may be accompanied by conscious perception of a certain color. The two conscious perceptions are linked somehow and always occur together. Many other linked sensory conscious experience combinations may occur involving the various sensory modalities (taste-colour, odour-colour, sight-taste, sound-odour). If the inferior parietal cortex is multimodally responsive and is where perception and consciousness arise, perhaps the links involved in synesthesia are caused by the pattern of connectivity developed here. A nonlinear explicit stable state (conscious episode) formed in one sensory modality may elicit formation of a nonlinear explicit stable state (conscious episode) in the linked sensory modality. I hesitate to say whether or not this is an abnormal development, as I am not sure that synesthesia is an abnormal condition. In sensory substitution, conscious sensation in one sensory modality substitutes for and produces conscious sensation in another sensory modality. For example, a video camera may be set up to transmit video information to a large number of electrodes attached to the skin on the back of a blind subject. The visual input from the camera activates the electrodes in various patterns (depending upon the changing composition of the visual input) and this cutaneous stimulation pattern is transmitted to the sensory cortex of the subject. After a period of learning, the blind subject becomes able to "see" what is happening around him or her. The incoming cutaneous information may somehow be linked or transferred to the cortical visual processing areas. The subject is eventually able to identify objects ("see" objects without touching them) and is even able to catch a ball ("see" motion). Thus conscious sensation in one sensory modality is linked to conscious sensation in another sensory modality. This might again be explained by the multimodally responsive structure of the inferior parietal cortex. Input from one modality (cutaneous) might easily activate neurons also responsive to another modality (vision) producing conscious perception involving the second modality (vision). Thus nonlinear explicit stable states (conscious episodes) produced in one modality cause formation of nonlinear explicit stable states (conscious episodes) in another modality. The white cane used by the blind might be another example of sensory substitution. With practice, the white cane becomes an extension of the subject's arm and allows the person to "see" obstacles as he or she progresses through the environment. This again might depend on the linking of cutaneous sensation and vision in the inferior parietal cortex.

VOLUNTARY NEW OR NOVEL INTENTIONAL ACTION AND CONSCIOUSNESS

One interesting thing about our production of voluntary new or novel intentional action is that it is always accompanied by consciousness. Our production of reflex and learned (programmed) action occurs without awareness or consciousness and is said to be automatic. As mentioned, consciousness is subjective-it is a particular personal perspective or point of view that is somehow created in our brains [Alter,2001; Byrne,2001; McClamrock,1994; Mandik,2001]. Since our voluntary new or novel intentional action is created from our particular point of view or perspective at the moment, it might be said to be created from our consciousness. Hence consciousness may be responsible for or is connected in some way with the composition of voluntary new or novel intentional action and is always present when such action is composed. There is some empirical evidence that was discussed previously that such a point of view or perspective (consciousness) arises after the choice is made to make a particular action, but shortly before the specific action begins [Haggard and Eimer,1999; Haggard,2005;Libet et al,1983]. This suggests that the causal brain activation required to produce a voluntary new or novel intentional movement must have arisen from preconscious or unconscious processes and this activation may have given rise to the consciousness, as well as the movement. Other experiments have shown that it takes time for sensory input to build up in strength before it becomes conscious [Libet,1985]. These facts provide support for the nonlinear emergent mechanism described previously for the production of consciousness. By this mechanism, perceptual activation is maintained and amplified by positive feedback (and additional factors that facilitate positive feedback, such as focussed attention) in order to generate consciousness. This may underscore the importance of focussed attention for the generation of consciousness. Perhaps focussed attention is a way of prolonging and maintaining specific sensory stimulation so as to facilitate and amplify operation of the positive feedback portion of the nonlinear emergent mechanism involved in the generation of consciousness. Focussed attention would thus make the mechanism for the generation of consciousness even more sensitive and efficient. Focussed attention also might help determine the domain of voluntary new or novel intentional action produced (skeletomotor movement, ocular movement, speech, writing, thought, or emotion). By lowering the threshold of activation of a certain dorsolateral prefrontal cortical system of voluntary new or novel intentional action engagement, focussed attention could direct conscious activation (an explicit stable state, point of view) arising in the inferior parietal cortex into the appropriate type of voluntary action. Since the generation of consciousness is more correlated with the lateralized readiness potential, (which indicates that the choice has been made to make a specific action), perhaps the qualia making up the content of consciousness might help determine the specifics (parameters) of the specific action selected to be made. Hence for skeletomotor and ocular movements, the qualia might determine the direction, velocity, and distance of movement. For speech and writing, the qualia might determine the words used and their sequence. For thought, the qualia might determine the thoughts activated, their modification, and their arrangement. For emotion, the qualia might determine the type and composition of the emotional reaction. The qualia arise from sensory input and so it is reasonable to think that they might determine the specifics of the voluntary response to this input. Hence consciousness may arise during the preparation to make a specific action and may play a role (its qualia) in determining the parameters (specifics) of the action. If an animal or machine could produce true voluntary new or novel intentional action (that is, action created and executed by the choice and free will of the animal or machine for a specific purpose), then such action may be said to arise from the animal's or machine's own particular point of view or perspective and consciousness may be deemed to be present. Some higher animals (especially mammals) appear to be able to do this; but no machine appears to be so capable, as every machine is built and programmed by a human and so has all its responses predetermined. If a physical mechanism can be found for the production of voluntary new or novel intentional action, perhaps it also explains how the particular point of view or perspective (consciousness) is produced.

PRODUCTION OF VOLUNTARY NEW OR NOVEL INTENTIONAL ACTION AND CONSCIOUSNESS

Current research indicates that the prefrontal cortex mediates (plans) our ongoing production of voluntary new or novel intentional action through the integration of three cognitive processes: active short-term memory (working memory), motor set (the selection, preparation, and readiness for action), and the inhibition of excess activity [Fuster,1997,2000]. These three processes may create and implement a particular point of view or perspective (consciousness) for a subject. As mentioned previously, there is some evidence that the dorsolateral prefrontal cortex possesses different specific regions for the engagement of the different voluntary new or novel intentional action domains that differ in their afferent (input) and efferent (output) projections depending on the action domain involved (Pandya and Yeterian,1990;Sieb,1995). Thus the dorsolateral prefrontal cortex appears to have different regions for the engagement of voluntary new or novel intentional skeletomotor movements, eye movements, speech, writing, thought, and emotion. Active short-term memory is the provisional retention of perceptual information for prospective action, a type of focal attention whereby perception is reorganized, re-represented, and maintained; becoming explicit, functional, and conscious [Luck and Vogel,1997;Todd and Marois,2004;Vogel and Machizawa,2004]. Specific perceptual activation is selected, re-represented, and maintained (stabilized) over some time interval (delay) so as to produce future action. Much of the research carried out and reviewed by Fuster [1997] utilized different types of delayed response tasks in which information was maintained and carried over a delay (a type of active short term memory, or working memory) and used to produce a certain response at a later time. Such action is thus mediated, deliberated, new or novel, voluntary, and intentional. Active short-term memory may be formed and maintained by positive feedback, a type of re-entry [Fuster,1997]. Reentry refers to reciprocal interaction (feedback) between elements and occurs throughout the brain [Tonelli and Edelman,1998]. Positive feedback occurs when this reciprocal feedback is excitatory. Positive feedback leads to exponential growth of activity [Scott,1996,1998,2000], as mentioned previously. Hence positive feedback between the dissipation and release of perceptual activity (dissipation leads to more release, leading to more dissipation, leading to more release, and so on) may lead to the exponential growth of perceptual activation. However, inhibition is also activated by these dissipation and release events (decay of activation, depletion of activity, change in input, refractory periods, etc.), limiting the growth, producing a balanced (stable) state [Scott,1996,1998,2000]. This stable state is a nonlinear emergent; ie. it depends on, but is entirely different from (is not defined by nor reducible to, is nondeterminant from), its initiating events [Newman,1997; Scott,1996,1998,2000]. It is a re-representation of perception. As mentioned before, such nonlinear emergence is responsible for a vast number of natural phenomena (candle flames, waves, nerve impulses, cells, nations, family groups, businesses, stock market, etc.)[Scott,1996, 1998,2000;Sieb,2004]. The emergent state is explicit, ie. it is fully established physically and can be directly utilized to produce other explicit states or effects (intentional character)[O'Brien and Opie,1999]. Since this explicit state is a new internal context built from perception (a new standpoint), it may be considered a new particular point of view or perspective for that system (subjective or phenomenal character). According to this reasoning, active short-term memory is a particular point of view or perspective for that subject arising from perception. This nonlinear explicit state (point of view, active short term memory) is utilized in the production of action (motor set). Since this state is created anew each time, it is always new or novel, and always produces voluntary new or novel intentional action.

These new or novel internal nonlinear explicit stable states (active short-term memories) have all the same properties that have been attributed to consciousness [Baars,1988; Clifton,2003,2004a,2004b;Koch,1998;Tonelli and Edelman,1998]. They, like consciousness, are self-generated. That is, they are generated in some way by processes occurring entirely within the individual. They, like conscious experiences, do not exist in any physical form in the external world. For example, our conscious experience of the colour red (or of any other colour) does not exist in any physical form in the external world. Our conscious experience of the colour red is created entirely within our brain and only exists there. Similarly for other conscious experiences. The nonlinearly-produced stable states, like conscious experiences, do not exist in any way in the external world and are created by neural processes entirely within the brain and so only exist in the brain. These stable states, like consciousness, form rapidly; but do take time to form and persist for a short period of time. These properties of consciousness and nonlinearly-produced stable states have been discussed extensively previously in this composition. These properties of consciousness also seem evident from our everyday experience with consciousness. Nonlinearly-produced stable states, like consciousness, require re-entry (reciprocal interaction) for their generation. Tonelli and Edelman [1998] have found that consciousness is impaired, if the re-entry mechanisms of the brain are disrupted. Re-entry is an integral part of the basic nonlinear emergent mechanism responsible for the generation of the explicit stable states discussed in this composition. Hence if these re-entry mechanisms are disrupted, the generation of nonlinearly-produced stable states is also disrupted. Consciousness may be disrupted by disturbance of the re-entry mechanisms involving the brainstem (especially the reticular formation) and cerebral cortex, the thalamus (especially the reticular and intralaminar nuclei of the thalamus) and cerebral cortex, the thalamus and the brainstem, and the different areas within the cerebral cortex. Disturbance of the first three types of re-entry may result in impairment of the level of consciousness (producing confusion or coma), while disturbance of the fourth type of re-entry might result in impairment of the content of consciousness (impaired generation of specific kinds of conscious experiences or qualia-of faces, motion, shape, etc.). Disruption of the re-entry mechanisms of the brain would also be expected to impair the ability of that individual to compose voluntary new or novel intentional action (psychomotor poverty). As for the generation of consciousness, focussed attention is probably required for the generation of the nonlinearly-produced stable states. This also seems evident from our everyday experience with consciousness. We must focus our attention on something before it is able to enter our consciousness. Similarly, attention probably must be focussed on something to build up the activation in the proper channels necessary to produce the nonlinearly-produced explicit stable states. Perhaps focussed attention also lowers the threshold for activation of the specific channels necessary for doing this. These nonlinear explicit stable states, like consciousness seems to have, have effects on other systems. This underlies their ability to generate various actions. Consciousness appears to have effects on systems that create and generate various new or novel purposeful responses. The generation of responses, once they are learned, does not require consciousness. For example, when adults tie their shoelaces, the movements involved are performed automatically and do not require consciousness. However, the generation of these responses before they are learned does require consciousness, as they may initially be considered new or novel. When learning to tie their shoelaces, children must initially create and generate the component movements involved consciously. Thus something new must be created (like nonlinear explicit stable states, consciousness) to generate voluntary new or novel intentional actions. New or novel responses, whether generated by consciousness or by nonlinear explicit stable states, may be thought of as being generated in accordance with the point of view or perspective of the person at that time for some specific purpose. Hence they may be thought of as being made by the choice and free will of the person. These responses therefore may be thought of as types of voluntary new or novel intentional action. Nonlinearly-produced stable states have an intentional character; that is, they are of or about something and they have a directedness. They are of or about the new or novel representation of certain specific active perceptual elements which serves as a standpoint (viewpoint, point of view, perspective) for the generation of specific voluntary new or novel intentional actions (thus having a directedness). Consciousness also appears to be of or about something (the generation of new or novel conscious experiences from certain specific active perceptual elements) and to have a directedness (these conscious experiences may be considered a standpoint, viewpoint, or point of view for the generation of specific voluntary new or novel intentional actions). Consciousness therefore also has an intentional character. If something is intentional, it is consequently representational (that is, it represents something). Hence these stable states and consciousness are representational and represent something; some kind of information (perceptual information) is represented in the neural activation making up these stable states or consciousness. It is interesting to note that both consciousness and nonlinearly-produced stable states are portrayed here as representing the same type of information. They both are presented as representing specific active elements of perception in a new or novel manner. These nonlinear explicit stable states, like consciousness, have a subjective character. They may be both considered as particular first person points of view or perspectives, and for the same reason; they both serve as a standpoint for the creation and generation of voluntary new or novel intentional actions. They both are defined by their subjectivity. If nonlinearly-produced explicit stable states and consciousness did not have subjectivity (were not particular first person points of view or perspectives), they would have no value or purpose for the subject. They would simply be an attachment to brain processing and have no purpose or function (epiphenomenal), they would be merely by-products. Their subjectivity confers a purpose or function to them, the ability to create new or novel effects or action. Nonlinearly-produced stable states and conscious states are differentiated by their content. The content of nonlinearly-produced stable states comes from specific active perceptual elements. Their content at any one time may be determined by the specific elements of perception active within a certain time window (integration period). The content of consciousness at any one time consists of various qualia or conscious experiences which are determined at any one time also by the elements of perception active within a certain time window (integration period). The content generated in subjective systems (like consciousness and this nonlinear system) is known only to the subject. It cannot be known or experienced by another. It is "what it is like" or "how it feels" to be that system at that particular time. It is that system's point of view or perspective at that particular moment. Future action is then conceived according to that point of view or perspective. Nonlinearly-produced stable states, like consciousness, are complex, bounded, and have limited capacity. This might be due partly to the complex interrelationships that exist between the elements making up the content at any one time. Thus for nonlinearly-produced stable states, the number of active perceptual elements, the intensity of their individual activations, and their interactions might determine the complexity, boundaries, and capacity of the resulting explicit stable state that is formed. Our consciousness at any one time is made up of a number of different experiences (each arising from a different active element of perception), which seem to have complex interrelationships with one another. The number and type of co-existing experiences, the intensity of their individual activation, and the way they interact with one another probably determines the complexity, boundaries, and capacity of overall consciousness at the time. The presence of one experience does appear to influence the presence or appearance of other experiences. For example, background conscious experience (background illumination or colour) can affect the conscious experience of a central colour (I believe this is the basis of the Land effect). Conscious experience of a certain colour might affect conscious experience of a sound or texture. For example, conscious experience of a white colour or a baby's cry might make a baby's blanket seem softer. For nonlinear-produced stable states, the activity contributed to formation of a stable state by one active perceptual element might influence the activity contributed to formation of the stable state from another active perceptual element. This is analogous to the effect the activity responsible for the generation of one conscious experience (from one active perceptual element) might have on the activity responsible for the generation of other accompanying conscious experiences (from other co-active perceptual elements). Conscious experiences might be judged as occurring simultaneously or serially, depending on the time window (integration period) within which they were created (whether or not the perceptual elements involved in their creation contributed to production of the same or different episode of consciousness). Similarly, the activation of one perceptual element might influence the activation of other perceptual elements (lateral inhibition or conversely lateral excitation), which might influence the spatial and temporal contributions of the various perceptual elements to a nonlinearly-produced stable state. Various perceptual elements might be perceived as occurring simultaneously or serially, depending on the time window (integration period) within which they are active and whether or not they contribute to production of the same or different stable state. The speed and intensity of our ability to release, develop, and shift focussed attention might also help determine our speed and capacity for generating various nonlinear explicit stable states or conscious experiences (since focussed attention is necessary for the formation of both). Active short term memory is dependent on focussed attention. The capacity of human active short term memory as determined by focussed attention appears to be limited to about 4 or 5 items at once; so here focussed attention might also put limits and boundaries on our ability to generate various nonlinear explicit stable states and conscious experience. Also, the generation of current nonlinear explicit stable states or conscious experiences might be influenced by previously generated stable states or conscious experience respectively, producing facillatory (priming) or inhibitory effects. Unconscious processes (like priming) undoubtedly affect the generation of nonlinear explicit stable states and conscious experience. All these factors may introduce complexity, boundaries, and help limit the capacity of nonlinearly-produced stable states and consciousness. These stable states, like consciousness, are variable, flexible, and seamless. Nonlinearly-produced stable states and consciousness may be formed to accommodate any type of situation that might arise. The individual must be able to cope with any situation that might arise in his or her environment by creating appropriate voluntary new or novel intentional action. Success or survival depends on it. Thus nonlinearly-produced stable states and consciousness are being created anew at each moment of time. No two states or conscious episodes are ever exactly alike because of the chaotic integration dynamics of re-entry. This variability and flexibility allows for generation of the most effective responses possible. One stable state or conscious episode grades smoothly and seamlessly into another to generate what appears to be a continuous flow of states or of consciousness, without any noticeable breaks in the flow. Thus consciousness has been compared to a river with a uniform, continuous, and uninterrupted flow-the stream of consciousness. Nonlinearly-produced stable states, like consciousness, are hard to describe in words and are therefore said to be ineffable. One has great difficulty in trying to define consciousness or these nonlinearly-produced stable states. It is not hard to guess what my definition is. I define consciousness and these nonlinearly-produced stable states as self-generated points of view or perspectives (subjective). These stable states, like consciousness, are transparent. They do not seem to have any tangible existence. We seem to see right through them, as though looking through a window, as if they were not even there, from objects and events perceived in the external world to responses made to these objects and events. The external world actually exists only in our minds, but appears to exist outside of ourselves in external space, viewed by us as through a window. Such may occur so as to allow us to have meaningful exchanges with our external world. We must interpret the external world in regard to our personal needs and this might not be possible if the world appeared to us as it really is. Similarly, nonlinearly-produced stable states are our interpretations of the external world. Nonlinearly-produced stable states are produced serially and are prone to interference. Consciousness also appears to be of this nature. Part of this serial production might be the result of the serial operation of focussed attention and active short term memory. Interference is bound to occur when what comes before can affect what comes after. Remnants of previously formed stable states or conscious experiences might remain to influence composition of a new stable state or conscious experience. Interference might result when the integration period for one stable state or conscious episode overlaps with the integration period for another stable state or conscious episode. The inhibitory influences operational during the creation of a nonlinear explicit stable state or conscious experience might produce some interference in final composition of the state or experience. Interference occurring during the generation of consciousness (or nonlinear explicit stable states) may lead to illusions, delusions, hallucinations, or confusion. Nonlinearly-produced stable states, like consciousness, are unified and coherent. That is, the components of each state are completely integrated or unified; that is, coherently bound together as one whole, there is a oneness about each state. Each part of such a state is like every other part of the state. If such a state is divided in any way, all separated parts maintain the same properties and identity. Such properties as unity and coherence (such as in nonlinearly-produced stable states and consciousness) might arise through discrete integration (integration over short periods, epochs, or episodes) rather than arising from continuous integration mechanisms. Two interesting points about unified and coherent states are that small changes in the initial conditions producing such states can have profound effects on the final state produced and once a unified and coherent state is formed, it is very resistant to external influences. Nonlinearly-produced stable states and consciousness are difficult to formally describe; that is, they are hard to describe scientifically (explain according to scientific laws and principles). This may be because the relevant laws and principles are at present incompletely developed. These nonlinear stable states, like consciousness, seem to be projected outwards. This may be because of their interpretive nature (of the external world). They have no visible cause-effect relation; it is as if the responses or effects they produce are caused by the external world . This gives an impression that they are projected outwards. Each nonlinearly-produced stable state, like consciousness, seems to have an intrinsic positive or negative valence; that is, each state or conscious experience seems to have its own positive or negative value to the individual. This valence might arise through unconscious processing via the relative activation of the reward and avoidance systems of the brain, which are activated during external sensory processing. Much of our emotion may be initiated by such unconscious processing. It is a tenet of consciousness studies that when two things have all the same properties, they must be identical (Velmans,2002). Hence if the internal nonlinear explicit states produced in the above manner have all the same properties as consciousness, then they must be identical to consciousness. This does appear to be the case. Thus consciousness may be the production of nonlinear explicit stable states involved in the generation of voluntary new or novel intentional action. Consciousness is essentially part of the mechanism producing voluntary new or novel intentional action. Consciousness is the natural expression of these nonlinear explicit states. This means that consciousness appears to produce physical action (have physical effects) because it is actually a physical state.

SUPPORTING EVIDENCE

Consciousness and the generation of nonlinearly-produced stable states is impaired if re-entry mechanisms in the brain are disrupted [Tonelli and Edelman,1998]. This is true of the re-entrant interaction between the thalamus and the reticular formation of the brainstem with each other and with the cerebral cortex and the re-entrant activation occurring within the cerebral cortex . Coma (complete loss of consciousness) or confusion (partial loss of consciousness) is produced by damage to the reticular formation and/or intralaminar thalamic nuclei; while selective loss of qualia (selective loss of color, motion, face, shape experience) occurs with damage to specific areas of the cerebral cortex. Positive feedback tempered by induced inhibitory influences is a basic nonlinear physical mechanism responsible for the production of a large number of natural phenomena. Hence why can this mechanism not also be utilized by the brain for the generation of consciousness? Re-entry appears to be a prominent activity that occurs in the brain. The formation of explicit stable states via this nonlinear emergent mechanism shows how information can be bound together in a cohesive and unified whole (as it appears to be in consciousness) which is then utilized to produce specific explicit states in other systems. Since these explicit states are always new or novel (as consciousness seems to be), they always produce new or novel activation of other systems. Hence these states are perfect (as consciousness seems to be) for the production of new or novel actions. Perception and focal attention are essential for consciousness [Rowlands,2002; Velmans,1999]. Perception is thought to occur in the inferior temporal and inferior parietal cortex [Mattingley, 1999]. Pathology of this cortex produces most of the cases of neglect-loss of perception and consciousness (and the production of voluntary new or novel intentional action) on the affected side [Mattingley,1999]. Active short-term memory has been shown to operate in the posterior parietal cortex [Todd and Marois,2004;Vogel and Machizawa,2004]. It thus operates in an appropriate area for the generation of consciousness. Damage to the prefrontal cortex and/or its connections leads to an impaired general ability to produce voluntary new or novel intentional action (of skeletal movements, oculomotor movements, speech, writing, thought, emotion-psychomotor poverty), but preserves consciousness [Joseph,1990]. This fits in with the described mechanism in which consciousness is formed in the inferior temporal and inferior parietal cortex and then transferred to the prefrontal cortex for the selection and generation of specific voluntary new or novel intentional actions. It also suggests that consciousness can still be formed even if only the potential to form voluntary new or novel intentional actions exists. Thus nonlinear explicit stable states (consciousness) might still be formed in the inferior parietal cortex, even if the dorsolateral prefrontal cortex is damaged and cannot generate voluntary new or novel intentional action. Damage to the supplementary motor cortex (skeletomotor movements), frontal eye fields (conjugate saccadic eye movements), Broca's Area (speech), Exner's Area (writing), temporal cortex (thought), or orbitofrontal cortex (emotion) impairs the ability to produce voluntary new or novel intentional action in that domain (since the prefrontal cortex apparently generates such action via these areas)[Fuster,1997;Pandya and Yeterian, 1990]. This also fits the mechanism described for the generation of voluntary new or novel intentional actions by consciousness. Electrical stimulation of the supplementary motor cortex of epileptic patients at low levels produces an urge to make a specific voluntary intentional movement, which at higher levels produces the actual movement [Haggard,2005]. Thus the electrical stimulation might act like consciousness (a nonlinear explicit stable state) in driving a specific voluntary movement. This provides further support for the mechanism described above for the generation of voluntary new or novel intentional movements. If similar stimulation could be applied to the frontal areas controlling the other voluntary new or novel intentional action domains, it might have analogous effects in each domain. Standardized intelligence tests (IQ tests) register how well the subject can integrate information consciously and create voluntary new or novel intentional action. This helps support the association between consciousness and the production of voluntary new or novel intentional action. A low score on such tests, might indicate a low ability to create and generate voluntary new or novel intentional action; while high scores might indicate a high ability to create and generate voluntary new or novel intentional action. Lower scores are taken as indicative of lower intelligence (a lower IQ or intelligence quotient). Higher scores are taken as indicative of higher intelligence or IQ. Intelligence might be considered as the ability to consciously compose voluntary new or novel intentional action. At any rate, the score on such tests might be indicative of the strength or degree of conscious integration of voluntary new or novel intentional action. Studies of illusions (the wagon wheel phenomena and others) suggest that the production of consciousness occurs in discrete epochs or time periods (episodes) rather than through continuous integration from the external world [VanRullen and Koch,2003]. Such production is also suggested by the properties of consciousness. Studies of voluntary movement production indicate that consciousness may arise after the choice is made to make a movement but before the specific movement is made [Haggard,2005]. Consciousness therefore may participate in the composition (determine the parameters, specifics) of a specific movement, a specific voluntary new or novel intentional movement.

CONCLUSION

Consciousness can be explained as a physical state of the brain, more precisely, as a succession of physical states of the brain. The "gap" between the subjective and the physical (How can the subjective arise from the physical? How can the subjective affect the physical?)[Velmans,2002] is removed because the subjective is a physical state [Carruthers,2002;Clark,1997;Lazarov,2003;Nicholson,2003]. Consciousness arises as a natural consequence of the establishment of these states. Consciousness is natural, material, and functional; not some mysterious, nonmaterial epiphenomenon. It may be explained and studied scientifically. It may occur in animals, machines, and natural systems; any system that has the ability to produce true voluntary new or novel intentional action or effects. The production of voluntary new or novel intentional action may be an objective indicator for the presence of consciousness. This is important for the composition, synthesis, and verification of consciousness research.

FUTURE RESEARCH

Future research might include the study of various animal species to determine their ability to compose voluntary new or novel intentional action. If they can, then they may possess some degree of consciousness and may allow study of the neural mechanisms involved in its production. Human studies of consciousness must involve the production of voluntary new or novel intentional action. Only if such action is truly generated, can one be certain that consciousness is really involved in the experiment. If true voluntary new or novel intentional action is not being generated, then one cannot be certain that consciousness is involved in the experiment and the effects measured may be produced by unconscious processes. If machines are built that can create true voluntary new or novel intentional action, then study and manipulation of the physical mechanisms involved in the production of consciousness might be facilitated. The nonlinear emergence of internal explicit stable states might be studied in natural systems to gain insight into the physical principles involved in the production of consciousness. Since the nonlinear mechanism described in this composition is responsible for the production of a large number of natural phenomena, its study in relation to the generation of these phenomena might have a lot to offer in the study of the generation of consciousness, since they appear to be generated by a similar basic mechanism. The former study might also help in the study of how voluntary new or novel intentional actions are selected, created, and generated. Since intelligence is the ability to consciously create voluntary new or novel intentional action, standardized tests might provide an index of intelligence, as well as the degree and effectiveness of consciousness present, ie. IQ might also be a measure of the degree or effectiveness of consciousness. Hence many of the intelligence tests that exist today may also provide a measure of the degree of consciousness. However, to provide a more accurate measure, they must be broadened to include all types of voluntary new or novel intentional action discussed. Since consciousness depends on the selection and maintenance of perceptual activity over a delay (of active short-term memory), studies utilizing delayed response tasks might be key to the understanding of consciousness. Such tasks have helped in the understanding of how voluntary new or novel intentional actions are produced and so might be of great interest in the study of consciousness.

PREDICTIONS

Consciousness will be found to be natural, material, and functional. It will be found to be explained by scientific principles. It will be found to function in the creation of voluntary new or novel intentional action and have an evolutionary history. Certain other animals (especially mammals) will be found to have a degree of consciousness. Conscious machines will be built. A degree of consciousness will be found in many nonlinear emergent natural systems. It will be possible to construct standardized tests to measure the degree and effectiveness of consciousness (IQ). It will be possible to manipulate and extend our consciousness, perhaps into what is now the paranormal. Our consciousness may persist after death, if we possess a physical energy that continues to interact with itself after we die.

REFERENCES

Afifi, A.K. and Bergman, R.A. (1986) *Basic Neuroscience*, Baltimore/Munich, Urban and Schwarzenberg.

Alter, T. (2000) Nagel on imagination and physicalism. In:*Online Papers On Consciousness,*ed.David Chalmers.

Allott, R.M. (1994) Motor theory of language origin:The diversity of languages. In:*Studies In Language Origins,*eds.Wind,Jan,andJonker;Abraham and Allott;RobinandRolfe; Leonard,John Benjamins,3:125-160. http://cogprints.ecs.soton.ac.uk/archive/00003286/

Baars, B. (1988) *A Cognitive Theory of Consciousness*, Cambridge University Press.

Brodal, A. (1981) *Neurological Anatomy*. New York:Oxford University Press.

Byrne, A. (April 2001) Intentionalism defended. *Philosophical Review* 110:199-240.

Carruthers, P. (2002) Reductive explanation and the 'explanatory gap'.

http://www.philosophy.umd.edu/people/faculty/pcarruthers/Reductive-explanation.htm

Chalmers, D. (2004) ed. *Online Papers on Consciousness*.

Clark, T.W. (1997) Function and phenomenology:closing the explanatory gap. In:*Explaining Consciousness,*ed.J.Shear, MIT Press.

Clifton, A. (2003) The introspection game-or, does the Tin Man have a heart? http://cogprints.ecs.soton.ac.uk/archive/00003483/

Clifton, A. (2004a) An empirical case against materialism. http://cogprints.ecs.soton. ac.uk/archive/00003481/

Clifton, A. (2004b) Blind mana? Ts bluff and the Turing Test. http://cogprints.ecs.soton.ac.uk/archive/00003480/

Davis, M., Hitchcock, J.M., Rosen, J.B. (1991) Neural mechanisms of fear conditioning measured with the acoustic startle reflex. In J. Madden IV (Ed.), *Neurobiology of Learning, Emotion, and Effect*, New York:Raven Press, 67-96.

Fried, I. et al (1991) Functional organization of human supplementary motor cortex studied by electrical stimulation. *J. Neurosci.* 11:3656-3666.

Fuster, J. (1997) *The Prefrontal Cortex. Anatomy, Physiology, and Neuropsychology of the Frontal Lobe*, 3rd ed,Lippincott-Raven.

Fuster, J. (2000) Cross-modal and cross-temporal association in neurons of frontal cortex. *Nature* 405:347-351.

Ganong, W.F. (1996) *Review of Medical Physiology*, Los Altos, California, Lange.

Gershenson, C. and Heylighen, F. (2004) How can we think the complex? In Richardson,Kurt,Eds. *Managing the Complex Volume One:Philosophy, Theory and Application,*Image Age Publishers. http://cogprints.ecs.soton.ac.uk/archive/00003439/

Haggard, P. (2005) Consciousness intention and motor cognition. *Trends in Cognitive Science 9(6)*.

Haggard, P. and Eimer, M. (1999) On the relation between brain potentials and the awareness of voluntary movements. *Exp. Brain Res.* 126:128-133.

Holstege G., Bandler, R. and Saper, C.B., eds. (1996) The Emotional Motor System. *Progress In Brain Research*, Elsevier.

Jones, E.G., Coulter, J.D., Hendry, S.H.C. (1978) Intracortical connectivity of architectonic fields in the somatic sensory, motor, parietal cortex of monkeys. *Journal of Comparative Neurology* 181:291-348.

Kuypers, H.G.J.M. and Catsman-Berrevoets, C.E. (1984) Frontal cortico-subcortical projections and their cells of origin. In F.Reinoso-Suarez and C.Ajmone-Marsan (Eds.),*Cortical Integration*,New York:Raven Press,171-194.

Joseph, R. (1990) *Neuropsychology, Neuropsychiatry, and Behavioral Neurology*, Plenum Press.

Kapp, B.S. et al (1990) A neuroanatomical systems analysis of conditioned bradycardia in the rabbit. In M.Gabriel and J.Moore (Eds.),*Learning and Computational Neuroscience: Foundations of Adaptive Networks*,Cambridge,Massachusetts:The MIT Press,53-90.

Koch, C. (1998) The neuroanatomy of visual consciousness. In:*Advances in Neurology. Consciousness:At the Frontiers of Neuroscience, eds. H. H.* Jasper, L. Descarries,V. F. Costelluchi, and S. Rossignol, Lippincott-Raven,77:229-239.

Lau, H.C. et al (2004) Attention to intention. *Science* 303:1208-1210.

Lazarov, G. (2003) Materialism and the problem of consciousness:the aesthesionomic approach. http://cogprints.ecs.soton.ac.uk/archive/00003161/

LeDoux, J.C. (1990) Information flow from sensation to emotion:Plasticity in the neural computation of stimulus value. In M.Gabriel and J.Moore (Eds.), *Learning and Computational Neuroscience:Foundations of Adaptive Networks, Cambridge, Massachusetts:The MIT Press,3-52.*

Libet, B. et al (1983) Time of conscious intention to act in relation to onset of cerebral activity (readiness-potential). The unconscious initiation of a freely voluntary act. *Brain* 106:623-642.

Libet, B. (1985) Unconscious cerebral initiation and the role of conscious will in voluntary action. *Behavioral Brain Science* 8:529-566.

Luck, S.J. and Vogel, E.K. (1997) The capacity of visual working memory for features and conjunctions. *Nature 390:*279-281.

Mattingley, J.B. (1999) Attention, consciousness, and the damaged brain: Insights from parietal neglect and extinction. *Psyche 5:*14.

Mandik, P. (2001) Mental representation and the subjectivity of consciousness. *Philosophical Reviews* 14(2):179-202.

McClamrock, R. (1994) Irreducibility and subjectivity. *Philosophical Reviews*.

McCrone, J. (1999) *Going Inside*, Chapter 13,Faber and Faber, UK.

McCrone, J. (2001) Subjective systems-how complexity science gives a new way of looking at the mind/body problem.
http://www.btinternet.com/~neuronaut/webtwo_features_complexity.htm

Newman, D.V. (1997) Chaos, emergence, and the mind-body problem. *Australasian Journal of Philosophy* 79(2):180-196.

Nicholson, D. (2003) Solving the mind-body problem-the real significance of the knowledge argument.Http://cogprints.ecs.soton.ac.uk/archive/00002951/

Pandya, D.N. and Yeterian, E.M. (1990) Prefrontal cortex in relation to other cortical areas in rhesus monkey: Architecture and connection. *Progress in Brain Research* 85:63-92.

Perryman, K.M., Kling, A.S., Lloyd, R.L. (1987) Differential effects of inferior temporal cortex lesions upon visual and auditory-evoked potentials in the amygdala of the squirrel monkey. *Behavioral and Neural Biology* 47:73-79.

O'Brien, G. (1998) Connectionism, analogicity, and mental content. *Acta Analytica* 22:111-131.

O'Brien, G. and Opie, J. (1999) A connectionist theory of phenomenal experience. *Behavioral and Brain Science* 22:127-148.

Rowlands, M. (2002) Two Dogmas of Consciousness. *Homepage.*

Scott, A.C. (1996) The hierarchical emergence of consciousness. In:*Toward a Science of Consciousness. The First Tucson Discussions and Debates,(eds.)*S.R. Hameroff, A.W.Kaszniak and A.C.Scott,MIT Press,659-672.

Scott, A.C. (1999) *Nonlinear Science:* Emergence *and Dynamics of Coherent Structures,*Oxford University Press.

Scott, A.C. (2000) *Modern Science and the Mind,*(University of Arizona Course:January-April,2000).

Sieb, R.A. (1987) A proposed mechanism for the production of skeletalmotor positioning movements by the basal ganglia. *Medical Hypotheses* 24:209.

Sieb, R.A. (1995) *Voluntary Action,* Edmonton:Richard Sieb.

Sieb, R.A. (2004) The emergence of consciousness. *Medical Hypotheses* 63(5):900-904.

Sirigu, A. et al (2004) Altered awareness of voluntary action after damage to the parietal cortex. *Nat. Neurosc.* 7:80-84.

Todd, J.J. and Marois, R. (2004) Capacity limit of visual short-term memory in human posterior parietal cortex. *Nature* 428:751-754.

Tononi, G. and Edelman, G. (1998) Consciousness and the integration of information in the brain. In:*Advances in Neurology. Consciousness:At the Frontiers of Neuroscience,*eds.H.H.Jasper,L.Descarries,V.F.Costelluchi and S.Rossignol,Lippincott-Raven,77:245-280.

Turner, B.H., Mishkin, M., Knapp, M. (1980) Organization of the amygdalopetal projections from modality-specific cortical association areas in the monkey. *Journal of Comparative Neurology* 191:515-543.

Van Hoesen, G.W. (1981) The differential distribution, diversity and sprouting of cortical projections to the amygdala in the rhesus monkey. In Y. Ben-Ari (Ed.),*The Amygdala Complex,*Elsevier:Amsterdam,77-99.

VanRullen, R. and Koch, C. (2003) Is perception discrete or continuous? *Trends In Cognitive Science* 7(5):207-213.

Velmans, M. (1999) When perception becomes conscious. *British Journal of Psychology 90(4):*543-566.

Velmans, M. (2002) How could conscious experiences affect brains? *Journal of Consciousness Studies 9(11):*3-29,69-95.

Vogel, E.K. and Machizawa, M.G. (2004) Neural activity predicts individual differences in visual working memory capacity. *Nature* 428:748-751.

Weinberger, M.W. et al (1990) Neural adaptive information processing:A preliminary model of receptive-field plasticity in auditory cortex during Pavlovian conditioning. In M.Gabriel and J.Moore (Eds.),*Learning and Computational Neuroscience:Foundations of Adaptive Networks,*Cambridge, Massachusetts:The MIT Press,91-137.

INDEX

A

academic performance, 127, 130, 136
academic progress, 127
academic settings, 121
academics, 126
acceptance, 65, 158
access, 86, 88, 179, 181
accounting, 168
accuracy, 20, 170
achievement, 34, 35, 123, 125, 127, 129, 132, 134, 167
acid, 103, 110
acquired characteristics, 141, 144
acquisition phase, 174
action potential, 16, 103, 106, 148
activation, 9, 37, 48, 90, 100, 111, 168, 171, 172, 173, 175, 179, 181, 182, 183, 184, 187, 189, 190, 194
activation energy, 48
adaptability, 104
adaptation, 19, 20
addiction, ix, 79, 80, 91, 94
ADHD, 108
adhesion, 102, 111, 117
adolescents, 93
adrenaline, 103
adults, 190
affect, viii, x, 49, 50, 55, 59, 63, 74, 108, 119, 120, 121, 122, 128, 131, 191, 195, 199
age, ix, 21, 98, 154, 155
agent, 169
aggression, 65
aggressive behavior, 64
aging, 19, 20, 21, 24, 29, 109
AIDS, 76, 93, 94, 111
alertness, 109
alternative, 13, 15, 17, 42, 81, 124, 126, 183

alternatives, 16
alters, 92
Alzheimer's disease, 116, 117
amplitude, 105, 172
amygdala, 199
anatomy, 143, 144
anger, 65, 69, 73, 169, 178
animals, 87, 98, 110, 116, 140, 141, 153, 156, 169, 170, 175, 178, 188, 195, 196
anisotropy, 28, 30
ANOVA, 128
anthropology, 144
anxiety, viii, 63, 64, 65, 66, 67, 73, 74, 75, 76, 77, 126, 133
aphasia, 175
aptitude, 121, 129, 132
argument, 14, 15, 18, 69, 99, 101, 126, 138, 145, 151, 155, 198
Aristotle, 140
arousal, 64, 81, 88, 90
arrest, 177
articulation, 122
artificial intelligence, 109
ASI, 126
aspartate, 113, 114, 115, 116, 117
assault, 77
assessment, 124, 131, 132, 154, 156, 159
assimilation, 180
association, 8, 20, 26, 27, 30, 36, 49, 81, 85, 104, 106, 110, 113, 120, 173, 178, 180, 195, 197, 199
assumptions, viii, 47, 50, 51, 61, 76
asymmetry, 123
athetosis, 174
atoms, 152, 158
atrocities, 170
attachment, 168, 191
attention, 50, 68, 102, 106, 108, 109, 115, 120, 122, 141, 166, 174, 178, 181, 184, 187, 189, 190, 194

D

E

F

G

H

I

J

K

L

M

S

W

Y

Z